beloved
WARRI

Other Titles from Potomac Books

My Life and Battles, by Jack Johnson

Tyson-Douglas: The Inside Story of the Upset of the Century,
by John Johnson and Bill Long

*Boxing's Most Wanted™: The Top 10 Book of Champs, Chumps,
and Punch-Drunk Palookas*, by David L. Hudson, Jr.,
and Mike Fitzgerald, Jr.

beloved WARRIOR

THE RISE AND FALL OF Alexis Argüello

CHRISTIAN GIUDICE

Potomac Books
Washington, D.C.

Library of Congress Cataloging-in-Publication Data
Giudice, Christian.
Beloved warrior : the rise and fall of Alexis Arguëllo / Christian Giudice.—1st ed.
    p. cm.
  ISBN 978-1-59797-709-8 (hardcover)
  ISBN 978-1-59797-799-9 (electronic edition)
  1. Arguëllo, Alexis. 2. Boxers (Sports)—Nicaragua—Biography. I. Title.
  GV1132.A76G58 2012
  796.83092—dc23
  [B]

                                                              2011045413

Printed in the United States of America on acid-free paper that meets the American National Standards Institute Z39-48 Standard.

Potomac Books
22841 Quicksilver Drive
Dulles, Virginia 20166

First Edition

10 9 8 7 6 5 4 3 2 1

For my beautiful wife, Tair.

"I did this with my bare hands."
—ALEXIS ARGÜELLO

CONTENTS

ACKNOWLEDGMENTS

Writing a book about a great fighter and man like Alexis Argüello has been a fascinating experience I will never forget. My first introduction to the classy fighter came in the early 1980s when my father met him in an Atlantic City casino and got me his autograph, which I still have to this day. I admittedly knew very little about him except for what I read in boxing magazines. I would meet him on three occasions over the next two decades—at the International Boxing Hall of Fame where he felt at home, and back in Nicaragua in 2008. Each time he was the same classy gentleman who treated me with the utmost respect.

When I initially arrived in Nicaragua, legendary boxing journalist Pablo Fletes welcomed me. He provided not only the background on boxing in Nicaragua, but he also took care of me and introduced me to the Managua that he knew and loved. During the visit, I also met with Alexis, who took me to his childhood home and told me stories about the streets where he grew up: "I didn't look for fights. I was a protector," he explained. I remember him walking up to his childhood home to say hello to a woman living there at the time.

Alexis's manager and lifelong friend, Dr. Eduardo Roman, welcomed me into his home in Laguna de Apoyo, and invited me to lounge in his hammocks as he retold stories of Alexis's forays into the sport, and the father-son bond they cultivated. He shared his love for Alexis, and how his home on the lake was where Alexis retreated to when he wanted to escape the chaos and pressures that came with being a champion. He took such pride in saying, "he thought of me as his father." His kindness and generosity will not be forgotten. I also was able to count on his friend Francisco, who drove me back and forth through Alexis's old neighborhood and to interviews. Through Dr. Roman, I was able to meet Dr. Henry Castillo, another longtime friend and supporter who loved Alexis like a brother. I also owe a debt of gratitude to Donald Rodriguez and

Renzo Bagnariol, who opened up to me about the successes and struggles that defined the last five years of their friend's life.

Nicaraguan sports journalists showed a love and appreciation for Alexis. Edgar Tijerino treated me like family as he invited me to his home for an unforgettable lunch. I am not sure if I could have finished the book without the generosity of his daughter, Tamara Tijerino. Not only did she translate most of the interviews, but she was able to answer any question regarding her father or Nicaragua. Not once did she ask for or accept anything in return. The warmth that I received from the Tijerino family, Dr. Roman, Dr. Castillo, and other members of the Nicaraguan Boxing Commission, such as Enrique Armas, made writing and researching this biography an easy and enjoyable endeavor. I also would like to thank Victor Boitano, Sergio Quintero, Mauricio Buitrago, Ray Mendoza, Nelson Pichardo, and Silvio Reyes from Don Elba Cigars for taking the time to sit down with me and recall their fond memories of Alexis. Being able to reference Alexis's two biographies written by Edgar and Miguel Angel Arcia also proved indispensable during the lengthy process.

There are certain people who never thought twice about assisting with some aspect of the book. Matthew Tarditi was one of them. He sacrificed precious time in and outside of Nicaragua to assist with interviews—even if it meant he was dragged to an interview during his check-in at a hotel in Managua. Thank you! Servando Echeandia also knew how much finishing the book meant to me, and provided valuable translation. Thanks also goes out to Jennifer Edenfield for finding time between lesson plans to translate interviews.

Since Alexis's last great fight was nearly thirty years ago, I had difficulty finding contacts who recalled the memorable battles with Aaron Pryor. However, a Miami contingent surfaced and patiently answered every question regarding that time period and provided valuable photos for the biography. Walter Alvarez, Ramiro Ortiz, Jimmy Resnick, Enrique Espinosa, and Frankie Otero were indispensable as each one helped me to fill in the empty spaces of Alexis's life in Miami. Dr. Marshall Abel gave his valuable perspective of the final seconds of the first Pryor matchup. Later, Bill and Yolanda Miller also sacrificed precious time to speak to me about their friendship with Alexis and Loretto.

When I first began the project there was one man who was always there to provide valuable insight, advice, and then generously locate contacts. Gerald Maltz was extremely influential in making this book a successful one. Gerald offered photos of Alexis's fierce training sessions, while Butch Flansburg, from the Florida Boxing Hall of Fame, also sent over photos without searching for anything in return. I noticed that same kindness and generosity from so many people who just wanted to see Alexis's story finally told, because they felt it was long overdue.

That being said, I couldn't have finished this project without the best cornermen in the business: Carlos Varela Jr. and his father, Carlos Sr., who spent countless hours revisiting bouts from the 1960s and 1970s. It was easy to see why Alexis held both men in such regard. Michael Schmidt also selflessly gave his time and assistance during the research process for this project. When I wasn't contacting the Varelas, I was talking to Don Kahn. From the first to the last interview with Mr. Kahn, I realized why he was the one man that Alexis trusted from the beginning up to their last weekend together. From sending photos to late-night calls, Don contributed so much to the making of this project that it is hard to properly thank him.

As far as past opponents, Ray "Boom Boom" Mancini is the epitome of class personified. For Mr. Mancini, it was always, "How can I help?" I was honored for such a great man to agree to write the foreword for this book. Former opponents Jim Watt, Art Hafey, Roberto Elizondo, Ruben Castillo, Bubba Busceme, and the late Billy Costello were instrumental in articulating the round-by-round analysis of their bouts with Alexis. Other boxers and promoters who shared their stories and insight who deserve thanks are Armando Muniz, Tony Balthazar, Danny "Little Red" Lopez, and promoters Don Fraser and Don Chargin.

As always, Steve Farhood has proven to be a great friend over the years, and his unwavering support is something I will always cherish. I also need to thank the passionate journalist Lee Groves for his generosity and willingness to open up his boxing collection (and magazine archives) and allowing me to revisit valuable footage of Alexis's early bouts. Lee also took his valuable time to proofread the book—Thank you my friend! When Jack Obermayer wasn't touring Jersey diners, he was busy assisting with the completion of the book. Thanks also goes out to Brad White, Jeff Brophy, Jimbo Amato, Rick Scharmberg, Michael Marley, and Ed Schuyler Jr. for the support they gave me over the years.

Whenever I needed a contact number, Edward Koenig was always there for me, as he always has been throughout my life. I have been blessed with a great group of friends—Cory, Greg, Keith, Brian Corbett, Dan, Ryan, Brian Faulk, Matt and Kevin—who have always supported my boxing projects. I would also like to thank Michael Andrews and Lou Papa for their enthusiasm for the project. Thank you!

Lastly, I could not have finished this without the support of my beautiful wife, Tair, my loving mother, unbelievably supportive sisters, Amy and Ali, and my father, who instilled a love and passion for boxing that has never left me. Whatever I have been able to accomplish with this project, I owe to the patience and love I receive from them every day.

FOREWORD

When I first heard that with my next win I'd have the opportunity to face the great Alexis Argüello, I felt a great surge of excitement as well as a confidence that could and would finally make my lifelong dream come true. I had known about and watched Alexis's career through the years with great respect and admiration.

I had seen his title-winning fight against Jim Watt of Scotland on TV and thought, though he had fought an efficient fight and won, that he didn't look very sharp or dominate as he had in other title fights in lighter weight classes.

I felt that I was catching him at the right time in his career. He was older than I was, not as fast or quick handed as I was, and maybe a little weatherworn from such a long and illustrious career. Also, I truly felt that he wouldn't be as physically strong as I was and that I could use that to my advantage. I was wrong on all accounts.

When we had the press conference in New York to announce the fight, I was a little taken back by his friendliness and graciousness. I had never encountered an opponent that respectful before a fight. And why shouldn't we be? This meeting was business, not personal. He had something I wanted, and he was going to do whatever he could to keep me from taking it. We would be fighting before a sold-out crowd in an Atlantic City casino ballroom, as well as a worldwide television audience.

The day after the press conference, I was going to drive from New York City to Grossinger's Resort in the Catskill Mountains—it was about a two-hour drive—and start my training camp. But before my group left, I wanted to make sure I got in my morning roadwork through Central Park. I knew I had to start right away, to get my mind, body, and spirit prepared for the battle ahead. I didn't want to leave anything for granted.

As I was finishing my four-mile run through the park, coming the other way was Alexis with his camp. Obviously, he was thinking the same thing. As we passed each other, again he threw me off by saying, "Good morning, Ray." I kind of half waved and said, "Hello." Round 1 went to Alexis.

I was training in the ski lodge at Grossinger's, the same place that Rocky Marciano, Muhammad Ali, and my idol Roberto Durán trained in. I felt a sense of history there. Training camp was going great. I felt strong, getting in top shape, and my mind was clear. I was away from all distractions and totally immersed into the fight and feeling very confident.

Through training camp, I'd watch tapes of Alexis's fights—his title-winning efforts against Rubén Olivares, Alfredo Escalera, and Jim Watt as well as his other great fights.

The one thing that stood out watching all of those fights was his ring artistry, how he kept his composure throughout any situation. Alexis never seemed to get rattled or out of position to fire back. He was very disciplined and economical in his style. He very seldom threw a wasted punch or left himself open when he missed.

After watching so many of his fights, I knew I had a daunting task ahead of me. But still, I felt confident that I could and would win.

Leading up to the fight, much of the talk was about whether I had enough experience to challenge such a great champion. I had recently beaten the number 6 and number 3 contenders in the world. What should've I done? Said no, thanks, and fight lesser opponents? Plus, I said, "Ask my father how many opportunities you get to fight for the world title."

But this man wasn't any champion. He was the great Alexis Argüello, "El Flaco Esplosivo," or the Explosive Thin Man. He was one of the all-time greats.

After the fight, which *Ring* magazine listed as one of the fights of the year and, later, one of the greatest in the decade, I knew I had what it took, and eventually I would be a world champion.

When the fight was over, Alexis came over to console me and offer apologies to my parents. He did it with so much grace and compassion that he not only won over my family, the people of Youngstown, Ohio, and the national viewing audience but also became an instant sports hero.

When people spoke of Alexis to me immediately following that fight, and for many years later, what consistently came out of their mouths was, "What a gentleman, what a class act." I had to agree.

Through the years, I'd occasionally run into Alexis at different events or we'd send greetings through mutual friends and acquaintances. And again, he was always consistent, gracious and warm.

When I first heard from the television that Alexis had died, I was stunned, then immediately saddened, knowing that we had lost one of the great ones. Not only a great fighter but also a great person.

I'll always have a love for Alexis, for the way he treated me before and after the fight. And for the times we'd see each other socially. For the loving way he treated my parents and family and the people of Youngstown. And just for being the man and champion he was. I will forever be appreciative of being so closely associated with such a gentleman and champion. I always say that when you look up the word "champion" in the dictionary and read of its qualities—class, grace, and humility—you will see a picture of Alexis Argüello.

Ray Mancini

Birth of a Champion

I knew boxing was my way out.
  —ALEXIS ARGÜELLO

During the 1960s and 1970s, boxing in Nicaragua wasn't profitable. In fact, most skilled fighters did everything possible to find a way out of the country and other opportunities to make a living. Less popular than baseball and soccer, the sport still had a loyal following throughout Latin America, especially in Panama and Mexico; however, without proper funding and exposure, the local Nicaraguan boxing champions would never be anything more than hometown heroes gracing the pages of *La Prensa*, *Barricada*, or *El Nuevo Diario*. Despite boxing's lack of exposure and support, young boys continued to fulfill their life-long dreams in the three main boxing havens in Nicaragua at the time: the Estadio Nacional (National Stadium, which was later named the Denis Martinez Baseball Stadium), Cranshaw Stadium, and the National Boxing School.

Because of the venues' sizes, the Nicaraguan Boxing Commission held most championship bouts at either the National Stadium or Cranshaw Stadium. Located directly behind the National Stadium on Calle Colon (Colon Street), Cranshaw was a soccer stadium that was converted for boxing matches. The National Stadium was built in 1948 and could hold thirty thousand spectators. A massive structure that takes up several blocks, the stadium was west of Paseo Naciones Unidas, east of Paseo Salvador Allende, and minutes from the Plaza de la Revolución and the Presidential Palace. While the young boys who brawled on the streets had some boxing idols they could admire, in comparison with the rest of Central America, the "Nica" tradition had little to boast about. While Nicaraguan boxers Eddie Gazo, Francois González, "Armando" (Jackal) Hurtado, Tony Huerta, Kid Pambelé, and Eduardo "Ratón" Mojica Rueda became local heroes, without government funding, their boxing prospects floundered. This situation often led to a lack of discipline. Nicaragua needed a world champion—someone to make the people proud, someone to represent the face of the country, and, more important, someone to make the people forget their daily struggles. That someone was Alexis Argüello.

On April 19, 1952, Andrés Alexis Argüello Bohórquez was born in Managua, one of five children and the third son to Zoila Rosa Bohórquez and Guillermo Argüello Bonilla, or "Cebollón" (Big Onion). Zoila and Guillermo were from Granada and had come to Managua in search of opportunity. Newborn Andrés Alexis was named after Zoila's father. By the time of Alexis's birth, the family already consisted of sisters Marina and Norma and two brothers, Guillermo and Ivan, who were fiercely protective of their younger brother. Later Orlando, Isabel, Eduardo, and Cesar added to the growing Argüello clan. Guillermo, a shoemaker, realized that as his family grew, their quality of life deteriorated. A large, hulking man, Guillermo had an infectious humor and way about him that attracted people.

Although Guillermo Senior tried many pursuits, he was never able to provide his family with the security it needed. Guillermo's associates during that time remember him as a jovial, welcoming figure, while Zoila, a strict and fair woman, ran the household. When one of the children challenged her in some way, that child received an unforgettable beating. In the Argüello home, she was feared. Each day, Guillermo gave Zoila ten córdobas (C$) to pay for breakfast, lunch, and dinner. The boys were expected to pick up the slack.

"My parents couldn't afford to have a camera. I never took a picture. My dad used to give $10 to my mom for breakfast, lunch and dinner," Argüello said. "Ten bucks to feed eight kids. My mom . . . it was tough for her to bring us up, but she did it. That's why she used to tell me, 'Alexis, you have to go hunt with your slingshot to bring home some iguanas and possum for food.' We used to go looking for lizards and iguanas. Sometimes, I got possum and sometimes I got chicken and I brought it home."

When not hunting possum or iguanas, Argüello headed to the local dance every Friday and Saturday night. "I liked some of the Latin songs. I was born in 1952. The 50s, 60s, 70s . . . it was a different kind of music back then."

The rail-thin youth grew up in Barrio Monseñor Lezcano near the restaurant Delicias del Volga. It was not a particularly dangerous neighborhood, and Alexis could wander freely without threat or harm. The dusty, unpaved roads were filled with children, who played a multitude of sports.

"The streets in Managua were a little more secure during those days," Argüello recalled as he retraced those streets decades later. "We had gangs, but you could walk anywhere and there would be no harm. Now, you walk into the wrong place and they pull a knife on you. A gun and they kill you."

Tall for his age, with strong Indian features, Alexis was a vibrant, intelligent, and amiable youth who never searched for confrontation and didn't allow his family's bleak financial outlook to affect him. He had a special relationship with his older brother Ivan. Although all his brothers dabbled in boxing at some point, Ivan and his younger brother Orlando were the ones who had made significant progress in the sport. Orlando even went to the Central American and Caribbean Games, but it was Ivan who eventually led his younger brother Alexis to the boxing gym for his initial foray into the sport.

"First one Alexis boxed in the family was me," said Ivan Argüello. "In my opinion, Orlando used to be a little better than Alexis, but he wasn't disciplined like Alexis. I needed to decide who to help, Alexis or Orlando. Orlando had everything, but he didn't have that discipline; Alexis had everything and that discipline. Both were excellent."

The Argüello home was a simple, one-story wood home bordered by similar houses on each side. Next to his house, Argüello recalled, "used to be a cantina nicknamed La Cantina de Cebollon before. People used to come and have some drinks. My father was a shoemaker. He used to manufacture shoes. I used to help him. I used to take water from here to the house for the sewers. I was 12 or 13 years old. I was a kid. I helped my father make a sewage system. I'd walk the water down these streets all the way home. Can you believe that?"

Argüello continued, "But back then there were no roads. It was all dirt. When the Sandinistas came, they put roads in the streets. Actually, I never got into a problem. I was a defender. I used to defend the kids. The smaller kids, the older kids used to beat them. But me, I never got into trouble, personally."

Young Alexis played every recreational sport from baseball to soccer to basketball, and he became a skilled outfielder in baseball. He also took his schooling seriously. During the late 1950s, it wasn't unusual for a child to forgo education and work for his family; however, Alexis experienced the ugliness of the school system as the reality of poverty set in. Early in the fourth grade, Alexis came home from Del Sagrado Corazón de Jesús and realized he couldn't go back because his family was too far behind in the annual payments. Alexis also suggested in various interviews throughout his life that his teacher had hidden the collection money. He was crushed. It was one of the first times in his life that Alexis recognized the dangers of politics.

"As a kid, I got thrown out of school. I didn't know why. But when I got home I realized it was because my father couldn't pay for school. Can you fucking believe it?" said an incredulous Argüello. "Back then, I asked myself, how could a guy have it in himself to kick a kid out of school because his father couldn't pay for it? If I saw that guy today I would kick his ass. That is detrimental to humanity. How could a guy throw a kid out on the street?"

Once his anger subsided, clearly a seed had been planted. No one in the Argüello family was politically inclined; no one protested or challenged Anastasio "Tachito" Somoza Debayle's dictatorial ways, or at least not in public as other families did. Alexis's humiliation, however, marked a turning point in his life. He realized that even when he followed the right path, people could still impede his way. Even in the face of poverty, that feeling of injustice stayed with him and would fuel his own political ambitions later in his life.

While Alexis spent most of his time doing odd jobs, such as working on a cattle ranch, and helping his father build a sewer system, he knew better opportunities were available. He began to grow as a leader in the family, and in order to help with the financial crisis, he decided to head to Ontario, Canada. Argüello had cousins in Canada, and his uncle, Teodoro Amador, was willing to take in and care for him. At the time, the counterculture was at its apex, and Alexis would experience a lifestyle—a new scene defined by drugs and music—that was foreign to him, and found it liberating to be on his own. When he left his family, though, he promised to return with his entire salary.

"My father spent $2,000 getting me to Canada, so I knew that I couldn't come back without it," said Argüello. "I cleaned bathrooms and worked in a Chinese restaurant. I ended up in Ontario, Canada, and I worked enough to make the money to come home."

Alexis was the first family member to travel extensively outside of Central America, and his experience in this foreign world provided the necessary insight to the characteristics of another culture. Prior to his trip to Canada, Alexis could only relate to Managua. After experiencing the nomadic lifestyle, one that he thoroughly enjoyed, Alexis returned less than one year later with several thousand dollars that he had earned during what he called the "hippie stage" of his life. Even his appearance had changed drastically. Argüello's long hair brought his mother to tears, so he cut it all off and returned to his clean-cut ways. He admitted it was merely a phase in his life, but he also hinted at the contentment he felt being away from the daily stress in Managua. The trip was a respite from the pressure of his home life. "Back then I went to free concerts in the park," he said. "I was a straight hippie, no drugs. I just enjoyed the music and the people."

Back in Nicaragua, as Argüello filled his idle time with sports and working on cars with his brothers, he had no viable prospects or direction.

"Our friendship started one day when we met on a patio," said Donald Rodriguez, a neighbor and longtime friend. "We used to play 2 to 3 hours back then and at night, like 7:30 p.m. he came where I was with my girlfriend, and he used to get there and ask me to go and ride the motorcycle I had back then. Or we went and played pool, or went out to eat something. That was normal. He always went out at night. Usually we just played baseball or pool or went to see a game at the stadium."

Boxing was not on Argüello's radar. In fact, while it was customary throughout Central America to bring troubled teens off the streets and into the gym to harness their anger and reckless natures, Argüello didn't fit into that category. He was a vivacious, outgoing adolescent who rarely fought in the streets, unless to defend himself. Then one day he asked his father for advice, and Guillermo told him to see Miguel Angel Rivas, known as "Kid Pambelé, " a popular Nicaraguan trainer and former welterweight down at Estadio Nacional.

"I started training at Estadio Nacional," said Argüello. "It was my father's idea. I went crying to my dad when I got kicked out of school, and he said, 'Go to the gym and see Pambelé! Maybe you can make something.' I responded, 'What the fuck am I going to do in a boxing gym?'"

Pambelé had a storied history that most Nicaraguans retell with pride. Decades before boxing became popular in Nicaragua, Pambelé traveled from gym to gym throughout Colombia and fought for small purses. No one kept detailed records back then, so as a transient boxer, Pambelé had the freedom to fight in whatever gym or on whatever fight card he wanted without threat of sanctions. He earned a cult status among Nicaraguans. Many guessed he must have amassed more than 250 fights throughout his career. Years later, legendary Colombian boxer and world champion Antonio Cervantes honored Rivas by adopting the nickname Kid Pambelé.

Thus, when Alexis wanted to see where he stood as a boxer, he would eventually turn to Pambelé, who would give his appraisal of the new student and decide if the young fighter was worth his time. At the time, Kid Pambelé was director of the National Boxing School, took on several boxers, and devoted most of his time to the local boxing gyms. Before bringing Argüello in, Pambelé consulted with former boxer Carlos "Kid Varelita" Varela, Sr., to assist him with his analysis.

"I was called by the Director of the National School, Miguel Angel Rivas or 'Kid Pambelé' to watch a sparring session with Alexis and other fighters," Varela recalled. "And he said to me, 'I want your opinion. I want to see if it is worth the time to train this skinny, little kid. I don't want to waste my time.'

"I was surprised. Alexis was using 16-ounce gloves and he knocked out two sparring partners. He knocked both of them out cold. Back then there were a lot of good amateur fighters. But they were not recognized."

Then a trainer, Carlos Varela did not need to observe another sparring session. He had seen enough of this wiry young fighter to understand that fourteen-year-old Argüello had the necessary foundation, and he simply needed polish and experience. In the mid-1960s, having both Pambelé's and Varela's support in Nicaragua meant that, as a boxer, you had potential. Not only did Argüello show the necessary resolve for a teenage boxer, but he also benefited from a significant height advantage over his opponents. In boxing terms, his tall, lanky frame and long reach put every smaller fighter who faced him at a clear disadvantage. If Pambelé and Varela taught him how to use his height and reach against his opponents, Argüello would always be one step ahead of his challengers.

Meanwhile, years before Varela and Pambelé educated Argüello on the subtleties of the fight game, both Argüello's brother Ivan and his brother-in-law Ratón Mojica had begun to toughen up Argüello.

Eduardo "Ratón" Mojica Rueda was a popular local boxer who drove a nice car and could afford the luxuries that Argüello and his friends could only dream of. Mojica, who was married to Marina, Argüello's oldest sibling, had known Argüello since he was five years old. Twelve years Argüello's senior, Mojica was well built, handsome, and aggressive. He began his professional career in 1958 and won his first fifteen bouts. Even though Mojica never won a world championship, the Nicaraguan boxing faithful treat him as if he did.

"Nicaragua never had a champion. An attractive fighter was my brother-in-law Ratón Mojica," said Argüello. "But out of stupidity he never fought for the championship. They offered him $30,000, but he wanted more, instead of winning the title and winning more money. He beat world champion Chartchai Chionoi in that gym [Estadio Nacional] right there in front of 30,000 people. In those days right after you beat a champion, you become a No. 1 contender, and Mojica was offered the money, but he wanted more and he lost the opportunity."

For many people the Mojica name is so deeply linked to Argüello's that some believe that the older fighter's greatest achievement was his ability and willingness to educate the young fighter. In the 1960s, Mojica would bring a teenage

Alexis to the local gym on the Northern Highway and use him as a sparring partner. He did not pull his punches, and this power alarmed Argüello, prompting the young man to complain that Mojica "hits me like I am the enemy." Mojica saw firsthand how timid Argüello could be at times.

"I was responsible for Alexis. When I was married to Marina, I looked at Alexis like my son. He would fight in the street, and also fight at school. Some days, Alexis came crying to me when classmates hit him," Mojica said at a tribute for Argüello in 2011. "I told him, 'When this guy tries to hit you again, hit him right here, [points] in his body. When you do this, you will win the fight.' He went back and started to hit those bullies like I told him to, and they would cry. Sometimes their parents would show up at the door and say, 'Look at what Alexis did to my son!'"

Mojica was merely toughening up Argüello, preparing him for the brutality of the sport, and many believe that he did so on behalf of his wife, Marina, who also showed a protective streak for her younger brother. Mojica would take Argüello to the gym and throw devastating hooks to his ribs in order to acclimate him to the rough environment.

"So he would learn," said Mojica at the tribute on the anniversary of Argüello's death in 2011. "If not, he wouldn't learn. He was heavier than me. My punches were lighter, but despite this he really felt my punches."

To Mojica, it was necessary, for he knew Argüello's opponents would not take mercy on the skinny young boy. Although Argüello understood the struggles his family faced on a daily basis, nothing prepared him for the daily mental and physical grind or the intensity of boxing.

"I became the first coach of [Argüello], because I took him to practice to the Victoria Gymnasium, where the beer company had built me a ring," Mojica recalled.

Argüello later told a reporter: "I used to get into street fights and I was good at it. Ratón took me to the gym and I got very interested in it. I wanted very much to improve myself. I wanted better things and I knew I would have to work very hard at fighting. I wanted to become champion. That was my ambition."

When young Alexis was preparing for a professional career, Mojica was in the throes of his own career. Mojica didn't have the time to expend on Argüello's training, but he realized his talents and called upon Pambelé to finish what he had started.

"When he first started out, Alexis was a bantamweight and he used to box a little bit more. But footwork wasn't his best quality. He tried to move, but he wasn't agile. The first to teach Alexis the basics was his brother," said Varela. "One day Alexis's brother Ivan and Ratón Mojica brought him to Estadio Nacional in pursuit of a boxing career. Mojica and Ivan taught him the fundamentals but could not train him. Mojica came in and told us, 'We cannot properly train Alexis.'"

It wasn't unusual for a professional boxer to help train a good prospect like Argüello. In fact, Mojica continued to provide opportunities for him once Argüello turned professional. His journey to become a world champ had begun. After working in Canada and assisting his father, Argüello knew that there was no room for error. With younger siblings to look out for, Argüello put his faith in Mojica and Pambelé to guide his career.

During his training, Argüello stayed close with his friend Donald Rodriguez and the local boxers with whom he trained. At the time, baseball was the dominant sport in the country, and the neighborhood boys could always be seen playing in the streets or on an open patch of land.

"Donald Rodriguez and Alexis were good friends, but they didn't have any other common interests besides the neighborhood. When you are well known, there are new friends just because you are making something big," said Dr. Eduardo Roman, who became Argüello's manager. "They were friends because they had a very clean type of friendship and because [Donald] knew him before the fame.

"In those neighborhoods, they always had fights. So [Alexis] used to fight; then he was doing it so well that he would defend his older brothers, Guillermo and Ivan. It helped that he had long arms and he would hit very hard."

After evaluating Argüello in the ring, Varela made a clear assessment of the fighter's strengths and weaknesses.

"Back when Alexis started out, his punch was his strength," Varela said. "He had excellent power and assimilation of punches. Also, when he hit, he showed good resistance. He was so strong. His weakness was that he didn't have good footwork. Even through the years, he didn't have good footwork."

The trainers also realized that the five-foot-nine Argüello was extremely tall for fighting out of the bantamweight division (118 pounds), and few boxers would be able to cope with his height and reach. Critics questioned Argüello's lack of strength, but when he turned his weight into his punches, the skinny fighter punched with unbelievable force. Argüello felt comfortable under Pambelé's tutelage and continued to blossom until people had to take notice. In fact, it was not long before he began to refer to Pambelé as "Abuelo," or grandfather.

What separated Argüello from the other amateur boxers was his discipline. Typically, it takes time for a teenage boxer to balance his priorities properly; few teenagers are willing to sacrifice their social lives for the grueling demands of a boxing career. Few Nicaraguan boxers were willing to spend their time and energy on a pursuit that seemed frivolous. Without any government support for boxers, teenagers didn't believe the sport warranted their time.

"I cleaned out all of the natural fighters in Nicaragua," Argüello recalled from the InterContinental Hotel in Managua. "Of course [I always had the punch], that was the remarkable thing: my trainer Kid Pambelé showed me the correct way to throw the punch.

"Kid Pambelé told me, 'It's good to be a good champion, but the idea is not just to win a world championship, but to defend it as much as you can.' He was a fighter, a brawler. He made a good boxer out of me. He was like my father. They don't make guys like that anymore. They're not around anymore. That is what the sport misses."

While eventually he would face the best Nicaraguan prospects of that time— such fighters as Pablo Emilio "Kid Clay" Buitrago and his brother, Mauricio Buitrago—from the start, Argüello showed a discipline and maturity that belied his age. "Since I was beginning as a fighter, that was the promise that I made on my knees to my trainer and my manager," he said, "that I would do whatever they wanted me to do. A man who doesn't have his word . . . is not a man."

Guillermo, his father, took an interest in his son's boxing career and often could be seen sitting in the stands or at the gym monitoring a training session. Conversely, Zoila could not bear to see her son get hurt and often lit candles the nights of his fights and prayed for his safety. According to family associates during that period, Zoila rarely would venture to one of her son's bouts. Whatever money Argüello made from the professional bouts, he would take it to his family. The excessive pressure weighed on Argüello, and from that point, the disciplined behavior that he exhibited went unequaled. He was winning medals and tournaments as he prepared for his first professional bout, but his family relied on his earnings.

"My father told me, 'Alexis, I don't want the medals. Fuck the medals. I want some green bucks,'" said Argüello, laughing. "But I don't blame him. I enjoyed it. I wanted to be somebody. I didn't think that I would get so far. I was so glad that I was so professionally oriented."

His mother, however, was less concerned about the financial aspect. "There's more pride in this business other than only to make the money," she told Alexis.

He recalled, "I gave her the money, and she told me, 'No, no, Alexis. It's not the money; where's your pride? Your pride?' That was a great lesson."

Along with Mojica's assistance, Kid Pambelé did much to develop Argüello during this time. Not only did he and Varela develop Argüello's powerful jab, improve his body punching, and sharpen his uppercut, but they would also buy Argüello fruit after workouts, give him money for sodas and the movies, and even counsel him on avoiding bad habits, specifically cigarettes.

Not everyone was sold on the young fighter, though. Few believed that the bony kid should be allowed to box. It would not take long for Argüello to change their minds. "The first thing I recall was a moment . . . I was a skinny guy and my first fight in Estadio Nacional," said Argüello. "I remember this guy when he saw me coming from my dressing room to the ring. A broadcaster said, 'Don't put this kid in, they're going to break his bones. They're going to break him.' I got scared."

Around this time, during Argüello's initiation into the sport, he received a sign. After returning from an early morning workout session, Argüello, who had never been sick, developed a fever. His entire body began to burn up.

"I promised to Kid Pambelé that I would take good care of myself and a month after that I got sick. I went running and I came back and went to sleep. I woke up two days later with a temperature about 110," Alexis told me in Managua. "I woke up screaming and delirious. The doctor [that Ratón Mojica had brought to give me an injection] said, 'Hey, kid, you're dying.' They put the injection in me and I had this dream that I got into a tunnel. I felt that. In the end I saw a bright light. I got at the light. I don't know what happened. I crossed the light, and then I woke up. I remember that vividly. That right there told me it was meant to be. I hope you understand this. How I led my life, no human could have done it."

Almost as if he was reliving the surreal moment, Argüello continued: "It could be magic. It was part of me."

To the young fighter the entire episode was a sign, a blessing, a test that God wanted him to go through, as he recalled, to "strengthen my body." The light at the end of the tunnel, he felt, was God's way of preparing and strengthening Argüello's slight and fragile build. It was a story that Argüello would tell countless times to show that he was chosen to do something that no one else could possibly accomplish.

Early Bouts: 1968–1974

I wanted to become a champion. This was my ambition.
—ALEXIS ARGÜELLO

It is not unusual for a boxer to engage in hundreds of amateur bouts against fighters who are just as hungry and determined as they are. In fact, some fighters engage in nearly three hundred bouts and enter the professional ranks with a gaudy record compiled over years of amateur status. Often, these bouts can aid or deter a young fighter. While a fighter who wins two hundred bouts in an amateur career can gain the necessary experience heading into his professional career, he can also deteriorate physically from the pounding received in these gym wars. Therefore, once he reaches the professional ranks, he is already damaged goods.

Often, fighters begin boxing at an early age; some even master the jab and hook by age ten. Since Argüello, at sixteen years of age, was a late bloomer, he skipped over this developmental stage completely. An early amateur career would have allowed him to perfect all of the techniques that he learned in the gym with Pambelé. It would have allowed him to learn how to pace himself over each round. However, amateurs could not receive purses, so Argüello felt he had to turn pro. He set his sights on winning prize money and gaining immediate financial help for his family.

Because Argüello often sparred with strong Nicaraguans, he wasn't at a distinct disadvantage once he became a professional in 1968. Boxing cards are usually set months prior to the actual date, but in Nicaragua and throughout Latin America, the bouts often lacked any organization. Argüello's first bout was against "Cachorro" (Puppy) Amaya in León, Nicaragua, on August 1, 1968. Some boxing records do not note his bout with Amaya because it was rare that anyone kept these types of statistics in the late 1960s. Argüello was boxing out of the 118-pound weight class, or bantamweight.

"This guy who offered me $100 to go fight in León, and I went to win the $100 for my mom," said Argüello. "I got knocked out in the first round. I just threw a right hand, and the guy made me miss, and went down and hit me right in my liver. And I didn't get up. I just sat there. I didn't do the right thing because I was only in it for the money. I didn't even take it seriously. I was supposed to be an amateur first, but I didn't do it. I just fought that one and I became pro. I didn't make an amateur career whatsoever."

Nicaraguan sports journalist Edgar Tijerino claimed the fight had little impact on Alexis's career: "No one remembers seeing that fight with Amaya. There are not even records about this fight. It was not an important fight. It was something that happened casually."

His assistant trainer Carlos Varela saw something unique in the fighter: "Even though Alexis lost, people were excited. They saw talent in him. He was a very sensitive boy, and actually I remember he wanted to stop boxing after this loss. We pushed him to keep boxing. We saw talent within him. He was a work in progress."

Argüello faced Israel Medina in Managua on November 18, 1968, and knocked him out in the first round. Argüello earned 100 córdobas as the victor; Medina settled for 80 córdobas in the loss. Nicaraguan promoter and sports broadcaster Evelio Areas had stipulated the specific amounts for the winner and loser of each bout.

"[Alexis] was very nervous before this bout," said Varela. "One of the things he always had was that he was always a little nervous. He came to me and said, 'I feel good, but I am nervous.' I remember Alexis made a mistake in that bout. He threw a right hook and then a right hand, but didn't bring it back in time. Medina threw a return left hook and surprised Alexis. But then Alexis returned with the left hook and right hand to knock Medina out. He finished him with the right hand, but the left hook did the initial damage."

Early on Argüello was fighting without a manager to shape his career. He worked part-time at a local dairy for $70 per month, and then he headed to the gym at 4 p.m. each day to train. The facilities were so poor back then that the arena could barely hold five hundred people. He eventually negotiated a deal with the milk sponsor, La Perfecta, and advertised for the company by wearing its name on his boxing robe. Argüello would also be sponsored by the electric company.

On December 14, 1968, Argüello won a four-round split-decision victory over Oscar Espinosa. He won his next bout by knocking out Burrito Martinez on January 25.

Argüello had to take something positive from each bout in order to grow as a fighter. Most fighters start boxing at age nine or ten and essentially spend their childhood near the bags; for Alexis, boxing came as a last recourse so his family wouldn't starve. Unlike most fighters who lacked the intense discipline needed to stay afloat in the sport, Argüello immediately looked at the sport as his job. Most young fighters move in and out of the gym at their own pace, but Argüello made a promise to his family and his trainers and vowed to keep it. So when Pambelé and Carlos Varela explained to Argüello that he gained something valuable from each loss, he listened. Although it wasn't an easy sell to a fighter down on his luck, Argüello refused to give up.

After beating Oscar Espinosa in December 1968, Argüello fell by split decision to him four months later on April 26, 1969, in Estadio Nacional. Espinosa, or the Scorpion, was a good technical fighter who moved well, and had better conditioning than Argüello at that time. Perhaps that fight sparked Argüello's competitiveness, because he didn't lose another bout until 1972. The streak gave him added confidence and ignited a fervor throughout Nicaragua that people hadn't seen since Ratón Mojica's early success. In 1969, Argüello also married his girlfriend, Silvia Urbina, a decision that his friends and family felt he rushed into. As Argüello noted, however, it was "love at first sight." Despite the financial pressures they faced, Urbina understood the sacrifices that her new husband had to make. In July and August 1970, Alexis decisioned Carlos Huete and then knocked out Ricardo Donoso in two rounds.

Still searching for a big payday, Argüello looked to Mojica to help him find his next bout. In September 1970, Mojica was preparing to fight Adolfo Osses in San José, Costa Rica. Costa Rican boxing promoter Levy Canne needed fighters to fill out his fight card, and Mojica suggested Argüello. Canne needed a challenger to fight lightweight Marcelino Beckles, but in boxing circles it was believed that no Nicaraguan fighter was on his level. This fact created a rift among Mojica, Pambelé, and boxing promoter Evelio Areas. While Mojica made his case to Areas, stressing that Argüello had a unique ability to resist punches and deserved a shot, Areas still questioned whether Argüello was experienced enough for a fighter of Beckles's caliber. For the fight, Mojica lent Argüello his boots and a gorgeous robe from Australia. In return, Argüello turned back naysayers and passed his first real test as he battled past the six-round bouts he was accustomed to and won by an eight-round technical knockout. For his performance, Argüello earned his biggest purse yet of $600. Miguel Angel Arcia, the author of *Alexis: La Leyenda*, noted that throughout the bout Argüello was in severe pain due to the boxing boots that he had borrowed from Ratón Mojica.

"He got good money for that fight, but he and Mojica went behind the backs of the commission and everyone else for that bout," said Varela. "Neither myself nor Pambelé went with him for this fight. Mojica came and took him to Costa Rica, and Alexis boxed well. He was a young guy, so what could we do? He was trying to get out of poverty. He realized this was his chance to do that."

Mojica, who lost a ten-round decision to Adolfo Osses that evening, recalled the coming-out party atmosphere for Argüello. "Levy Canne, the Costa Rican promoter, came to Nicaragua. He was looking for someone to fight at bantamweight. I told Evelio Areas that Alexis could fight him, and he started yelling, 'He's going to get killed. You have no idea who Marcelino Beckles is! Beckles, an international star, will kill him.' Since [Alexis] was my brother-in-law and he could withstand my punches, I had one-hundred percent confidence in him. But we ended up making the fight, and I had to give Alexis my boots, because he had none. He stops Beckles in eight rounds, and the next day in the newspapers, it said something like 'One candle burns, while another one dies.' I don't know why."

Many Nicaraguan sportswriters identify the bout with Beckles as a turning point in Argüello's career. By knocking out an experienced fighter, Argüello put himself at the pinnacle of Nicaraguan boxing and earned recognition from critics.

"When Ratón went to fight in Costa Rica with Adolfo, he asked for Alexis to be on that card to fight on the undercard. I went to this fight, and Beckles was a big favorite. When Alexis won, that was when we started the friendship," said sportswriter Edgar Tijerino. "The key was that Alexis actually won the bout and that, at the time, Costa Ricans thought Beckles was supposed to have a great future."

Argüello, who sparred with locals Mario Martinez, Luis Cortes, and Francisco "Toro" Coronado, walked through his next four challengers: Mario Bojorge, José Urbina, Julio Morales, and Armando Figueroa. By this time, the eighteen-year-old Argüello was fighting ten rounders. Every fighter needs to progress slowly from four- to six- to eight- to ten-round bouts and build up stamina and to gain experience so that when they fight twelve- and fifteen-round bouts, they will be prepared both mentally and physically to handle the grind. Despite a few mishaps in earlier bouts in his career, Argüello had entered a comfort zone. By going undefeated in 1971, Argüello gained the momentum he desperately needed. Fans thoroughly enjoyed Argüello's two consecutive ten-round unanimous decision victories over Julio "Ratón" Hernandez in March and April 1971.

"Those were great fights," said Varela. "They were classics because they went after each other round after round. In those two fights, Alexis couldn't knock him out. You never saw one boxer clinch. Alexis had a better jab and overall boxing skills, but Hernandez was a warrior."

Edgar Tijerino added: "In those wars, neither fighter stopped punching."

Unfortunately, it wasn't unusual for Argüello to knock out his close friends or the guys with whom he had trained. He knocked out brothers Mauricio and Kid Clay Buitrago over a two-month span and then would face another close friend Ray Mendoza on September 4, 1971.

When Argüello fought Mauricio Buitrago on May 1, 1971, people had already begun to marvel at his skills. Hernandez had forced Argüello to the limit, and many people believed that Buitrago also had showcased excellent qualities. Yet he only lasted seven rounds against Argüello's vaunted left hook. "Me and Alexis were friends; it was like a brotherhood with the local boxers. In fact I knew him for six years before we got into the ring. Me and Alexis had the same style. He was a very good fighter," said Buitrago from a Nicaraguan gym. "I sparred with my brother to prepare for this fight. I was very careful. In the first three rounds, it was calm, but we became more assertive after the fifth round."

Three fights later, Argüello faced the other Buitrago. Each national prospect presented some problem for Argüello, but few were as dangerous as Kid Clay. Despite making a valiant effort, Clay could not avoid Argüello's left hook and went down in the third round. Argüello jarred loose two teeth early in the fight. The punch opened a cut over Kid Clay's left eyebrow, and eventually Dr. Rodrigo Portocarrero stopped the fight in the fifth round.

"Clay had a very unorthodox style that gave Alexis trouble so the fight was not a technical fight," said Carlos Varela. "This was a tough fight from the beginning to the end. For that fight, Kid Pambelé, myself, and Efraín López Galeano were in Alexis's corner."

Years later, Mendoza said, "[The Buitrago brothers] were fighters who really prepared themselves, and they were strong and had the guts to be boxers and prove themselves. "They didn't step into the ring only to win money. They stepped into the ring to win money and the fight. Those were the types of fighters that were in Nicaragua in those times."

When Argüello walked into the ring to fight his close friend Ray Mendoza on September 4, 1971, he already had eighteen wins against two losses. Argüello was familiar with Mendoza because they trained together. Although Pambelé trained both fighters, he made an agreement to work with Argüello for that bout. Argüello needed four rounds to dispose of Mendoza.

"Mendoza was a southpaw [difficult to fight] and there was this impressive thing," remembered Varela. "Alexis hit Mendoza with this left hook and knocked him out in the fourth round. The punch confirmed to us that Alexis could hit with power with both hands."

At a tribute to Argüello in 2011, Mendoza recalled the day he fought the legend. "Yes, I didn't want to fight him, and he didn't want to fight me, because we were great friends, but the the shrewd promoter, Evelio Arias Mendoza, who's a bit old now, wanted to turn us into a rivalry, and that's why we fought," said Mendoza, who trained with Tony Huerta for the bout. "We didn't want to fight, but we did, and he beat me. He bested me and won the fight."

Mendoza continued, "It was a very emotional fight for me. I was beating him until the third round, but I changed the fight plan we had—that we prepared for him—and I started boxing him in the fourth round. Then, with his long reach, and that size, he measured me and measured me, and he hit me with a one-two."

That revelation excited Argüello's cornermen and supporters but frightened his opponents because it meant that he no longer had to rely on one punch to hurt his opponent. Few boxers could boast about having power in both hands, and this development meant that Argüello was maturing. After easily knocking out Mendoza, Argüello met his toughest challenger, Kid Clay, in a rematch on October 2, 1971, and ended up with a ten-round unanimous decision victory. Argüello had aggravated a prior injury in his left hand early in the bout and showed his courage by fighting the last couple rounds with only his right hand.

Back in the ring two months later, Argüello made quick work of Panamanian Vicente Worrel Jr. Then Argüello only needed three total rounds to knock out Guillermo Barrera and Rafael González.

Just when it appeared that Argüello had begun to mature, he encountered a setback. Dealing with the stress and tumultuous ebb and flow of a professional boxing career is one thing, but a hand injury can completely derail a fighter's career and disrupt any psychological edge he may have. For Argüello, the hand injury he suffered in his next bout would prove nearly catastrophic. On January 14, 1972, Argüello fought Mexican Jorge Reyes, who came into the bout with a record of six wins and four losses. Argüello was winning the bout early on, but he broke his left hand in the second round. By the sixth round, the hand was useless. The bout was recorded as a sixth-round knockout victory for Reyes.

"In the first six rounds, Alexis was winning the bout, and I think that he could have beaten him with one hand, but Dr. Martin Flütsch did not think so, so he stopped the fight," said Edgar Tijerino, who covered the bout. "The way that his cornermen covered his hands made him fragile. They did not do it the right way. He had surgery and they put a plate [a platinum wire] in his hand. Dr. Jaime Granera said that after the surgery, Alexis could fight."

Trainer Carlos Varela saw firsthand how passionate Argüello was for the sport: "He was out-of-control crying because he injured his hand so badly. He thought his career was over and he was crying on my shoulder. I told him, 'No kid, we'll get you a good doctor and you will have a good career. This is not the end.'"

Former member of the Nicaraguan Boxing Commission Sergio Quintero recalled, "During the fight in the fourth and fifth rounds he broke his hand, but because of his enormous pride, Alexis kept fighting and wanted to finish the fight. I thought his career was personally over. Thanks to orthopedic surgeon Dr. Jaime Granera Soto, he was able to fix his hand, which was broken in two places."

After the bout against Reyes, Argüello traveled to see Dr. Granera at San Vincent de Paul Hospital located in León. He had broken two knuckles on two fingers of his left hand. Granera put Argüello's hand in a cast for the next four weeks. Argüello suffered the same injury again when he returned to the ring, and he went back to Granera for consultation. This time, Argüello underwent a second surgery, in which Granera installed a small nail in Argüello's finger and cut off a bone from his pelvis to apply to the knuckle for support. Although Granera's timeline becomes distorted, as Argüello never took more than three months off from the ring, clearly Granera had a major impact on Argüello's career. Later, to show his appreciation, Argüello would buy a refrigerator for the San Vincent de Paul Hospital and bring the world championship trophy to Granera.

"Alexis came to me when he was 20 years old, and told me, 'I want to be an example for the youth and new generations,'" said Granera.

If anything, Argüello showed his fans his capacity to absorb and cope with extreme punishment. Fighters who can handle adversity early in their careers show a greater capacity later on, and this case was true with Argüello. As he progressed, his resistance to pain became one of his legendary traits. "During the time when he came back, Alexis was a little scared to throw his left hand," Varela recalled. "Then, Granera taught me how to wrap his hands (and protect them), and after that Alexis began to let go during training."

Other issues plagued Argüello's life, which his broken hand only exacerbated. He was struggling through the worst financial crisis in his life and, at times, actually had to stick his hand in an ashtray to pry a quarter from the bottom of it.

Argüello waited almost two months for his hand to heal, and Granera had done an excellent job. Argüello thanked him and assuaged his fans' worries, quickly dispatching Fernando Fernandez in August and Jorge Benitez in September in his return bouts. The new boxing dynamo's supporters breathed a collective sigh of relief as Argüello clearly had not lost any of his power since the Reyes incident.

ROUND 3

A Second Father

Alexis used to introduce me as his father.

—Dr. Eduardo Roman, vice president of ENALUF

It all started with a book on World War II.

Well, not exactly, but the relationship between Dr. Eduardo Roman—the vice president of Empresa Nacional de Luz y Fuerza (ENALUF), the national power and light company in Nicaragua—and the future world champ nearly didn't happen. In Nicaragua in the 1960s and 1970s, it was common for a wealthy businessman to search out athletes like Argüello in an attempt to manage them. These relationships between businessmen and athletes often begin with a journalist acting as a go-between. In 1968, wealthy landowner Carlos Eleta was enticing the Panamanian boxing hero Roberto Durán in a similar manner. Elsewhere, investors pooled their money in order to support a fighter financially, as in the cases of Muhammad Ali and "Sugar" Ray Leonard.

Unlike some boxing insiders who followed the sport religiously, Dr. Roman didn't grow up with any real understanding of the fight game. Dr. Roman was born in Jinotepe, in the southwestern part of the Nicaraguan Diriamba Highlands, but after his parents divorced, he spent most of his childhood with his grandmother's family in the picturesque city of Masaya. Roman's family owned coffee plantations and cattle ranches; politically, the family was split on Somoza supporters and the opposition. Although Roman eventually earned his doctorate in economics at Indiana University–Bloomington in the United States, in his early days at the military academy in Nicaragua he established key contacts with the hierarchy of the Panamanian military. After getting his degree in the United States, Roman returned to Nicaragua. He eventually became vice president of ENALUF; however, before long he branched off into boxing. Roman had only boxed once when he was a curious eighty-eight-pounder practicing at a local gym. When the sport piqued his interest again as an adult, he had to start from scratch.

For all intents and purposes, Dr. Eduardo Roman, who was married to Miriam Lacayo, saw all he had to see in a three-round bout in Estadio Nacional in 1970. Days afterward, he approached Argüello, who eventually grew to love his new benefactor unconditionally. Back then, Roman had an intermediary bring the confident teenage future champ into his office so he could propose an offer. However, it didn't go as smoothly as Roman planned.

"In Nicaragua, we used to have some old boxers who were very well known. Pambelé was a welterweight. We had another fighter named Francois González, who was more of a stylist. They would travel around Central America to win fights. The problem was that boxers didn't get very good help, and they weren't disciplined people," said Roman from his home in Laguna de Apoyo. "At that time I thought about getting a boxer who had good discipline and who was dedicated. So I found this thin guy named Alexis Argüello.

"No one told me about him; the news reporters were to blame, because they used to write that he was a big, explosive guy. Then I went to see him. And he was good."

According to testimony that Argüello gave Miguel Angel Arcia in his biography *Alexis: La Leyenda*, the fighter nearly walked out on Roman after a three-hour wait because he felt that a future world champ should not be kept waiting. Roman brought him back and offered to pay him handsomely in exchange for his dedication to and focus on the sport. Roman had witnessed the downfall of too many young fighters, so in return the only thing he demanded was Argüello's willingness to sacrifice and train hard.

"I was vice-president of ENALUF and Dr. Martin Flütsch was the doctor for the boxing federation. Dr. Martin Flütsch was studying medicine in Mexico while I was also studying in Mexico. We were friendly. He wanted to help Alexis and to bring him here to get help," Roman recalled. "I went to one fight and I saw Alexis and I thought he had a good possibility because he was thin and tall and hit hard. I told Flütsch, 'Give this guy this card and tell him to look for me.' And he went to look for me two days later. When he came to see me I asked him, 'What are you doing besides fighting?' And he told me he was working for his father. I told him he won't work anymore, but he will train hard."

Argüello agreed. They shook hands, and a lifelong friendship had begun. From the outset, Roman wanted to make it clear that he cared more about Alexis the man than Alexis the fighter. He also understood that he was dealing with a fighter whose confidence inside the ring belied a sensitive soul outside of it. Argüello took everything to heart. He was the antithesis of Roberto Durán, another Latin American icon who was also growing in popularity in nearby Panama.

"I was with him [Alexis] since he was 18 years old . . . ," said Dr. Eduardo Roman. "I asked him where he lived and what did he make. He told me 300 córdobas per month. But he didn't have a manager at the time. He was paid by the people who made the fight. When I got him he was no longer fighting three- or six-rounders. Now he was fighting ten-rounders. I told him that I would pay him 1,500 córdobas and the 300 córdobas [for training purposes] and would get him a trainer. We started that way until the end. I never charged him anything, not the 33 percent that managers normally do."

A great manager doesn't have to be a boxing historian or even an astute boxing analyst. In fact, a good boxing manager doesn't even have to be a boxing fan. A good manager needs to understand the mind-set of the teenage kid in front of him, gain his trust, and understand exactly what people to put around that fighter in order for him to succeed. Roman helped shape Alexis the man without infringing upon the Alexis the fighter, but the process wasn't always easy.

"I tried to teach him how to act outside the ring, and how to behave with people, but he always had good behavior and was very gentlemanly," said Roman. "He learned how to become a gentleman in the ring. He even learned English."

Roman bought Argüello books, encouraged him to learn to speak English, and effectively shaped his boxing career with experienced opponents. Roman prided himself on never taking advantage of his fighter. He refused to accept the typical 33 percent most managers take, but instead settled for travel and hotel expenses. Showing his appreciation, Argüello would often say, "He is everything to me—father, friend, manager. I fight to see the happy look on his face when I win."

"I will never forget this as long as I live," Argüello told a reporter. "The first thing Dr. Roman gave me was not a contract to be my manager—we still have no contract—but it was a book about the Second World War, because he knew I always wanted to read."

Roman wanted to develop Argüello's mind. He facilitated the young fighter's return to school, where he eventually earned his high school degree.

"Ruben Dario Pastora was the director of the San Francisco high school in Nicaragua. That school received all of the students who were expelled from other schools. Alexis passed, but he did not do that well," Roman recalled. "The press attacked the school and him for accepting him. Because they considered that you need to get five years of high school in order to pass, but he didn't do that. He got to fourth or fifth grade in primary school, and then I helped him to get reenrolled."

His plan paid dividends as Argüello progressed from a skilled boxer to an introspective icon. What separated Argüello from other fighters was his capacity to obtain, process, and continually learn new information.

"He was a poor boy and he needed all the salary I gave him. Sometimes I would give him money when he needed it. They were a poor family. He had a scar on the back of his hand. It was made by one of his brothers. When they were eating, Alexis tried to get a piece of meat from the dish of one of his brothers, and his brother stabbed his hand. He was hungry. That is the condition of a lot of people in this country," said Roman. "They don't know what they have to do to eat. They don't know what happens to them when they get sick. They don't know how to live. Poverty is something that for people who have never experienced it, they can never understand it. I know these poor people. We have a coffee plantation, and I used to go around and see what these people ate. It is unbelievable. Some people never see the people or things I see."

Even after his early losses, Argüello knew exactly what he needed to do differently. Most fighters don't have that ability or willingness to assess a bad performance and learn from it. If Argüello had let an early loss set him back emotionally, then he might never have achieved greatness.

"I gave him books, because he was intelligent but not very knowledgeable. I noticed his intelligence, memory, and reasoning. I wanted him to get the necessary culture. You might notice the difference between his answers in the beginning of his career and in the end," said Dr. Roman. "Even if he was not a boxer, he would have made the highest point in any career, but many Nicaraguans didn't or don't have the help he did. Without my help, he probably would have had three fights and you would never have heard of him. In this underdeveloped world, we don't have infrastructure."

In order for Argüello to face strong opposition, Roman needed to negotiate with the current promoter, Roger Riguero, who promoted fights at Arena Kennedy on Panama America Highway. Roman recalled, "I asked the promoter Riguero, 'Why don't you get some better fights for Alexis so he will be able to fight ranked boxers and be ranked himself?' But he told me no, because he was making plenty of money on Alexis already. 'All right,' I said to him. 'Get better fighters. If you lose money, I'll make up the difference.'"

Roman continued, "Riguero used to exploit the fighters. He used to pay them cents, nothing. I remember one time seeing a fighter walking on the highway after a fight and he was hitchhiking. I told him, 'Take this money, get a cab and go to my office tomorrow.'"

Argüello fought and annihilated Cuban José Legrá on November 24, 1973. At the time Legrá had fought more than a hundred bouts and had earned a No. 1 ranking. In fact, he recently fought and lost a close decision to Eder Jofre that May. So everyone was shocked when Argüello deposited him with relative ease.

"Against José Legrá, Alexis hit him so hard in the second round that the guy collapsed, that he bounced completely off the canvas," said Varela. "He bounced up, lifted his head off the canvas, and then bounced back down. It was the condition of Alexis that stood out. He always had superior condition. When he faced tough Mexican fighters like Sigfrido Rodríguez, he kept fighting. Rodriguez was a seasoned fighter . . . who gave Alexis as good as he got."

Leading up to that climactic encounter with Legra, Argüello faced the best fighters Mexico had to offer. Prior to Argüello's memorable bout with Sigfrido Rodríguez, a tall resilient fighter, where he knocked the Mexican down seven times, the future world champ destroyed Mexican Octavio Gómez on June 30, 1973. "It was the most spectacular knockout," said Varela. "He hit Gomez so hard with a left hook that he actually lifted him off the canvas. Gomez actually landed on his shoulder blades when he hit the canvas. The photo was all over *La Prensa*." From the end of 1972 to the beginning of 1974, Argüello went 12-0, with eleven knockouts. Yet, the younger fighter still experienced brief setbacks as he was knocked down in the first round by unknown Nacho Lomeli on August 25, 1973. Both he and Lomeli shared a "Rocky" moment as they landed the punch at the same time and both hit the canvas simultaneously. Pambelé frantically turned to Varela, "Alexis is on the floor. Alexis is on the floor." Yet, Argüello appeased his corner when he got up at the count of four and quickly dispatched Lomeli with a right hand.

"We were so surprised, and referee Ferny Carpentier started to count with both hands as both men lay on the canvas," said trainer Varela. At this point everyone had fallen in love with the young prospect. What made it easier for the Argüello camp was that Alexis was so willing to learn. When his trainer asked him to throw a punch a certain way, he did it; when he was asked to get up at 5 a.m. to run for forty-five minutes, he ran for two hours. Although Argüello's father still had an impact on his life, Argüello also showed the utmost respect and appreciation for Roman's interest in him. Most looked to the Famoso Gomez,

Legra, and Rodriguez fights as evidence of Argüello's growth, but it was his bout with Kid Pascualito in the midst of his knockout streak that provided him a world ranking. Varela commented, "I told him, 'Tonight you will be ranked. Don't follow me and Ratón Mojica and waste your money.' And he didn't. In fact, he wouldn't pay a sparring partner unless they finished the round."

"If he wasn't clear about something, I would tell him to retell it to me," said Roman. "There are millions of fighters who don't use their brains; this was not the case of Argüello. He understood. When we asked him to train, he would do two times what we asked. I eventually told him, 'Alexis, I want you to be a boxer, not a runner.'"

During this period, Argüello faced his most lethal opponent. The date of December 23, 1972, will forever be remembered as as a night when thousands of Nicaraguans lost everything. That evening, Christmas lights dotted the trees, jolly Santa Clauses filled the streets, and people relished the thought of celebrating the joyous holiday. Nobody could have planned for what was to come; nobody could have comprehended the possible repercussions. An unbearable heat wave stifled Nicaragua as families made their final preparations for the Christmas holiday. As the crowds emptied from the downtown stores and made their way home, they had no reason for concern. Typical of Nicaraguans' passion for parties, the Christmas season was filled with late-night cocktails, raucous storytelling, singing, and impromptu poems from a country of poets.

Argüello woke up before midnight and took his newborn son, Alexis Junior (A. J.), into his room to sleep in the bed with him and his wife, Silvia. It was an act that would save his son's life. After a false alarm minutes earlier, at 12:40 a.m., an earthquake measuring 6.2 on the Richter scale shattered the lives of the 300,000 inhabitants of Managua, the Nicaraguan capital. A. J.'s crib was crushed completely, and only one room of the Argüellos' house was left standing as Argüello took Silvia and his son and sprinted out to the street. Across town, the Argüello family home, made of wood, did not suffer the same fate.

Nicaraguan writer Gioconda Belli, who lived in an apartment near Lake Managua, recalled the damage in her memoir, The Country Under My Skin: "The pavement was undulating, as if riding on the back of a slithering serpent . . . overhead a sinister moon shone, huge and orange in a sky that glowed red from the fires. It felt like the sun had plunged into the city." Belli, who lived in a middle-class neighborhood, helplessly looked for answers.

Ten thousand people died. Argüello and 275,000 countrymen were left homeless. It was the second earthquake in forty-one years; the previous one in

1931 had left 2,000 people dead and caused $70 million in damages. Although the capital returned to normal after the first earthquake, to this day it has not recovered fully from the 1972 disaster. Argüello's home, which he had purchased with his purse earnings, was in ruins. He went to see his new manager and father figure, Dr. Eduardo Roman, for advice and a loan.

"When I met him, he was married to a woman named Silvia, and they had a very hard life," recalled Roman. "After the first and second times he came to see me, they had the earthquake in 1972. The house completely collapsed, and he came over to see me and said, 'I need some help to get a new house.' I asked him how much he needed and he said $140. I gave him $140 to buy the same type of house he once had."

Argüello and his countrymen could only cling to memories; meanwhile, he and his people relied on each other for support as the charred remains piled up around the city. Families with enough money to travel fled to coastal towns such as Granada to recover. Argüello was one of the fortunate Nicaraguans who had help and could one day rebuild his home on the same land where the house had collapsed. A day after the earthquake, as Nicaraguans assessed the damages, a local man crystallized the desperation of the people when he said, "What can we say now? Nicaragua needs everything. Water, food, medicine, blood, and so far all of Central America and Latin America is bringing help as fast as they can." Nearly three-fourths of the capital had succumbed to either the quake or the subsequent fires. Juan Castenera, manager of the Communications Satellite Corporation's station nearby, summed it up when he told newsmen that the devastation was like "the end of the world."

Many Nicaraguans feared another earthquake would occur. Argüello took his family between Urbina's family's home in Estelí and one of Dr. Roman's homes over the next couple of months. Three months later, Argüello returned to the capital on March 30, 1973, to knock out Fernando Fernandez, and he continued the torrid pace by knocking out six of his next seven opponents. "After the earthquake he lived in Estelí in the northern part of Nicaragua. He lived there because by then he already had a son and he was afraid that something might happen to his house in Nicaragua," said longtime friend Donald Rodriguez. "A lot of people from Managua went to other cities because they were afraid of another earthquake, but then he came back, started training again, and life continued on." In order to build up a budding prospect in boxing properly, it is essential to pit the fighter against a host of easy opponents and then slowly move him to fight better competition. As Argüello headed into 1974 with a record of thirty wins and three losses, he had fought well enough to earn a bout with a legitimate top-ten challenger. Having already fought the best fighters Nicaragua had to offer, Argüello was mentally and physically ready to face elite fighters. One of those elite fighters in the mid-1970s was World Boxing Association (WBA) featherweight champion Ernesto "Ñato" Marcel.

After acclimating Argüello to eight- and ten-round fights, Dr. Roman used his influence in Panama to negotiate a title bout with Marcel, one of that country's most underrated fighters, but "move, chase, miss" would become an unfortunate theme throughout the evening. However, the Marcel negotiations did not go off without a hitch. Before securing the bout with Marcel, Roman had to agree to pay $7,000 to Filipino southpaw Bert Nabalatan to step aside. Riguero had signed Argüello to face Nabalatan during the final months of 1973, but when the Marcel opportunity surfaced, Argüello's camp scrambled to make the title bout their first priority. With little boxing acumen or background, Roman called upon a former classmate, Rubén Darío Paredes, who helped promote the sport of boxing in Panama and one day would become that country's military leader. To Roman, Panama and Mexico had created the ideal boxing blueprint for the rest of Central America to follow. Having grown close to several members of the Panamanian military while at the military university in Nicaragua, Roman felt he had more political power in Panama than in his own country, and he often leaned on them for advice.

"I was at the military academy in 1953 and my class was 1953–1957 and I had many Panamanian friends. Some of them were in second class, third class, fourth class, and the last class. I didn't graduate there because I left the military academy, but I had a good friendship with all of them except General Omar Torrijos," said Roman. "Well, in the second class, there were many Panamanians who were the best people under Omar Torrijos years later. My classmate was Rubén Darío Paredes, who was the right hand of Torrijos, and before that there was General (Florencio) Flores. Paredes was number 567, and I was number 568. We had a good relationship."

Roman wanted to ensure that Argüello had access to the best boxing minds, so Roman also called his cousin Edgar Escobar Fornos, who worked at the Nicaraguan Embassy in Mexico, to recommend a good but affordable trainer. Days later, Escobar sent him Mexican Pepe Morales as head trainer to work with Kid Pambelé and Carlos Varela and prepared Argüello for his next fight. Morales took Argüello to Panama City, Panama, two weeks early so he could become acclimated to the heat and hostile environment. Roman explained his decision to bring in Morales within the context of helping his career: "Look, Alexis, Pambelé taught you the basics. You need someone to take you to the next level, like you were going to the University."

In boxing circles, Marcel, whose manager was Panamanian promoter Harmodio Icaza, had fought valiantly. Despite a controversial technical knock-out loss to his countryman Roberto Durán in May 1970, he returned to prominence when he outboxed Antonio Gomez over fifteen rounds in Maracay, Venezuela, on August 19, 1972, to win the WBA featherweight title. Now he had to defend the crown.

A gifted athlete, Marcel embodied and, at times, perfected the skills that had eluded Argüello to this point in his career. Ñato (pug nose) grew up on Fourth Street and Bolivar in Colón, Panama. Marcel's real education came from the spirited basketball and boxing lessons he received from the country's finest athletes. Many claimed Colón was the "Cradle of Champions," and Marcel reflected the skilled athletes who hailed from this coastal town. Despite his prowess in basketball, Marcel harnessed his energy toward boxing.

There was no better place to hone his skills than the boxing hotbed of Colón. The province had a knack for hatching and matching the finest boxers in Panama, and Marcel started in the back of the line of fabulous boxers. With help from trainer Felipe Vega and the boxer Pedro "Manhattan Kid" Ortiz, Marcel entered the amateur ranks when he was sixteen years old in the minimumweight, or 105-pound weight, class. Now, as he was closing out his career, he was a world champion at 126 pounds. Marcel even made a promise through the press: "This will be my last bout." It was a bold statement, and some questioned its validity.

As soon as Roman began to manage Argüello, he must have envisioned an eventual showdown with the Panamanian Marcel. Roman had cultivated a strong relationship with Dr. Elias Córdoba, president of the World Boxing Association, which was located in Panama. Panama's military leaders Rubén Dario Paredes and Omar Torrijos helped him cement the long-awaited title bout. The bout against Argüello was scheduled for February 16, 1974, and Marcel was making his fourth title defense of his WBA 126-pound featherweight title. In preparation for the bout, Argüello sparred with his brother and skilled boxer Orlando, Peru's Armando Torres, Panama's Rafael Ortega, Mexico's Juan Martinez, and Nicaraguans Luis Cortés and Miguel Angel Arcia, while Varela, Pambelé, and Pepe Morales worked his corner as trainers. Nicaraguan Luis Cortés was also fighting on the card. Cortés, a good friend of Argüello's, would eventually move from working as Argüello's sparring partner to his second assistant when the

Varelas no longer worked in the corner. "Cortés and Alexis respected each other because they came up at about the same time," said Varela Sr. The bout would take place in the stifling heat of the New Panama Arena in Panama City. Marcel walked into the bout at 39-4-2 with twenty-three knockouts, against a host of experienced opponents, while Argüello, 36-3, had built his impressive record knocking out Nicaraguan prospects. Marcel was Argüello's first true test that would show where he belonged in the 126-pound division. Marcel would earn $80,000 for the Argüello bout, his highest purse since the $50,000 he had earned in the rematch against Antonio Gómez. Argüello settled for $7,500.

At the weigh-in, which back then was conducted the day of the bout to avoid any significant weight gain, a controversy arose. Argüello's trainer Pambelé began to argue with some Panamanian military figures over Marcel's weight. During that time, Gen. Omar Torrijos had his men "oversee" the proceedings. The military and the athletes had to coexist; financially, it was a glorious time for professional sports in Panama. When looking back on the events that transpired, camps recall different scenarios.

"This fight was irregular because Marcel didn't make weight," said Varela. "But because a lot of people were involved, the fight happened. That's what a lot of people don't know. The people from Panama argued with Pambelé. The military guys told him to shut up. And that's the truth. A lot of money was involved." Varela continued: "Things like that happened back then. It was not strange. Roman didn't say anything because he was a rookie. He was still learning his craft."

In a typical title fight where one of the fighters comes in significantly overweight, the camps get together and come up with a compromise. Usually, the champ immediately loses his belt, despite the outcome of the bout, and has to pay a hefty fee to his opponent for not making weight. Argüello, the challenger, had little, if any, leverage. The bout took place on Marcel's turf, and Argüello was forced to comply with his rules. In other words, Roman wanted to learn from his Panamanian counterparts and use these connections later. Causing dissension before the fight could fracture his close ties with the Panamanians. Despite Pambelé's objections, Roman denied seeing anything corrupt about the way the weigh-in was conducted.

"I heard they sometimes put their foot on the back of the scale, tricks like that," said Roman. "But I didn't see anything like that during the weigh-in. They were very professional."

After the weight conflict faded, Argüello, at 122½ pounds, walked into the ring. He appeared gaunt and awkward compared to the stockier, yet smaller champion, Marcel, who entered at 125¾ pounds.

From the opening bell, Marcel relied on his usual ring tricks, which had served him well in his previous forty-five bouts. Over the first two rounds, Marcel the professor shimmied his shoulders, danced, and used his speed and experience to bottle up the dangerous challenger. Relying on a lead right to offset the incoming Argüello, the champ eluded powerful blows with ease. If Argüello had only one speed, Marcel had five gears and shifted when necessary. Marcel was busy providing the boxing lesson that Argüello, now age twenty-two, sorely needed. In order for Argüello to learn how to approach a bout with a slick, skilled fighter, he had to get through Marcel.

Argüello, the student, showed he was mentally prepared for championship-caliber fights in the third round when he hurt Marcel and forced him to seek shelter along the ropes. The Nicaraguan contingent screamed as Argüello patiently placed hooks in Marcel's ribs. Not to be out done, Marcel bullied Argüello and jammed him with four vicious uppercuts, as if to remind the young fighter that this bout was his show. The brilliant third round reflected the theme of the evening: Argüello had the ability to do in the ring what Marcel had already perfected.

Fighting at a blistering pace, Marcel moved to his right and counterpunched to offset Argüello's strength. Argüello was still raw and immature and had yet to grow into his 126-pound frame. In the sixth round, inexperience reigned as Argüello allowed Marcel to square up against him and potshot him at will. Tailor-made for Marcel, Argüello continued to absorb a consistent beating a round later. If Argüello had not experienced hell in a boxing ring before, Marcel presented him an up close and personal snapshot.

Against Marcel, Argüello said he "realized that it wasn't strength, but intelligence that commands in the ring. One round cannot be the same; they vary. You have to use strategy and brilliance to hit, and not get hit, when you become a master, and I accomplished that [later on]." As Roman watched his fighter get outclassed, he was busy cementing his fighter's future plans.

Although Argüello showed flashes of brilliance, he could not sustain the pace for fifteen rounds. He fought in spurts, which meant that although he nearly knocked out Marcel on two occasions, he couldn't string several spectacular rounds together. With this bout, one of boxing's tenets—a challenger can't come into a world champ's hometown and win by decision—also held true. In other words, Argüello knew that he needed to knock out Marcel in order to become his country's first world champ. Midway through the bout, however, Argüello faced adversity.

"In that fight in the eighth round, Alexis came back to the corner and he was crying because he said he couldn't move. We kicked the Mexican trainer Morales out of the ring and took over. We told him, 'That's it. We're taking over.' We took the stool out from under Argüello, and kept him standing for the rest of the bout, and kept massaging his legs with cold water," said Varela.

"Alexis didn't want to continue. I told him, 'Are you crazy? Nice people paid a lot of money for this. You're not going to fight? You don't have any pride.' I pushed him back in the ring."

Whatever his corner did to motivate Argüello between rounds worked. Argüello ravaged Marcel's body in the eighth and had him reeling in the ninth. Broken, exhausted, and trying to survive, Marcel's refusal to engage stunned the partisan crowd. No longer was he the confident champ looking to end his career with one final masterpiece; now, he clinched, threw harmless punches, and tried desperately to find his second wind. If Marcel appeared desperate in the two previous rounds, he was nearly out on his feet in the tenth as Argüello landed thirteen unabated punches to end the round. By all accounts, clearly the belt would change hands.

Critics who claimed that Argüello was too immature for the crafty Marcel were quiet by the eleventh round, but then Marcel, revived and hungry, resurfaced in the final three rounds to dash the Nicaraguan's hopes and finish his masterpiece. Whether or not he had purposefully conserved energy in the previous nine minutes, the champ set a precedent for how to finish a fight. And in those thirteenth and fourteenth rounds, Marcel landed several vicious combinations against a now-defenseless Argüello.

For Argüello, every second of that bout proved to be a learning experience that he had to endure. Eventually the innate understanding of how to close a bout, as Marcel did, would become a staple of Argüello's repertoire throughout the rest of his career.

"Alexis didn't have enough experience to finish Marcel," Varela said. "He had him hurt in the ninth, tenth, and eleventh rounds. But the rest of the fight Alexis lost the Rounds 12 through 15."

By using a variety of awkward angles and superior speed, the enigmatic Marcel kept Argüello at a safe distance to win a unanimous decision that winter. The judges' scorecards read: Harmodio Cedeno, 146–142; Juan Carlos Tapia, 146–140; and referee Servio Tulio Lay, 146–140. The win over Argüello was the final piece of Marcel's boxing oeuvre. Honoring a promise he made to his mother, Marcel never climbed into the ring again. Marcel's performance proved that his lateral movement and boxing acumen gave Argüello fits. Whenever Argüello began to rally, Marcel jabbed and stepped away, a maneuver he also had applied to steer clear of Roberto Durán's ambushes when they had fought in 1970.

"In Nicaragua at the time we had very few good boxers and they left Nicaragua for a better life, because it was not a good place for boxing. Alexis felt pressure before that fight with Marcel to represent his country," said Roman years later. "The problem was that his mind was only on the knockout, and not to box. He was just looking and looking for that knockout punch. Marcel knew that and ran around the ring because he knew he was a better boxer. Alexis didn't know how to box."

Argüello broke down after the fight. He finally succumbed to the overwhelming pressures that he faced in trying to make his people proud.

"After the fight, Alexis was crying and apologized to us for disappointing us. We told him that we weren't disappointed and told him that one day he would win a title," said trainer Varela. "He was a very sensitive boy. After the fight, Alexis called me and Pambelé to the hotel and said, 'I failed and ask for your forgiveness.' We told him, 'There's nothing to apologize for. You fought bravely.' I told him, 'Alexis, you're young and the next world champion will be you.'"

Even when Argüello became champion of the world, he always wanted to please everyone; it was a trait that both aided and worked against him. But when the disappointment from the loss to Marcel faded, Argüello recognized his mistakes and made the necessary changes. Even then, Argüello understood the ramifications.

"Against Marcel, I found out that I didn't have the qualifications to be a world-class fighter, not yet," said Argüello. "After that I proved that I had it. I put more enthusiasm, more desire into my training because it would be my second chance to win a world title. I did it with more dedication; I sweated more [for my preparation for then world featherweight Rubén Olivares] than I did when I fought Marcel. I put my heart and my brains into that fight. After I fought with Marcel, I put six or seven fights into gaining that No. 1 spot."

The difference between Argüello and other young fighters in Nicaragua was that he accepted each loss as a lesson. As he learned, Argüello never made the same mistake twice.

"In Marcel, I encountered a smart fighter who really knew how to handle a heavy hitter," said Argüello. "He had good movement, good coordination with speed, and great balance. In that fight, I learned that boxing is knowledge, conditioning, and know-how to do things like approach your opponent or to put him against the ropes in a position where he can't move. It's something that a fighter has to mature in order to conquer and accomplish what he wants."

Although Argüello lost this bout, his performance against Marcel did not go unnoticed. Sports fans recognized how close he was to becoming a great fighter. Roman joined Argüello as he, too, was receiving on-the-job training.

"When I went to Panama, General Rubén Paredes came up to me two days before the fight and told me, 'Your fighter is not ready for Marcel,'" said Roman. "I got suspicious, because he gave me that advice to try and influence my mind and possibly for me to let Alexis know some of the conversation. I was only thinking about Alexis's well-being, but what he told me was right. Alexis was not ready for that type of fight, so after that fight I changed everything."

After the fight, Roman traveled to the Hotel Panama. He convinced Marcel's gifted trainer, Ramón "Curro" Dossman, to train Argüello for his next two fights. As Roman later stated, "At that point Alexis only knew how to throw punches."

Before Argüello went back to work, though, there had been rumors circulating in Panama that Marcel had agreed to lose, or "throw," the fight. Although some Panamanians still adhere to the notion that Marcel intended to lose, it was never proved.

"In one round Argüello hit me and I got dizzy and I felt that way for about three rounds, and people thought I was selling out because President Omar Torrijos had spoken with [Nicaraguan dictator] Anastasio Somoza about getting a title shot for Argüello. But I wanted to retire as a world champion and that's what I did," said Marcel. "I'm happy with my conscience so I don't have to worry about what other people think. I know people thought I sold out against Argüello, but I know the truth. After the fight, Argüello told me, 'You are very difficult to box, and I didn't want to take any chances on the inside with you.' I told him, 'I have more experience than you, but you have good strength and can be champion one day after me.'"

Marcel would not be lured out of retirement, not even to fight Spider Nemoto for $150,000 in Japan. He had made a promise to his mother to leave the ring with his faculties intact and didn't need to fight anymore, even though he admitted to missing the fame. However, the Argüello camp benefitted from his retirement because under manager Harmodio Icaza, Marcel had the option to face World Boxing Association champ Rubén Olivares in the next bout. With Marcel stepping aside and Icaza quickly finalizing the retirement on his end, the door opened for Argüello to take that spot.

Campeón!

Olivares was a master in the ring.
—Alexis Argüello

Argüello went back home after the Marcel bout and dedicated himself to becoming Nicaragua's first world champion. Boxing fans were not disappointed in his performance because most people didn't believe he was physically ready to take on Marcel in the first place.

"After the fight with Ernesto Marcel, Alexis told me in tears that he lost because the other one was a lot better than him, but he was still going to be a world champion, someday," said longtime friend and confidant Donald Rodriguez. Regarding what Argüello thought about fame, Rodriguez said, "I think he got the impact of the fame but he thought about it in a positive way. He always was gentle with the people, reporters and everyone. The people loved him. And then he started to have the nickname 'the Ring's Gentleman' because of the way he acted. He was proud of his fame, but he was always gentle."

Boxing insiders recognized the consequences of the Marcel bout, and Argüello knew that challengers rarely received two chances at the world title. Yet, his manager, Dr. Roman, had cultivated ample contacts in the boxing world, and even though he had decided to put Argüello in against a seasoned champion so early in his career, the loss was essential to Argüello's growth. Roman was also negotiating a bout with the great Mexican featherweight Rubén "El Púas" Olivares.

"When I fought Marcel, it was my first introduction to the international stage," said Argüello. "I was a national fighter, and to get into that [next] level, I needed technique. I thought with Marcel that I could beat him with my punching power. But I found out that night that Marcel was extremely quick and extremely smart not to exchange punches with me, and he did a helluva job. He did it quickly.

He used speed and intelligence and was a smart fighter, and that night I found out that using strength was not enough; you have to be smart too."

In some ways, Marcel and Argüello led parallel careers; both fighters suffered multiple losses early in their careers only to learn from their mistakes and go on to win world titles. After the loss to Marcel and his first bout working with his new Panamanian trainer Ramón Dossman, Argüello stopped Enrique Garcia in three rounds on April 27, 1974, and then trained for his next bout less than a month later. During the months leading up to the showdown with Olivares, Argüello had to steel himself for a fifteen-round war. Olivares's style was based not on elusiveness and movement but on warfare and pressure.

Dr. Roman had used his influence, and luck, to wrestle Dossman away from Panama. The move paid dividends. Not only was Dossman a well-respected trainer, but he was also responsible for perfecting the styles of the supreme boxers Ernesto Marcel and Panamanian legend and two-time lightweight champ Ismael Laguna. Realizing that change was necessary for a fighter, Roman closely monitored Argüello's growth. If Dossman could develop Argüello's boxing skills and impart even a little boxing knowledge, it would be beneficial. Around the same time, Argüello's friend and former sparring partner Luis Cortés became a familiar face in the corner as an assistant trainer.

That May, Argüello would face a heavy hitter from Nova Scotia, Art Hafey. Fighting out of the featherweight division, Hafey used a fierce left hook to win his first thirteen of fourteen bouts, his one blemish being a draw. Of those first bouts, Hafey inserted himself into the hardscrabble West Coast boxing fraternity by knocking out nine of the fourteen challengers. Hafey had developed into a boxing globetrotter and accepted the challenge to fight the great Olivares, who was now an astounding 73-1-1, in Monterrey, Mexico, on September, 15, 1973.

"Before I fought Olivares I faced 'Famoso' [Octavio] Gómez. I was not ready, and I got dropped two times during this bout. Gomez had a nice left hook. I won the fight, but I was too inexperienced to face a guy like that," said Hafey. "I should have never taken that fight. Turns out Olivares asked Gómez about me. Gómez told him that I would be an easy fight and to take it. Fortunately, he took it. That night it was a different Art Hafey. At the time I was mentally digesting a lot of material."

Instead of deriding the Canadian spark plug, the Mexican contingent welcomed him with open arms. Having been a boxing vagabond, Hafey knew that he was walking into enemy territory, but he was pleasantly surprised. Olivares did not fare as well. The champ hardly acknowledged the challenger and was knocked out within five rounds. According to the matchmaker for the Olympic

Auditorium, Don Chargin, Hafey was sent to Nicaragua as collateral. In the 1970s there was a fierce competition between the Olympic Auditorium and the "other" Los Angeles boxing bastion, the Inglewood Forum, two fight arenas that matched the best fighters in the world.

"They had more opponents at the Inglewood Forum, and they told Alexis that he wouldn't get those opponents at the Olympic. I had signed Alexis to fight at the Olympic, but when the Forum found out about it, they made a deal and agreed to send Art Hafey to Nicaragua," said Chargin. "Now, Alexis really wanted Hafey because he was beating people. And they knew he wanted Hafey; they said, 'We'll give you Hafey, if you stay away from the Olympic.'"

Inglewood Forum promoter Don Fraser denied the allegations when he said, "We were competing for fighters with the Olympic Auditorium. At times they were very hostile against us. I didn't understand why. Olivares had all his fights with us; so did Alexis. We were able to get Danny [López] and Bobby [Chacón] over a couple times and they got upset. They were not too happy with me. But that was the boxing business. [As for the Hafey controversy] Art's manager was Suey Welch, who was very close with George Parnassus, who was promoting fights at the Forum. That was it."

Argüello finished off several unmatched challengers before talks of a bout with the hard-hitting Hafey, who had burnished his reputation as a debilitating puncher on the West Coast boxing circuit. Argüello lobbied for the bout. Hafey, who had lost a split-decision rematch to Olivares eight months earlier, felt prepared for any fighter placed in front of him, but he was concerned about traveling to Nicaragua, where he didn't think he would receive a fair shot. He earned $15,000 for the twelve-round featherweight bout set for May 19, 1974.

"Prior to the fight with Alexis, I fought Olivares. A short time after that they took me to fight Alexis. You don't do that to a guy still ranked in the top ten. You don't take him over to get beaten. At the time I didn't realize it," Hafey recalled. "I was too ignorant. . . . Promoter Mickey Davies was very upset about what had happened. . . . I didn't have any knowledge of the decision to take that match. I had no idea who Argüello was. A capable manager wouldn't have taken that match. I was still in the top five after the loss to Olivares; why jeopardize that?"

Hafey traveled to Managua with Los Angeles promoter George Parnassus, his assistant Don Fraser, and their lawyer, Norm Caplan. Hafey conceded that "they took a contract with them to Argüello thinking I would lose. They had Alexis sign a contract to fight Olivares at a later date . . . Parnassus and the guys had big plans for Alexis. They used me as a steppingstone for a crack at the title."

Despite the furor and supposed underhanded dealings, Hafey met Argüello when he landed in Nicaragua. With less than a week to prepare, Hafey felt completely out of his element in the heat and the unfamiliar surroundings.

"After I arrived this guy comes up to me and says, 'Hi, how are you?' Here I am looking up at this 5-foot-11 guy," said Hafey, who is only 5 foot 2. "Then I realized I was fighting this guy. I was in shock. I was wondering how he was going to make the 126[-pound] division. I can tell you that when he got into the ring he wasn't a featherweight. They must have fixed up the scales."

That evening in Masaya, an hour outside the capital city, Hafey (35-5-4) struggled with what he considered an unkempt ring, an overweight Argüello, and a violent fan base. Realistically, he was physically overmatched against the growing Argüello. Hafey was spit on as he entered the ring and endured insults from the pro-Argüello contingent. Hafey managed to survive the first four rounds. Then, in the fifth, Parnassus said, "That's enough," and called an end to the bout.

"I was afraid that I would get shot by guys with machine guns if I knocked him out," said Hafey, who lost by a knockout in five rounds. "I had him shaken a couple times. But that night I had to deal with so many things. The referee wouldn't allow me to fight, and every time I got underneath Alexis, he got between us and told me to keep my head up. It was ridiculous what I had to deal with. The canvas was terrible. I was tripping over things sticking out of the canvas. I had short legs, and Alexis had long legs, so he was able to step around them. I was stumbling all over."

Argüello remembered a different scenario: "George Parnassus, Olivares's manager, didn't want me to fight Olivares because he knew I would beat him. So he sent a Canadian guy, Art Hafey, to fight me. Hafey was a tough guy that beat a lot of guys, and he came to Masaya [where the fight was held], and I knocked him out in five rounds. I broke his nose, and pulled out a couple of teeth. That was the biggest mistake that Parnassus did was to bring that fighter to fight me in my country. That was a spectacular fight—technically I looked like a good boxer— and then we went for the championship of the world." Consequently, Hafey would go on to be labeled the best fighter never to get a shot at a world title.

After his destruction of Art Hafey, Argüello fought two bouts in Masaya. First, he decisioned Oscar Aparicio in twelve rounds that August to win the Central American Featherweight title, and then he came back in September to knock out the lightly regarded Otoniel Martinez in the first round. Both fights were held at the Roberto Clemente Stadium, named for the Puerto Rican baseball icon who died in a plane crash while bringing aid to the Nicaraguan earthquake victims in 1972.

Now, after a patient Dr. Roman negotiated with the stubborn Olivares camp, Argüello was in line for another title shot. "Ruben didn't want to go into Alexis's backyard. You don't know what you're going to get from the officials. In Los Angeles, Ruben was the favorite and 90 percent of the crowd was rooting for him. But Alexis didn't want to fight in Mexico City, and I don't think we could find a viable promoter who could put up the money for that bout," said Forum promoter Don Fraser. "I don't think Olivares was concerned when he saw how big Alexis was because he was a good-sized fighter himself. There was no fear in that. It was a good matchup. The main thing for that bout was the money and the guarantees. We were reasonably sure that we would make money. Alexis was well known, and Olivares was a big favorite of the Mexican fans."

Born on January 14, 1947, Rubén Olivares grew up in the Colonia Bondojo district of Mexico City. Before he turned fifteen, Olivares paid twenty-five centavos to watch a local bout between his friend Dumbo Perez and Chucho Hernández, at Arena Coliseo in Mexico City. After witnessing a crushing left hook from Hernández, to end the bout, Olivares was captivated. Excited by the machismo, the camaraderie, and the adulation, Olivares had discovered his niche. Perfecting a short, compact left hook, Olivares gunned down his first twenty-three opponents and then impressively disposed of another Mexican prospect, Julio Guerrero, who was also highly regarded as a big puncher.

From late 1967 to 1968, Olivares had fought and conquered fourteen opponents. Conversely, at the same time, Argüello suffered his first loss in his professional debut. Instead of withdrawing from the sport, Argüello took that first-round knockout loss to Cachorro Amaya in his September 1968 debut as a boxing lesson.

Dr. Roman had made all the right moves in shaping Argüello's career leading up to the championship bout. With all of Los Angeles behind him, Olivares (77-4-1) signed to fight Argüello in November 1974. The bout was reported in the press on September 9, and Inglewood Forum promoter Don Fraser confirmed it. Olivares had won the vacant WBA featherweight crown from Zensuke Utagawa on July 9 and had not yet officially defended his title. The fight with Alexis had been originally scheduled for November 16, but it was postponed to November 23 when Olivares caught a cold. After an exhausting negotiations process where Olivares turned down the initial offer to fight for $120,000 in Masaya, Nicaragua, he finally agreed to a November 23 date for $100,000 at the Forum. According to Roman, Olivares tried to buy out of the contract at the last minute, but Roman immediately declined. The fight was set for 3 p.m. in order to satisfy TV commitments to Central and South America.

Before Argüello left for Los Angeles, he received encouraging words from an old friend.

"I used to be stablemate with Rubén Olivares in Mexico. And when Olivares visited Nicaragua, I worked as his sparring partner," said Varela. "Always, he had that personality and he thought he would win by knockout. I told Alexis, 'Olivares is a very good in-and-out fighter. You have to control him with three punches, and you have to keep him away from you. He's a tremendous fighter.'"

A week before the fight, Argüello, who had not yet become the darling of the TV circuit, was ranked No. 3 among WBA featherweights. He was earning mixed reviews during his sparring sessions at the Main Street Gym in Los Angeles. Danny "Little Red" López, a featherweight and Argüello sparring partner, sized up Argüello: "I think Olivares will beat him." Former 1950s featherweight champ Gil Cadilli responded, "I don't think Olivares can take a punch like he used to. This guy's got everything going for him—height, reach, youth. . . ." Veteran manager Willie Ketchum chimed in: "This guy's young and hungry. He'll knock out Olivares." As others extolled praise for the challenger, Argüello focused on his opponent.

Before the bout, he faced an unsettling confrontation with U.S. Immigration agents. Two weeks before the bout, immigration agents accosted Argüello, stablemate and fellow Nicaraguan Mario Martinez, manager Curro Dossman, and assistant trainer Luis Cortés during a traffic stop and forcibly took the men back to their Olympian Motor Hotel to fetch their entry papers, which were all in order. The incident left Argüello clearly shaken. Nevertheless, he dealt with the unfortunate situation with grace and class, the same way he approached the ring. Argüello quickly moved on and focused on his career.

"I was surprised when they harassed him like that," said promoter Don Fraser. "But I couldn't do anything. I didn't know why they would single him out like that. It didn't make the front pages because nobody really made a big fuss about it. Alexis certainly didn't. He wasn't the type of guy to cry about something like that."

Meanwhile, Olivares, who trained at the International Youth Boxing Gym in Montebello, California, was looking to the future and his third world title in three weight classes. "I've seen [WBC 130-pound champ Kuniaki Shibata] fight, and I think I can beat him," said Olivares. "I would have no trouble making 130 pounds."

If Argüello, at age twenty-two, was merely starting out, Olivares had already reached the zenith of his career. Lists of boxing's all-time greatest featherweights couldn't exclude the great fighter. Ironically, the two had previously met in the ring. In June 1971, Argüello helped Olivares prepare for his bout with

Nicaraguan Vicente "Yambito" Blanco, whom he knocked out in five rounds. That fight was held in Managua, and the sparring session with Argüello marked the first time that the two fighters collided.

Few would disagree that the Inglewood Forum provided a comfort zone for Olivares. It was reported that for his sixteen fights in the venerable arena, the gross gates had reached $2,877,419. For this title fight, Olivares would earn $80,000, or much more than Argüello's $15,000. The odds, however, had evened up by fight time. The Nicaraguan and American boxing diehard fans knew what Argüello was capable of after his performance against Ernesto Marcel.

When he was preparing to fight Rubén Olivares, Argüello remembered their confrontation at the Elks Building: "He comes up to me before the fight at the weigh-in and tells me, 'Don't worry, I'll take it easy on you. I won't make you suffer. I'll knock you out quick.' At the weigh-in, I had my pants off and he took his pants off and I got in there with my speedo, those tiny things, and I weighed in at 125¾. After I weighed in at 125¾, my trainer gave me a broth of liver. It was so damn hot that when the doctor put the thermometer in my mouth, he starts telling people that I am not able to fight. I told them nothing could keep me from the ring."

Everyone in the Forum was pulling for Rubén "Púas" Olivares on November 23, 1974. Olivares walked into his seventeenth bout at the Forum, with a nearly unblemished 14-2 record (eleven knockouts). The five-year disparity in age between Argüello and Olivares put the Mexican champ at a severe disadvantage against the lanky but fierce young contender from Nicaragua. That evening in the Inglewood Forum, the fighters stood in opposite corners. Physically, Argüello towered over Olivares by four inches and benefited from a 2½-inch reach advantage. Undaunted, Olivares told local reporters: "I have trained for a 15-round fight, but sometimes when I hit people, they go down."

The Forum busted at the seams with a strong Nicaraguan contingent. Some, though, still saw it as Olivares's crowd. Roman claimed that the ratio was close to fifteen thousand Mexicans chanting, "Mexico!" to a thousand Argüello followers.

Why wasn't Argüello the bigger draw? "You have to ask yourself, how many Nicaraguans were around?" asked Olympic Auditorium promoter Don Chargin. "All of Mexico idolized Rubén. As he [Argüello] started to win and develop fight fans, the hardcore fight fans rooted for Alexis. The nationalistic fight fans rooted for Rubén, and I mean the real Mexican fight fans."

Although Argüello was not a West Coast mainstay, he evoked a genuine love for people and had won over some of the locals. They had watched intently every punch and feint at the Main Street Gym during his training sessions.

"When he first got to Los Angeles, his reputation was here before him," said Don Chargin. "We all knew about him because of a Nicaraguan writer who would send stuff over. This was before computers, so he would send us clippings. We would read about him in the boxing magazines. Stuff like, 'Watch out for Alexis Argüello; he's going to be world champion.' You can't keep a talent like that quiet.

"Alexis went from a fight prospect to a great fighter right from the outset. Anybody that saw him was just enamored by him and the way he carried himself, the looks, everything."

Deep down Argüello knew he could conquer the Mexican legend, a belief that eluded most of the pro-Olivares crowd. In the dressing room prior to the matchup, Argüello received a visit from an old friend.

"Alexis came to Los Angeles to fight for the title. I went into his dressing room before the bout, and he looked like such a frail fellow because he had to make weight," said Art Hafey. "He came in at 124½ which made him weaker." As had so many fighters before him, Hafey pondered what could have been: "The way I punch to the body with no limitations, I would have been allowed to do that in Los Angeles. It would have been on fair grounds."

On November 23, 1974, Argüello (35-4, thirty-three knockouts) bounded down the aisle as the hostile crowd yelled insults, while Olivares (77-4-1, sixty-nine knockouts) entered to a hero's welcome. Argüello proudly donned Nicaraguan navy and white. A sense of quiet determination enveloped the fighter. Olivares, who was managed by Pancho Rosales, didn't stand out, but he didn't have to, judging by the bodies he'd left in his wake. Despite having a proclivity for an indifference to training, Olivares sparred 114 rounds in Mexico leading up to the bout. Olivares was a man, and Argüello still had to prove he could become one. Nearly 14,500 fight fans filled the Inglewood Forum to produce a gross gate of $186,210. Oddsmakers had Argüello as a 10-9 favorite.

"Olivares tells me that he will knock me out early, but I didn't know what he was saying," said Argüello. "It was a lot different in the ring. I got it in my head that what he was saying was bullshit. I put it in my head that I was the best. I promised my country that I wouldn't fail."

The bell for Round 1 reverberated throughout the arena, and Olivares charted a rapid path to his left and circled Argüello. Although Olivares was the champion, many wondered, could Argüello use his height against the longtime champ? Could he handle Olivares's power? By using a classic boxing style, Argüello, who appeared stiff and clearly overwhelmed by the sheer magnitude of the bout, made it impossible for Olivares to break through his guard. Olivares managed to break the ice, however, with a short left hook that only glanced off Argüello's chest. He quickly pulled it back.

"When we got into the ring, it was a different fucking story from the beginning to the end," said Argüello. "It was like a roller coaster. I got in my mind what he told me. I kept thinking, Bullshit, he can think whatever he thinks. But I got into the best shape of my life. That's a guy who can accomplish anything that he wants. I promised this country that I couldn't fail because I failed the first time, I couldn't take that chance. In the first round he was something that I could never believe. The guy was masterfully destroying me. He would throw his punches and then get out of my reach."

Almost a minute into that first round, Olivares threw a weak left hook to bait the challenger and woke Argüello with a straight right in the same offering. Argüello's head was forced back, but he quickly composed himself. The young student felt the immediate force of his professor's power and survived. Argüello landed two short uppercuts that barely dented Olivares, but he would have to go back to that same punch in the later rounds.

As the champ squirmed into and away from Argüello's power zone, he studied the young challenger. Olivares was so slight in build that the casual fan might have questioned his place in the ring across from such an imposing figure. With Beatle-like hair flopping over his ears, a body devoid of definition, along with a 5-foot-5-inch frame, Olivares had an impish quality about him. His pale skin and strong Indian features highlighted his Mexican heritage. He hadn't entertained decisive thoughts of a brawl as the first round came to an end.

Argüello jumped off his stool at the start of the second round and beelined toward the champ. Despite the immediate prospect of an exciting Latin brawl, no significant action ensued. In comparison with Olivares's lack of definition, every bit of Argüello's 126 pounds was molded neatly onto his sculpted frame; he stood away from the champion with an air of respect.

Once the feeling-out process ended, Argüello began to stalk the champ. After cautiously preparing each move and each punch in his mind, Argüello landed a straight right that forced Olivares back to the corner. If Olivares thrived on furious bursts, Argüello depended on a controlled strategy.

With seconds remaining in the second round, Argüello missed a four-punch combination. His inconsistency and inexperience were glaringly evident to the champ. Few men were ready even to embrace the idea of confronting a legend like Púas. Was Argüello in over his head? Olivares receded to the opposite corner, out of harm's way. When Argüello entered the Mexican's comfort zone, Olivares nailed him with a straight right and then seconds later followed with a short right to the body. The host of Mexican fans anxiously awaited the forthcoming warfare.

If Argüello stalked Olivares in the second round with conviction, at the outset of the third the introspective challenger carefully monitored each opening as he headed toward Olivares. Transforming from the aggressor to the cautious challenger, Argüello fell into a trap. The face of the fight changed dramatically as Olivares slashed Argüello with a straight right along the ropes. No damage was inflicted, but Olivares's looping right hand found its mark as the round ended. Although Argüello didn't acknowledge it, he felt Olivares's power.

For the first time in the fight, the men faced off in the corner. Olivares shoved Argüello there and landed telling blows. The arc of Olivares's looping punches often left him open for counters, but now he was so focused that Argüello had no chance to return fire. Each punch cracked his chiseled ribs, prompting no response. He just pressed on. The round ended as the war began.

The keen featherweight champ boxed and moved beautifully in the fourth, rarely leaving space for the fighter. Each man took a breather and a step back in the fourth round. Argüello was still pulling punches, not yet ready to give himself over completely to battle, while Olivares, clearly in the early stages of a boxing lesson, used his jitterbug moves and slippery feet to move away from his methodical foe.

The fifth round opened. Olivares took a circuitous route; Argüello unleashed a classic straight right hand inside Olivares's punch. Argüello pushed Olivares back with the punch, then punished him again with a right. Seconds later Olivares scampered for cover, and Argüello urged him back into the corner and ambushed him. He inflicted no real damage, but the roles were slowly changing. This fact was not lost on the pro-Olivares crowd.

Although Olivares was still ahead on points as the bout neared the midpoint, his eye began to swell and redden. With Olivares still controlling the ebb and flow of the fight, Argüello made him step back and consider the next step. Caution wasn't his forte. Seconds after the sixth bell rang, Argüello forged ahead with urgency and nailed the Mexican champ with a straight right. Argüello's purpose was clearly defined: straight right, push him back, another right, jab, and left hook. Olivares was no longer jitterbugging around the ring. The young fighter had reached him and successfully flushed his energy.

With fifty seconds remaining in the round, Olivares crowded the challenger and suffocated him with a barrage of punches. Nevertheless, Argüello withstood the attack. As he recalled, "From the fourth to the seventh or eighth round, I put a lot of pressure on him."

By the midway point of the seventh round, Argüello gained control as Olivares anxiously brushed his injured eye. For the final forty seconds of the round, both men charged each other. As if questioning each other's bravery, the Latin warriors faced off. Olivares intensified his commitment to getting rid of the twenty-two-year-old challenger. He fought off Argüello to make space and then landed a jutting right uppercut followed by a left to the body. As the bell sounded, Olivares clipped him with another left hook.

For Argüello, the slick movements of Marcel's had given him trouble in February, and by comparison, the Mexican champ was more powerful, yet easier to hit. Argüello's camp knew that a twenty-seven-year-old Olivares no longer had the longevity and stamina to endure fifteen rounds of hell.

Not much had changed from the previous round as the eighth round took shape. Olivares sapped Argüello's wealth of energy with a crisp combination. As blood streamed into Olivares's eye, he became desperate and immediate, bullying Argüello while spitting rights and lefts as the challenger covered up. All Argüello could do was stay in matador fashion and ineffectively stave off the onslaught. Referee Dick Young warned Olivares not to hold and punch, but it didn't register. As usual, Olivares landed one more shot to end the round and impress the judges.

Argüello remembered the battle: "He was a master fighter; he had such a technique that he moved like a butterfly and whatever angle he wanted to hit me at, he did."

The fight moved back to the center of the ring in the ninth round. For Olivares, a new spirit replaced earlier frustration, experience trumped immaturity, and the champ was back in a position to succeed.

The first two minutes of the tenth round belonged to Olivares as he smothered Argüello with a left to the ribs and a right to his neck. Then, in the middle of the ring he sneaked in a sharp right over Argüello's guard. He continued to hold the back of Argüello's head and powder him with uppercuts. Argüello, nearly defenseless, bent over from a body shot, then stood up straight, and took a jab to his face. He could do nothing to stave off the determined champ.

As the chant "Olivares! Olivares!" stirred the crowd, the champ met their approval with a sharp right hook to Argüello's neck, then landed a vicious left hook as he walked into the challenger. One more left hook snapped back Argüello's head, and a straight right punctuated a beautiful stanza that would have brought down any other challenger.

With a minute remaining, Argüello lunged and missed with a huge but lazily thrown left hook, the exhaustion apparent as he fell off balance. Moments later, the crafty Mexican squared himself in front of Argüello, masterfully blocked incoming punches, slipped hooks, and landed an uppercut that Argüello never saw. The young fighter's expression grew dim.

Argüello couldn't move; Olivares was glued to him. For seconds, he appeared helpless, an amateur fighter in the crosshairs of a legend. Everything that he offered—the vaunted left, the straight right—was mere fodder for Olivares as he walked through the punches without blinking. As the round ended, the referee forcefully had to intervene and stop the battering. Back in the corner, as Argüello gently took his seat, his stare lacked the same conviction.

As Argüello told it, "When I passed the tenth and the guy had hit me with everything, I started feeling that he was getting more steady. My trainer was telling me that the guy was beating the shit out of me. But I was giving it up; I was fucking fighting. Give me a chance . . . I'm getting into it. I'm getting into it, and he started to use the ropes, because he was falling into the ropes. I'm telling myself, 'He's mine.'"

At the outset of the twelfth round, Olivares bullied Argüello and forced him into desperate corners as he landed six unanswered body and head shots. A huge right momentarily stunned Argüello with 1:30 remaining, and he was battered throughout the latter half of the round.

It was only the second time Argüello had to fight past twelve rounds since his fifteen-round loss to Marcel. A silver lining roused the Nicaraguan faithful in the thirteenth round. It came early, when Olivares walked directly into a straight right and went down from a short Argüello left hook. Olivares rolled over on his stomach and lay in agony. Barely reaching his feet by referee Dick Young's nine count, Olivares bided his time as Young fixed his mouthpiece. Yet, instead of clinching, Olivares implored Argüello, "Engage, bastard!"

"In the twelfth, I hit him with a good left hook in the chin and the guy went down. Actually, I didn't feel it was a heavy punch," said Argüello. "It was a precise punch. And with no strength. A punch that you see—the body opposes the punch. It's the precision that you connect the punch that gives you the advantage. And when the opponent doesn't see the punch, that's what screws him up."

Still recovering, Olivares recklessly ambushed Argüello and threw wild, off-the-mark punches. Argüello patiently placed his shots, created space, softened him with a crushing uppercut, and had the presence to land a lengthy right uppercut that sent Olivares face down. A downtrodden Olivares put his hands on his knees and watched as the referee counted him out with 1:20 left in the thirteenth round. The rapid turn of events belied the previous five one-sided rounds; at the time of the stoppage Argüello was behind on two scorecards (Dick Young, 3–8; Judge Larry Rozadilla, 5–6) and even on the final one (Judge George Latka, 5–5).

"Even though Olivares was beating me in the first ten rounds, I turned it over," said Argüello. "What the reporter said was true: 'When Olivares went down, the Mariachis stopped singing.' The Mariachis got quiet when they saw Olivares on the floor."

There was a new featherweight champion. A party ignited throughout Central America to celebrate Nicaragua's first world boxing champion. As his cornermen hoisted him to the rafters and carried around the ring, Argüello had realized his dream and fulfilled a pact to his parents. Exiting the ring, Olivares looked over. "Take good care of that title," he told the new champion.

"I made a promise to my mom and dad to do the right thing," said Argüello. "I did it for my folks. They went through so much that I wanted to buy a house for my mom.

"When I got past Olivares, I realized that I could play with anyone. There was no one on my level. I was a master in the ring. I returned to my country as a hero. There were about 10,000 people at the airport. They were there to say hello to a guy who represented them as a Latin. I think that they did the right thing because I represented them with dignity, respect, and love to the country."

The Forum was shaking as Nicaraguan supporters hoisted their new champion.

"I traveled to the fight with my family," said owner of Doña Elba Cigars Silvio Reyes. "It was such a big event. When Alexis won, we felt these things coming from behind. The Mexicans were throwing bags of piss on the crowd. But you know what, we didn't care. We had a new champion!"

Fight fans and experts weighed in on the victory.

"I drove to Los Angeles to see Olivares fight Alexis," said former boxer and boxing commentator Sean O'Grady, who was a teenager at the time of the bout. "Everybody in the crowd was for Olivares but also quite a few for Alexis. Olivares beat the tar out of him for thirteen rounds. Then, Olivares looked down for a split second, and it was over. Boom! It was spectacular. I saw Alexis do that time and again."

Promoter Don Chargin weighed the legacy of Olivares against the ramifications of an Argüello victory: "I remember the Mexican fans couldn't believe it when Argüello knocked out Olivares. Rubén had that great personality where he was always smiling and did nothing wrong. He was just like them, a two-fisted drinker. He mixed with people; he was a guy of the people. They were stunned when he lost. People actually cried."

Promoter Don Fraser claimed that no Forum fighter had a following like that of Olivares. "The difference between Bobby Chacón, Rubén Olivares, and Argüello was that Chacón and Olivares were Mexicans," he said. "Alexis wasn't as accepted by the Mexicans. When the fight with Olivares ended, there was no question, no controversy. Olivares's people accepted it."

Immediately after the fight, there were rumors of a rematch being negotiated. However, Argüello's camp had already committed to a defense against Venezuelan stalwart Leonel Hernández that March.

In the dressing room after the bout, Eduardo Roman and WBA president and friend Elias Córdoba enjoyed the journalist's role when they asked Olivares if any one punch had hurt him.

"I asked Rubén if there was one punch that hurt him," said Roman. "Rubén said, 'One punch? I wish it was just one punch. All the punches hurt me.' And then I asked him about the referee making a long count, I asked him what the referee asked him. Rubén told me the referee said, 'Can you continue fighting him, champ?' To which the champ replied, 'Yeah, next year.'"

Although Argüello often eschewed the party scene for much needed rest, he went to a party in his honor after the bout.

"After he beat Olivares, it was crazy in Los Angeles, it was crazy. There were many Nicaraguans," said Roman. "There were two or three thousand people who threw him a big party in Los Angeles at a local bar. These Mexicans come into the bar and said, 'These fucking Nicaraguans. Argüello, this sonofabitch. We are going to break this up.' And then a Nicaraguan in the bar knocked him down with a punch. I will never forget that. Then the other Mexican picked him up, and say 'Let's go, brother.' They loved Alexis."

Nicaragua was still years away from the internecine war that would ravage the landscape and its people, and the spirited battle that Argüello waged blinded them to the coming struggle while the celebration began. Argüello went back to the gym and the people who helped transition him from a gregarious boy to world champion.

"One day I went to visit the gym and Alexis, the champ, was there. Pambelé told Alexis: 'You're not going to thank Varelita?' He hugged me and thanked me for everything. I told him, 'Now I can call you champion,'" said Varela.

ROUND 5

King's Reign

He's the best fighter I've seen in 20 years.
—MADISON SQUARE GARDEN MATCHMAKER TEDDY BRENNER
    ON ARGÜELLO

In the mid-1970s, the featherweight division proved to be as competitive as any division in the sport. Argüello had a plethora of capable challengers to choose from. Whether he sought a rematch with Rubén Olivares or a title defense down the line against a heralded Danny "Little Red" López or Forum favorite Bobby "Schoolboy" Chacón, there were few pushovers. After earning an easy unanimous decision in a nontitle tune-up against Oscar Aparicio in Nuevo Poliedro in El Salvador on February 8, 1975, Argüello fought again in five weeks, a testament to his dedication to conditioning. Many believed the ring was the only place he felt comfortable; a life full of contradictions would later impede his happiness.

On March 15, 1975, the sculpted, confident, twenty-six-year-old Leonel Hernández walked onto his home turf of El Poliedro in Caracas, Venezuela, in front of twelve thousand screaming countrymen as he looked to take down the featherweight giant, Argüello. Hernández had lost a razor-sharp decision to Panama's Ernesto Marcel two years earlier, but Hernández hadn't faced any top-ten-caliber opponents since then. Both men came in within a pound of the 126-pound limit, and Argüello wasted little time before he unleashed the patented right cross that he had often kept dormant for several rounds in past fights. Early on, Hernández (28-4, seventeen knockouts) employed head movement, but that maneuver didn't stop Argüello from keeping him on the end of his sharp jab. The partisan crowd rose accordingly as Hernández found a rhythm and landed consecutive right hooks to close out the second round.

Hernández was still buzzing after an emotional second round. He recklessly entered Argüello's danger zone and walked into short, crisp uppercuts. Impervious to the punishment, the brave Hernández landed a right hook that cuffed Argüello as they moved from the corner. If Hernández had been more disciplined, it might have been a different outcome.

Still, it was Argüello's ability to open up and hit Hernandez at will that changed the look and pace of the fight. This fighter wasn't the analytical Argüello, content to bide his time round after round and wait for that brief opening. Instead, as the crowd rose with each glancing blow by Hernández, this Argüello carried the pulse of the fight. He brilliantly picked off shots with his right glove and never wavered from throwing the sharp jab. Even when Hernández pinned Argüello in the corner in the fifth round, Hernández couldn't take advantage of the situation. If the tides were turned, the erudite Argüello would have made his opponent pay dearly and possibly would have ended the bout early.

Trained by Curro Dossman, Argüello finally caught Hernández with a potent left to the body late in the sixth, but the Venezuelan challenger slipped away. The crowd appreciated Hernández's deft defensive skills, yet the local fighter couldn't prevent a cut from opening under his right eye. The riveting cat-and-mouse game that satiated the fans to that point was slowly coming to a halt as Argüello inched closer to victory.

The fight reached a zenith in the eighth. Although Hernández continued to fight valiantly off the ropes, the rope-a-dope placed him in dire need of relief. As he tried to walk out of the corner, Argüello caught him flat-footed with a right cross on the side of his jaw that sent him falling sideways to the canvas. Hernández was up by referee Ferny Carpentier's count of five and back in the eye of the storm.

Argüello hurried over, missed a left hook, and then proceeded to trap the challenger. Argüello threw twelve to fourteen punches, but only a couple, including a vicious left hook, landed. Hernández, whose left eye was swelling and right eye was bleeding profusely, was slipping some of his punches, and his movement made it difficult for the meticulous Argüello to land a crushing shot. But as Hernández's head bounced back and forth, a right uppercut slipped through his guard and jarred him. Referee Carpentier had observed long enough. He moved over and stepped in to halt the action at 2:52 of the eighth round. Argüello had successfully defended his WBA World Feather-weight title and was carried around the ring with the Nicaraguan flag draped over his back. It was hard to miss the brief incandescent smile of relief that shot across his face

In the dressing room, Hernández stated, "This guy hits hard!" Although he would earn rave reviews for later bouts, many believe that Argüello was at his peak when he bested Hernández.

Three months after the Hernandez defense, Argüello watched as Rubén Olivares prepared for his attempt to win the WBC version of his belt in a momentous Forum clash with Schoolboy Chacón that would set gate records. The infusion of South and Central American titleholders had reflected the influx of international talent during the mid-1970s. Of the fourteen world champions in that decade, eight hailed from South and Central America.

While Olivares took a technical knockout victory over Benjamin Ortiz in Tijuana to secure the return match with Chacón, Argüello returned home in May to face Panama's lightly regarded Rigoberto Riasco (19-4-4) and make his first hometown title defense. Argüello's lopsided second-round knockout of Panama's Riasco at the Estadio Flor de Caña, Granada on May 31, 1975, surprised no one. Riasco, a slick boxer, wilted under a barrage of uppercuts in Round 1 and was damaged goods a round later. Two minutes into the second round, referee Ferny Carpentier, fresh off officiating the Hernández bout, ended the slaughter as Riasco's head was uncomfortably jolted back from a five-punch combination.

Instead of enjoying his newfound fame, Argüello wasted no time and signed to fight a nontitle ten-rounder against Rosalio Muro at the San Francisco Cow Palace in mid-July. He also made plans for his third title defense, set for October 12, 1975, against Japan's Royal Kobayashi. Rumors abounded that there was a $100,000 offer made by West Coast boxing promoter Aileen Eaton for an Argüello defense against Danny Lopez, but these negotiations fell through.

Although the fight would have pitted two West Coast stars against each other, the size difference had López's supporters questioning the matchup. "To this day, Danny [López] is the same little kid we used as an amateur," former Olympic promoter Don Chargin recalled. "We were too smart to put him in against Alexis. That would have been a terrible fight for him."

Danny López concurred: "I might have sparred with him a couple times. Everybody got up when Alexis came to town. The gyms were packed. Everything was good. He was a guy with so much charisma. We never fought. But I am pretty sure he would have clobbered me. He was too strong, too good of a boxer. I might have been on the losing end of that one. Being a friend of his, we never met up."

That June, Olivares trained diligently and knocked out Bobby Chacón in two rounds for the WBC featherweight crown to set a record gate of $401,000 at the Forum. A month later, Argüello fought Rosalio Muro (8-1), a lightly regarded challenger. On July 18, referee Vern Bybee saved Muro from any further punishment at 2:54 of the second round. Argüello next set his sights on Royal Kobayashi and would earn $125,000 for the title defense. Negating any possibility of a rematch between Argüello and Olivares, Ghana's David Kotey earned a split-decision victory over Olivares for the WBC featherweight crown.

Argüello traveled to Tokyo, Japan, that October to face Kobayashi, who was undefeated in eighteen bouts. To assist Argüello with the sparring sessions, Nicaraguan boxer Francisco "Toro" Coronado and boxing journalist Miguel Angel Arcia made the journey. Few, if any, writers gave Kobayashi a fighting chance, since he had never faced a credible challenger or many fighters with winning records coming into the title bout. On October 12, 1975, in Sumo Hall, the highly inexperienced Kobayashi had the heart but not the physical or mental capability to deal with a champ of Argüello's stature. In the first round, Argüello, replete in white trunks and a placid demeanor, ransacked his challenger with a left hook. Despite the adulation from the hometown fans after every punch, Kobayashi could not break through Argüello's defense, and a reckless pattern of flailing punches only set him up perfectly for Argüello's left hook.

Kobayashi had one shining moment at the end of the fourth round as he cornered Argüello and landed three lunging hooks. A round later, Argüello sent Kobayashi to a knee after landing a vicious body shot. Then Kobayashi rose, but he couldn't protect himself against an eight-punch barrage and a left hook that shattered his ribs. Argüello's combination ended the bout, as referee Carlos Padilla called the bout at 2:47 of the fifth round. Argüello successfully defended his 126-pound title for the third time.

Argüello changed during this period. Having sacrificed his adolescent years for the mundane life of intense training regimens and sweaty boxing gyms, Argüello was now experiencing problems outside the ring with his wife, Silvia Urbina. Argüello had difficulty balancing his newfound fame and constant traveling with his family life, and it left him feeling depressed. "When he was the champ, problems started," said Donald Rodriguez. "It was hard for him to find stability. He was always at the gym, 4 a.m. runs, and people always wanted to be around him."

One of Argüello's strengths was his ability to mix socially. He rarely felt out of place in any environment, and many observers attributed this ability to his learning to speak English. Not one to gamble, drink, or flaunt his wealth, Argüello received a $150 monthly stipend from Nicaragua's president Anastasio Somoza, owned a Mercedes and an MG, and had a closet filled with nearly two hundred suits.

Now Argüello, a private person, was a celebrity in Managua, where his every move made front-page news. Local scribes claimed that Argüello was spending late nights in the club district, Plastic City. The tension from his personal life may have infected his training habits, because on February 1, 1976, he barely survived a ninth-round knockdown against Mexican José Torres (24-3, twenty-two knockouts), squeaking out a split-decision victory. "When the fight with José (Torres) happened in Mexicali, (Alexis) went down," said Tijerino. "Alexis won the fight legit, but Mexicans were saying that because he was knocked down that he should have lost the fight. But because you lose one round, you don't lose a fight."

Soon Argüello and Silvia divorced, and he briefly retired. Journalists in Nicaragua claimed that he did so to avoid the financial burden of the divorce; however, the only fact that they confirmed was the deep emotional crisis he faced. Not everyone had sided with Argüello after the painful separation. In the face of the criticism he received from local journalists, Argüello tried to stay above the fray.

"A small section of the population was upset with Alexis," said Nicaraguan sportswriter Edgar Tijerino. "But idolatry prevailed as almost always happens here. So with the continuation of his career . . . it all passed."

Emotionally, Argüello felt destroyed by the breakup, and before finalizing his divorce with Silvia he often consulted with Dr. Roman to find some closure. Roman happily obliged with advice. "When Alexis told me he wanted to divorce Silvia, I quickly said, 'All right, I will do it.'"

After his divorce, Argüello, who was seventeen years old when he married Urbina, had begun another relationship with a teenager named Patricia Barreto, with whom he had fallen in love at first sight when he met her at a disco in Nicaragua. Roman recalled, "Patricia Barreto had a higher class than Alexis because she went to a school that was run by nuns. She was from a low-income family, but she had a higher social level because she went to a Catholic high school." Yet, Argüello stated to a reporter that he feared being "exposed" if he continued to fight during this time.

Instead of waiting for bigger paydays, though, Argüello decided to make it a family affair and took on José's older brother, Salvador Torres, in June. While the boxing brothers of Edwin and Adolpho Viruet and Wilfred and Roberto Benítez were highly touted, José and Salvador were also considered dangerous prospects. The fourth title defense would take Argüello back to the famed Inglewood Forum. Torres, a capable challenger, only had seventeen fights before he stepped in against Argüello, who was nearing the fifty-win mark with forty-three knockouts. Ranked No. 5 by the WBC, Torres's most notable fight thus far was a majority-decision loss to Canadian featherweight Art Hafey a year earlier. Sandwiched between the bouts with the Torres brothers, Argüello destroyed Modesto Concepción in Managua in April, and then he was temporarily placed on a South African card to defend against Arnold Taylor, but the fight never materialized. The *Los Angeles Times* also reported a tentative bout with WBC featherweight champ David Kotey for September at the Forum. First, Argüello had to get past the durable Torres, a fight that would earn him $50,000 and the additional ancillary rights to Torres's $10,000 purse. In an ironic twist, Olivares was fighting on the undercard.

Making weight for the Torres fight did not seem to be a problem as Argüello was down to 128 pounds only days before the bout. With Dr. Eduardo Roman out of commission because of an automobile accident, Argüello was working with three trainers and conducted most of his training sessions at the Main Street Gym. Unlike most fighters, who only take one day off from their training, Argüello dedicated only five days during the week for training. Although this regimen concerned some in his camp and his lack of dedication had been severely criticized in the newspapers, Argüello tried to allay any fears: "I'll be ready. I know what I have to do. I haven't let my people down before, and I won't now. Torres is a tough, strong fighter like all Mexican fighters. But I will be in good condition."

On June 19, 1976, Argüello, now 44-4, weighed in at 125¾ pounds, while Torres (14-2-1) came in a half pound lighter. The critics who had lambasted Argüello in the press saw, in the fight itself, a sharp featherweight breaking down the overmatched Torres. Five consecutive Argüello jabs penetrated Torres's defense as the final seconds of Round 1 ticked off. At the outset of the second round, Argüello punished the youthful Torres after forcing him to the ropes. First, he went to the body with a hook and then straightened up and landed a hook to his head. Torres learned that he could not brawl with a ring technician like Argüello, a fact that the champ reminded him of as the round ended. Argüello lifted Torres partially off the canvas with a straight right cross and then deposited him on the mat. Referee Larry Rozadilla had seen enough, as a game

Torres flailed in several attempts to regain his senses and balance. The fight was called at 1:25 of the third round.

"We needed somebody for that fight, so we got Torres ranked and he had a good reputation," promoter Don Fraser recalled. "We didn't do well with that fight, [only] enough to make some money."

The period after the Salvador Torres bout marked the biggest gap between fights in Argüello's career. While the rest of the combatants in the division waged battles, Argüello moved between his home in the Linda Vista neighborhood in Nicaragua and Miami, content to stay away from the ring. The *Los Angeles Times* had reported in October that Argüello had retired and was planning to go back to school in Nicaragua. By this point he had married the teenage Barreto after a brief courtship. Everyone close to Argüello understood the possible repercussions of the situation as he rushed back into marriage. To honor Dr. Roman, Argüello was finishing his plans to build the Eduardo Roman Boxing Gym in the Barrio Monseñor Lezcano where he was born. To add to the intrigue about his future, Argüello vacated the WBA featherweight title that fall because of weight problems; in other words, he had outgrown the division. Few put credence in Argüello's brief return to school or in his retirement, and by February he announced plans to return as a junior lightweight in the 130-pound division. In the interim, Panamanian Rafael Ortega used his speed to win Argüello's vacant WBA Featherweight belt.

In June 1977, Argüello stepped into vaunted Madison Square Garden for his New York debut. Madison Square Garden represented to New York what the Inglewood Forum symbolized to Los Angeles. To box at the Garden was an honor for any fighter. Argüello made the most of it. He headlined a card that included four ten-rounders with notables such as Harold Weston, Andy Price, and Sean O'Grady. On June 22, in front of 7,364 fans ($67,143 gate), Argüello (47-4) faced Ezequiel "Cocoa" Sanchez (22-6-1) from the Dominican Republic. In what amounted to an over-the-weight junior lightweight matchup, Argüello came in at 132 pounds, while Sanchez weighed 133½ pounds. The lack of a recognizable challenger didn't diminish the attraction as a pro-Dominican crowd flooded the arena.

Having fought only three rounds in 1977—making quick work of Godfrey Stevens and Alberto Herrera in February and May, respectively—Argüello appeared unsteady and rusty as he chased Sanchez around the ring in the first round. Sanchez lifted his supporters with impressive counterpunching in spurts during the second round, as Argüello struggled to get untracked. Although

Sanchez was well conditioned and durable, he was reduced to reaching and desperation midway through the third round. Argüello was at his best in that third round as he finally attacked Sanchez's body, and he landed a rarely used uppercut. Argüello's Madison Square Garden debut marked many fight fans' first real glimpse of the great fighter.

By the fourth round, Argüello had softened Sanchez with a combination and a short hook to ignite the first knockdown early in the round. Referee Tony Perez could have ended the bout on several occasions as Argüello ravaged Sanchez and knocked him down for a second time with a straight right. The bell to end the round saved Sanchez, who likely was about to be counted out. After viewing the damage from the previous round, ring doctor Harry Kleiman walked over to Sanchez's corner to advise the referee to halt the fight. Referee Tony Perez obliged. Argüello knocked out one of Sanchez's teeth during the bout. The performance prompted Garden matchmaker Teddy Brenner to say Argüello was "the best fighter I've seen in 20 years."

Prior to the bout, an incident at the Statler Hilton Hotel sullied this New York visit for Argüello. His wife Patricia Barreto accosted him and screamed, "I got married to you to get a good life, but you are giving me nothing!" Argüello pulled out a wad of money from his pocket and gave it to her. A recent addition to the fighter's team, Don Kahn remembered that "Alexis had a problem with Patricia. She was pregnant, and women want to do things but don't understand that when their husband is in training, he can't do those things. She wasn't letting Alexis go to places, and that's when the argument started. But Alexis didn't lose his temper with her, and he didn't lose his concentration. The marriage only lasted a couple years."

Although Alexis and Patricia welcomed their son, Andrés, a few months later, the impulsive marriage had lost its luster. During the time that his marriage with Patricia was unraveling, Argüello began his lifelong relationship with Kahn, a man he would trust unconditionally for his entire career.

"Our friendship started in New York when Alexis fought Cocoa Sanchez," said Kahn. "I was sent by Madison Square Garden to pick him up at La Guardia Airport. I was telling him about the New York experience in boxing. We started to get to know and liked each other. He liked the way I worked. I ended up taking him to the gym. We were always joking and talking."

Argüello eventually brought Kahn to work in his camp, but their relationship was more of a friendship than a typical trainer-fighter partnership. Feeling comfortable around Kahn, Argüello knew that he needed a person he could trust and confide in like Kahn. When Argüello wanted to vent on a personal matter or joke to lighten the mood, he turned to Kahn. It marked the beginning of a beautiful friendship that would last the vagaries of a complicated boxing career.

Two months later on August 3, Argüello fought for Teddy Brenner again at the Garden. The famed matchmaker played a vital role in shaping the Nicaraguan's career. This time around, however, Argüello was content to play second fiddle to Puerto Rican defensive genius Wilfred Benítez, a boxer who possessed more natural ability than any fighter in the world. In front of 11,236 faithful fans, Benítez fought a listless bout as he waited until the fifteenth round to dispose of overmatched Ray Chavez Guerrero. While Benítez was under-whelming in his performance, Argüello made quick work of the Dominican Republic's José Fernández (28-9-3), who had dropped five of his previous thir-teen contests. Argüello recorded three knockdowns before the slaughter was stopped at 2:06 of the first round. The three-knockdown rule, which in 1977 had not been enforced by all sanctioning bodies and jurisdictions, states that if a boxer is knocked to the canvas three times during a round, the fight is over and recorded as a technical knockout for the victor.

"That fight against José Fernández was only his second fight in New York," said Associated Press (AP) journalist Ed Schuyler Jr. "Boxing people knew him, but the guy just going to see the fights might not have known him. Don't forget a lot of those fans in New York were Puerto Ricans and Panamanians. Hell, a lot of people don't know where Nicaragua is now."

Then Argüello (54-4) padded his record with a ten-round unanimous deci-sion over Benjamin Ortiz in Roberto Clemente Stadium in San Juan, Puerto Rico. By moving up in weight, Argüello did not lose his penchant for early knockouts or for using the closing speed of his right hand. Still, in a handful of junior lightweight and over-the-weight contests, Argüello had not yet fought a true threat. His next bout on September 29, 1977 with Philadelphia southpaw Jerome Artis would be the first serious challenge in his new weight division. A light puncher, Artis (16-1-4) had compiled only six knockouts in his twenty-one bouts. Fighting on the undercard of a heavyweight tilt between Muhammad Ali and Earnie Shavers, Argüello never allowed Artis to get into a rhythm. After registering a knockdown at the outset of the second round, Argüello finished off Artis at 2:00 of the same round for his forty-fourth knockout victory in a near-flawless career. Referee Lew Eskin confirmed the knockdown: "Artis did not want to fight. He was just staying out of trouble."

Journalist Tijerino went back to Argüello's hotel room after the fight, and received news of his impending retirement. During the brief conversation, Argüello said, "I am going to retire. I am not going to continue." The fighter lamented the fact that he let down his mentor Dr. Roman, who was prepared to put him in to fight for a second world title, but there was no one who could talk him out of it.

Days later, Argüello appeared at Club Las Colinas to reveal his plans.

"After this fight, Alexis came back to Nicaragua and announced at a press conference—before he fought for his second title—that he was retiring," Tijerino recalled. "He wasn't emotionally ok, and he had depression. I wrote in *La Cronica* that 'Alexis announced his retirement.' But I didn't think he was going to do it, because it was just a moment—a mind-set. Then he came back to keep fighting."

Despite his impulsiveness, Argüello would call a press conference in Nicaragua to confirm his plans to retire, but quickly reneged and did not follow through on his retirement plans. After a nondescript tune-up, fifth-round knockout victory over Enrique Solis that December, Argüello was involved in a minor auto accident with trainer and cutman Al Silvani in Nicaragua. While suffering minor injuries, both men confirmed that the upcoming title bout with current WBC super featherweight champ Alfredo Escalera would go off as planned on January 28, 1978.

During this time, Escalera was carving his own impressive body of work in the 130-pound weight class. A native of Carolina, Puerto Rico, Escalera shared his hometown with the skilled lightweight Esteban De Jesús. While De Jesús was busy finishing his glorious lightweight trilogy with Roberto Durán, Escalera was preparing for the toughest challenge of his career.

"Anastasio Somoza was very friendly to us. Argüello needed a new trainer. We got him Al Silvani. Al went to Nicaragua to work with him a couple times. Then he went to Puerto Rico when he fought [Alfredo] Escalera," promoter Don Fraser recalled.

In the late 1970s, boxing experts salivated at the possible showdown between lightweight (135 pounds) champ Roberto Durán and Argüello, but both fighters were on the move. While Argüello searched for his second title at the junior lightweight division, or 130 pounds, Durán could hardly make 135 pounds anymore. Argüello settled for a bout with Escalera, and Durán tried to position himself for the biggest money fight of his career opposite Olympic golden boy Sugar Ray Leonard. During this period, it was Durán who galvanized boxing fans, seducing them with his elixir of vitriol and natural skills. Although Argüello never expressed his frustration, he must have felt slighted by the global appreciation for a guy who was his polar opposite. By the time they were clearly past their primes, though, each fighter would have won at least three world titles.

In January 1978, Alfredo Escalera defended his WBC super featherweight crown against Argüello in Bayamón, Puerto Rico, at the Juan Ramón Lubriel Stadium. "El Salsero," a nickname Escalera earned from his salsa-dancing days, had defended his crown ten times already, outpointing contenders such as slick Philly native Tyrone Everett, Venezuelan stalwart Leonel Hernández, and, on two occasions, Japan's Buzzsaw Yamabe. Many claimed that Escalera received a gift decision against Philadelphian Tyrone Everett and retained his title in an extremely controversial outcome. The division lacked formidable challengers, so when Escalera signed to fight Argüello, the boxing world tuned in. Escalera recognized the danger of facing Argüello; however, his manager, Paul Ruiz, had little doubt that his fighter would rise to the challenge.

"There was no negativity between Alexis and Alfredo, and the first time they saw each other was the press conference," said Ruiz. "Also, Escalera was a tough guy, but a gentleman. He didn't like to put the other guy down. So they were both the best gentlemen."

The fight was billed the "Bloody Battle of Bayamon," and thousands came out to support their hero, Escalera. Leading into the bout, there was one guarantee: both men would come forward for fifteen rounds. Each had his quirks. Escalera loved to shock his fans, and he was always looking for a good time. Conversely, Argüello appeared tight, pensive, and withdrawn. In fact, both his manager, Dr. Roman, and the Nicaraguan journalists noticed the change in him. It was unusual for Argüello, let alone any fighter, to appear indifferent and detached leading into the biggest fight of his life. Even his closest confidants couldn't get him to engage with them in any way.

"Before the fight with Alfredo Escalera, Alexis was in a conflicted moment, and he didn't know where he was heading," said journalist Edgar Tijerino. "Dr. Eduardo Roman said it was a mystery, and he also didn't know where Alexis was headed. But he always faced the media, and went out to fight a great fight."

Years later, Dr. Roman took a broad stroke and skirted around the issue: "Sometimes you can see an amazing doctor or engineer who have some type of common behavior. It is the same with boxers. They have that common behavior because they are in this type of hard profession. You see a lot of the worst in boxers because of how hard they live, and they don't have a lot of sex, so it influenced the way they act with people. Alexis was a boxer and it got him to thinking very similar to other boxers."

Escalera, however, livened the atmosphere whenever he walked in a room.

"By that time, I considered Argüello a great fighter," said boxing journalist Michael Marley, who covered the title bout. "And that made the difference. Escalera walked in with a snake around his neck and even brought that snake to the weigh-in. He was one of the more popular Puerto Rican boxers. He wasn't beloved like three-time champ Wilfred Benítez or [Felix] Tito Trinidad, but the people loved Escalera because he always gave it his all. On paper, he was no match for Argüello."

A hard, incessant rain poured down the day of the fight. The combatants stayed dry under a tin roof erected several feet above the ring, but it often leaked onto the canvas. Now working with the stoic Mexican trainer Cuyo Hernández, Argüello (57-4) was the favorite. The corner team consisted of Hernández, the head trainer, with Kahn and Pambelé as the assistants. Referee Arthur Mercante was doing his twenty-eighth title fight and would be busy throughout the contest. Argüello came in at 130 pounds, and Escalera was half a pound under the weight limit. Critics who analyzed their styles realized that Argüello brought power in both hands, while Escalera aggravated foes with his speed, punched at awkward angles, and favored movement.

That style frustrated Argüello from the outset. The lanky Escalera pinpointed Argüello's chin through his tight guard, and Escalera's herky-jerky motion made it difficult for the challenger to land clean shots. Neither fighter controlled the action as they traded shots to end an action-packed first round. However, three minutes later Argüello had begun to find a rhythm, landing short left hooks. A brawl ensued for thirty seconds, and somewhere during that frantic second round, Argüello sliced a cut over the corner of Escalera's left eye, which aggravated the Puerto Rican champ for the remainder of the bout. During one violent exchange, referee Mercante confirmed that Escalera was sent to the canvas, and although the punch had little impact, it added intrigue to a chaotic round. Many wondered if Escalera's undisciplined approach would effectively offset Argüello's short, precise, and more accurate style.

"After Argüello knocked him down in that second round, I told him, 'Flaco, don't take any chances with this guy. He's still strong,'" trainer Don Kahn advised. "It was a difficult fight and I told Alexis to fight smart and don't let up until you see him go down."

Escalera came out for Round 3 with huge gobs of Vaseline purposefully left on his face between rounds, a clear corner tactic. Typically, a referee will send the fighter back to his corner to have his handlers either remove the substance or rub it into the fighter's face, but referee Mercante didn't admonish the fighter or the corner, so the round continued. Defense was not an option as Escalera held his gloves low and carelessly sauntered in and out of Argüello's zone. Argüello's jabs had begun to eat away, though, at the fierce cuts around Escalera's eye by the third round. Escalera still showed glimpses of power and walked through some of Argüello's early shots, but a vicious left uppercut and right hand only increased the blood flow from Escalera's damaged eyes. Cuts zigzagged his once clean face.

By the fifth round, cuts had worsened in Escalera's mouth and on his lower lip. Each time Argüello landed a clean hook, a spigot of blood shot out. Although Escalera was still partially effective, Argüello's ability to stay calm and collected gave him a decided edge. Argüello thought about each punch, while Escalera threw punches with abandon. While cuts have been known to make fighters reluctant, they had the opposite effect on Escalera. He didn't paw at them or shy away from the violence; he invited it, a quality that few great fighters have. On the inside, the warriors continued to jaw away. "I am going to kill you Flaco," warned Escalera. "Not if I kill you first, Negro," Argüello retorted.

"Escalera was a guy who would fight anyone, anywhere," said Ruiz. "But that night everything went wrong. He was fighting with his training mouthpiece, so he had to fight with his lip hanging out."

Taking a breather in the sixth, the fighters rallied a round later. In fact, the seventh round proved to be climactic as Argüello reproved Escalera at every juncture, and even tripled up on his hooks. Escalera spit blood along the canvas and sprayed the front-row journalists as he moved away from the powerful challenger. Argüello found him, pushed him off, and landed a fluid five-punch combination that didn't visibly deter Escalera's onward push. After the combination, Escalera got nailed with a huge right hand that nearly swiveled his head; somehow, he managed to land his own left hook to the jaw. In a rare moment of exasperation, Escalera walked into a left hook and then slumped on Argüello's shoulders. He scanned his corner listlessly, hoping for some relief from the torture. When the merciless round ended, Argüello held up his glove to show respect, and the indifferent Escalera looked past him and walked away. Although both men had shown the utmost respect outside the ring, they taunted and provoked each other throughout the fight.

"They were like savages. I was scared of seeing Escalera's face, his lips were ripped off, and his eyebrow was cut," said Tijerino, who covered the bout. "A lot of people supporting Escalera were calling for the people to stop the fight. They were trying to stop it for Escalera because his face looked so bad, and they didn't want him to have any more punishment."

Between rounds, the doctor was summoned to Escalera's corner, and surprisingly he noted that the cuts weren't severe enough to end the fight. If Escalera hadn't been put through enough torture in the seventh, Argüello exacerbated the situation by hurting him again in the eighth.

Argüello had completely figured out the champ by the ninth; Escalera's staple right to the body and left to the head had almost no effect on him. Still, Escalera was active enough to earn the round, one of the few in the fight. During training both he and Ruiz had emphasized the "sprints," where Escalera got his second wind; thus, he woke up in the ninth. For the third time in the fight, in the tenth round referee Mercante stepped in and warned Escalera of backhanded punches, but at this point it didn't matter. Despite being nailed with a surprise uppercut that opened a cut under his right eye, Argüello latched on to that prize jab and kept sticking it to the myriad cuts that covered Escalera's face.

"In the twelfth round, Escalera's lip was all messed up, but he never gave up," Kahn noted. "In fact he caught Alexis with a good punch, and Alexis felt it. So I told him to jab and jab. But the kid was strong and until they stopped the fight, he kept coming and coming."

Between rounds they cleaned up the harmless cut that surfaced under Argüello's eye. Escalera jumped at Argüello with a hook to start the thirteenth round and absorbed a huge right and left hook. Mercante called time and brought Escalera over to the doctor. While cradling Escalera's face, the doctor examined the cuts. With 2:36 left in the round, Mercante stopped the slaughter.

"At the end his top lip was hanging off; the doctor came over and said, 'You can not make it,'" said Escalera's manager, Paul Ruiz. "I said you know how Alfredo fights, but that was it. It was a bad break."

Argüello was winning by five or six points on all three scorecards when the fight was called. Members of the Nicaraguan contingent crowded Argüello, the new WBC super featherweight champ at 130 pounds, and held up the dark-blue-and-white flag for the world to see that their guy had won his second world title in a new weight class. Escalera, who made $125,000 for the affair, pronounced his intentions to a reporter: "I am going to retire once and for all from boxing." Argüello, meanwhile, made plans to conquer the division.

"The Puerto Rican press and people knew that Escalera would need a miracle to beat Argüello," said Marley. "That night there was a wicked rainstorm. The press box wasn't covered and it was like a swamp at ringside. I remember writing that the very good fighter got outclassed by a great fighter. It was a war of attrition. You could see Argüello's mind at work. He was like a Swiss watch in everything he did. He was like a chess player who was always two or three moves ahead of you. But the next day was like a national depression in Puerto Rico. They gave grudging respect to Argüello. For him to come to Puerto Rico and beat their guy was a powerful statement."

Despite the victory, the Argüello camp may have underestimated Escalera's skills.

"We didn't think that Escalera was going to be so hard," said Roman. "He was a very good boxer. But Alexis was completely committed to training. He was always in good shape because he knew that the day he wasn't in shape, he could lose. So he always had good condition. The gym in San Juan was full of people. The Puerto Ricans were very nice to him. Sports people, the people who were interested in boxing, were always very nice to him."

Escalera's manager echoed Dr. Roman's sentiments that the Argüello camp underestimated his fighter's capabilities.

"In the first fight, Alexis never fought a guy as strong as Alfredo. When you bang like that, you feel it. Flaco could punch, but he didn't like to get hit back," said Ruiz. "Now, Alfredo didn't care if you killed him. He would beg to fight."

After the fight, Escalera's camp took their fighter to get stitched up at a nearby hospital. Although Escalera had put up a great fight, he suffered the consequences of facing a killer like Argüello. When he was released, Escalera went out and celebrated to release the pressure of the bout. Ironically, Argüello stayed in and didn't partake in the celebration.

"We went to the hospital after that first fight. [Despite reports] Alexis didn't," Ruiz said. "Alexis healed too quickly. You are not going to fight that soon after if your ribs were broken. Alexis only had discoloration around his eye. I never saw something like that in the ring; two masters in the ring."

The next morning, both fighters were supposed to meet one last time, but they went their separate ways.

"The morning after the 'Duel at Sunset' was a painful one for all of us around Alfredo, for all of us with the exception of Alfredo," said Ruiz. "It seemed that all the pressure of such an important fight was finally taken off his shoulders and his simple life was once again given back to him. His humor came back and, yes, he did invite Alexis to breakfast but he [Alexis] did not accept the invitation."

Despite the personal issues that Argüello was dealing with, he had been able to block out any interference and focus on Escalera. In contrast to the outside influences, Argüello had complete control inside the ring.

"Experience-wise, I was much better when I fought with Escalera than when I fought with Marcel," said Argüello, "and I thought I could solve the problem with one punch."

The new champ didn't take time to revel in his success; there would always be an opportunity later on to enjoy his celebrity. The strain of the sport had taken its toll on him. "I stayed away from that life because, well, after fights I was too tired," Argüello said. "I needed to rest. Whether it was my tooth was falling out or it was my eye. . . . Who wants to party when you can't eat or even put soap on your head? Forget about it. I told them to go, and I would rest."

Now a two-time champion in both the 126- and 130-pound weight classes, Argüello didn't waste time. He continued to plug away and move closer to the lightweight and welterweight divisions where big money fights with such marquee fighters as Sugar Ray Leonard and Roberto Durán awaited. After winning his second world title in an exhausting bout, Argüello did not need to extend himself in his next match, a nontitle contest against lightly regarded Mario Méndez in Las Vegas. Fighting as the opener to the heavyweight title bout between Larry Holmes and Earnie Shavers, Argüello was expected to handle Méndez easily. After disposing of the Mexican southpaw in three rounds on March 25, 1978, at Caesars Palace in Las Vegas, Argüello (58-4) signed to make his first defense against another southpaw, Rey Tam. A unique pattern of lefty challengers developed.

No longer was Argüello a secret. After the Escalera bout, Argüello began to earn votes as the top fighter in the world. In the article "Pound for Pound: The Best There Is!" writers and boxing insiders heralded Argüello as on a par with the indomitable Roberto Durán. Respected trainer Angelo Dundee lit up when he talked about the classy Nicaraguan fighter.

"I love watching the kid fight," he said. "Argüello sets you up beautifully and just doesn't let up. He's so cool in there, never going wild, even when pressured and hit. He's the best body-puncher I've seen in a long time. He hits you where you live, taking all the fight out of you. Argüello is the best I've seen in a long time."

Argüello balanced his power with patience and used his intuitive sense to understand when a fighter was ready to be knocked out. Few, if any, fighters were blessed with that innate sense. Filipino Rey Tam (23-0-1, twelve knockouts) from Baguio City had little of the panache or skill of his compatriot and Hall of Famer Gabriel "Flash" Elorde. Elorde was one of the top junior lightweights of the 1970s when the division was packed with abundant talent. Ranked No. 4 by the World Boxing Council, Tam was a decent fighter who found himself in the presence of a great one. The fight was scheduled to take place at the Inglewood Forum on April 29, ten days after Argüello celebrated his twenty-sixth birthday. Those who chose to investigate the significance behind Tam's No. 4 ranking came up empty-handed; in fact, Tam had not fought anyone worthy of a top-fifty ranking. His controversial ranking would be eclipsed only by his lack of effort.

Argüello, fighting for the third time at the Inglewood Forum, had grown familiar with the surroundings. Los Angeles represented a haven for the Nicaraguan, and he became a mainstay at the Main Street Gym.

Forum promoter Don Fraser shared top billing with Don King for the bout, which was televised on *Wide World of Sports* for the American Broadcasting Company (ABC). Argüello would add $115,000 to his account for this bout. Three days before the match, confusion over Tam's visa and subsequent entry into the country nearly postponed it, but Fraser ironed out the details, and Tam was ready by the fight date. Tam came in at 129¾ pounds, while Argüello walked in a shredded 129½. Tam struggled mightily as he shed 2¼ pounds in order to make weight. Fighting in front of fifteen hundred onlookers and millions of TV viewers, Argüello, who was becoming a TV sensation, early on didn't show Tam much respect.

Tam wasn't the type of slippery, awkward southpaw who often gave Argüello problems. Nor was he the macho southpaw willing to take two punches to land one. As Argüello was polishing his boxing skills, Tam was a mere pit stop. There was no customary feeling-out process as Argüello struck early and often with uppercuts and right leads. Anyone who couldn't see that Argüello was a methodical technician wasn't studying the fighter close enough. Because Tam didn't understand the peril of standing in front of the killer, Argüello used his near seventy-inch reach and sledgehammer jab to remind him. By the third round, Tam became hesitant after absorbing multiple hooks and jabs from Argüello.

In the third round, Tam made the mistake of motioning Argüello to the ropes. With his beautiful defense, the WBC champ bounced off the ropes and landed an uppercut, the best punch of the fight. Tam pressed the action with those lefts, but he often got the worst of it as Argüello countered effectively.

With 1:20 left in the fifth round, the champion Argüello initiated the final assault with a grazing uppercut followed by a left hook that nearly decapitated Tam. A disoriented Tam stumbled around the ring but didn't fall. Argüello chased him and landed an uppercut to his neck, a running left hook, and a right hook to the hip. Then he was bottled up by a brief respite as Tam clinched.

With Tam reeling, Argüello sent his beaten opponent back to the ropes with two more right hands and one vicious punch to the neck. In a move eerily prescient of the famous 1980 "No Mas" bout between Sugar Ray Leonard and Roberto Durán, Tam decided that he was finished, held up his glove, and surrendered. Few questioned the decision when referee Rudy Jordan stepped between them and officially halted the bout at 1:54 of the fifth round. Without changing his expression, Argüello put his hand in the air and went over to check on Tam. "The punch [that hurt him] was to the body," Argüello explained after the fight.

One newspaper said Tam took the easy way out. But because few expected Tam to put up much of a fight, the crowd didn't protest the poor effort from the overmatched challenger.

"That fight against Tam was a co-promotion with King," said Fraser. "We put it on *Wide World of Sports*. We brought in Tam, a Filipino who couldn't fight that well. Oh, and did he have trouble with the visa. After that fight there wasn't a backlash, and there were no riots. Nobody expected the Filipino to win it."

Argüello, represented by Don King Productions, wouldn't face another capable puncher until his rematch with Escalera the following year. Meanwhile, on May 19, Argüello had signed to meet a Panamanian who, unfortunately for everyone associated with boxing, was not Roberto Durán. Argüello met Diego Alcala in San Juan, Puerto Rico, on June 3, 1978, in a bout staged by Don King. Alcala (30-8-2) had few of the attributes of the typical Panamanian challenger. In fact, in the boxing community many understood that he had done less than Tam had to earn the No. 3 position in the junior lightweight division, and they attributed his ranking to WBC politics To add to the absurdity, Alcala was ranked only the seventh best junior lightweight in the lightly regarded division of the Central American Boxing Federation (FECARBOX). In over a year and a half Alcala moved from No. 5 to the No. 3 spot among the WBC junior lightweights. During that period, Alcala beat three nonentities, each of whom had suffered at least seven losses, and his manufactured record had left out at least two losses. He was neither a big puncher nor a skilled boxer. Although Alcala showed quickness, he lacked the fearlessness and willingness to engage that so many of his countrymen exhibited. Panamanian warrior and featherweight champion Eusebio Pedroza he was not. When facing Argüello, whether it was a legitimate move or one meant to agitate the champ, the Alcala camp chose to press Argüello on a glove issue.

"Against Alcala in Puerto Rico, a representative of Alcala came over and started bothering Alexis and telling him that he was wrapping his hands wrong," said Roman. "For the first time, Alexis was so mad. I told the man if he didn't stop bothering Alexis, we would tell the promoter that we wouldn't fight. Alexis was very professional, but he was still mad when he went into the ring. . . ."

At thirty years old, Alcala evidently had nothing to offer the great champ and briefly stumbled from an ordinary Argüello left hook to start the bout. Less than a minute later, the Panamanian challenger was sprawled out between the middle ropes. A short uppercut and a left hook to the neck had Alcala flailing, but it was the next uppercut that caught Alcala flush and ended the fight. One more punch and the challenger could have been seriously injured. For those who made the bout, it was an embarrassing ending to a clear mismatch. Argüello only needed a little longer than a minute to dispose of the challenger.

While the champ received $100,000 for his short work, Alcala took home $15,000 for his less than stellar effort. After the fight, Argüello was clearly miffed at the lack of effort Alcala exerted. Argüello said, "I can't remember an easier encounter. I didn't even work up a sweat." When asked if Durán was on his radar, he replied, "No, not yet. Maybe early next year." Durán was busy mulling a $400,000 offer to fight WBA welterweight champ, Colombia's Antonio Cervantes.

Prior to making short work of Alcala, Argüello had turned his attention toward the undercard bout with Alfredo Escalera facing Rogelio Castaneda. It had been only little more than four months since Argüello had bested Escalera for the WBC belt. Now not only did Argüello openly cheer for Escalera, but he also sneaked into his corner to offer instructions. Yet Argüello did not give a ringing endorsement after the fight when he said, "I'll give Alfredo a rematch, if he wants it, but if a light puncher like Castaneda was able to do so much damage, imagine what someone with a punch can do."

ROUND 6

Movin' on Up

I'll tell you one thing, when I get out of this division, I'll be happy.
—ALEXIS ARGÜELLO

In early July 1978, in a move designed to make boxing more palatable, Madison Square Garden Corporation president Sonny Werblin signed Don King as the new copromoter of its historic boxing institution. The contract was nonexclusive and allowed the Garden to work with various independent promoters. The news struck a chord with Garden matchmaker Teddy Brenner, who had little respect for the menacing, three-hundred-pound former convict. Werblin added that the move would "certainly put us in a better spot," which translated to more leverage at the bargaining table, and would position the group to bring in big fights with Top Rank's Bob Arum on the other end of the negotiating table. King would continue to be an independent promoter, but he would provide essential leverage for the Garden to hold heavyweight title bouts. Several possible bouts with Roberto Durán, Carlos Palomino, Larry Holmes, and Wilfred Benítez were mentioned for the initial copromotion with the new staff.

Meanwhile, King copromoted Argüello's next bout, a nontitle scrap with Dominican Vilomar Fernández whose elusive style had severely agitated all of his thirty opponents. Argüello went to New York to train with master cutman and cornerman Al Silvani at Bobby Gleason's Gym on West Thirtieth Street. According to those close to him, Argüello didn't feel the affinity with Silvani that he had with other trainers. Part of the problem was the language barrier, and they only spent a few weeks together before the fight. But as one trainer noted, "We did the work, but Silvani was the main man." Talks regarding a matchup between Argüello and Durán, meanwhile, had intensified.

"In the present state of life in this world," Silvani told reporters, "I would say that pound for pound, Argüello is the best fighter in the world. He has the necessary jab and the necessary right cross; he's got the left hook to the body, to the head. He's got the right uppercut. He weaves. He has a lot of foot movement. He has the hardest punch in the division. You can't call for more than that. He will take Durán in the early part of next year."

Yet Argüello was not only concerned with boxing. He added two Dobermans to the flock of animals at his Managua home. The dogs would join his parrot and a pair of monkeys.

"You would go to his house and it was like a zoo," said Roman. "Sometimes I would not go there because of the monkeys."

Argüello earned top billing on the seven-fight card, which also featured former super featherweight champ Alfredo Escalera on the undercard. Then, just when Argüello began to make his argument that he was the top fighter in the pound-for-pound category, he stumbled. Fighting for the fourth time at Madison Square Garden, Argüello wanted to impress against Fernández (22-6-2, seven knockouts). A crowd of 11,875 produced a $166,032 gate. Although the unheralded Fernández had six losses on his résumé, he aggravated big punchers with his slippery, skillful style. The unflappable lightweight king Roberto Durán had needed thirteen rounds to dispose of Fernández in January 1977.

Prior to Argüello's bout with Fernández, the conversation with reporters turned to Durán. Argüello did not back down when he told a reporter, "I feel strong at this weight. Very strong! I feel I can take Roberto Durán right now." However, despite the champ's plea to face the Panamanian, Argüello was clearly aware that Durán, who had set his sights on the 147-pounders, was already acclimating his body to the welterweight division. The Argüello-Durán fight would never materialize.

The Fernández bout, held on July 26, 1978, didn't stray from expectations. This time around Fernández had the benefit of meeting an uninspired Alexis Argüello. Argüello came in at 135¼ pounds, while Fernández entered at 134¾.

Occasionally, the nontitle label alone can elicit average performances and apathy from world-class fighters. In fact, Durán fought a ten-round nontitle clunker at the Garden in 1972, appearing listless and apathetic during a dreadful loss to Esteban De Jesús. Durán suffered a careless first-round knockdown and plodded aimlessly through the rest of the bout. Although De Jesús was a step above Fernández, Argüello had the opportunity to show the Garden faithful that he did not take any nights off, especially against a notorious "runner" like Fernández. The backstory added intrigue as Argüello had deposited Vilomar's brother, José, in one round in 1977, and his reputation was growing in the Big Apple.

If patience was a virtue for Argüello during his previous sixty bouts, he took it to an extreme at the outset of this one. The bouncy and loose Fernández accentuated Argüello's tightness by circling him and raking him with combinations in the second round. A round later, Fernández connected on a right cross to Argüello's throat, easily the most potent punch of the evening. It was still early, but if Argüello subscribed to the notion of training for every fight "like a championship fight," this one looked to be an exception.

Lacking any of the conviction or venom that defined his earlier bouts, Argüello watched helplessly as Fernández piled up points. In one instance, the Dominican landed a flush overhand right and quickly feinted, leaving Argüello to heave a lunging right hand that missed by miles. In the fourth round, Argüello pushed a weak, pawing jab, and Fernández beat him to the punch. The crowd recognized that Fernández was forcing Argüello to assent to his style.

Argüello's trainer, Al Silvani, screamed in Argüello's ear during the majority of the break, anything to kindle a fire under his charge. Argüello did not heed the exhortation in the fifth and was stunned by a telegraphed winging right cross. Fernández added an exclamation point to the round with a sharp combination that left an indelible mark on the judges. What Argüello deemed an unwillingness to fight, others recognized as a beautiful boxing display.

The momentum shifted in the sixth, as the champ unleashed a fierce attack. Pushing Fernández from one side of the ropes to the other, Argüello landed a devastating right uppercut followed by a left hook to the body that forced the challenger into a matador style. Fernández put his hands in the air and slithered down the side of the ropes, out of harm's way. Yet he was only afforded a brief respite as Argüello trapped and blistered Fernández with triple left hooks to the body. Fernández, fortunate to survive the round, went back to the corner and plotted his revenge.

Unable to continue at that pace or capitalize on his success, Argüello slowed in the seventh. As fans and the three judges tallied their scorecards heading into the eighth, few would have believed that Fernández was still on his feet let alone comfortably winning the bout. For the first time in his career, Argüello lost his composure in the eighth round. Standing alone in the middle of the ring, Argüello uncharacteristically dropped his guard and put his palms up as if to say, "C'mon, let's go." Fernández responded with a little jig of his own. Argüello put his right hand up in the air and shook it, but the posturing only wasted precious time. It was clear that Argüello needed a knockout in the last two rounds to salvage a victory.

Boxing scribes were already placing their vote for Upset of the Year by the ninth round, and nothing occurred during those three minutes to change their minds. Argüello absorbed two flash right hands that he normally would have picked off, and at this point, his legs had become useless. He resorted to following Fernández again, a recipe for disaster.

In the tenth and final round, Argüello found his target on several occasions, but it was too late. Claims that the fight meant the world to Fernández and little to Argüello already had been confirmed after the first couple rounds. Ironically, Fernández confronted Argüello in the final seconds of the bout and recklessly brawled with him. As the bell sounded, a dejected Argüello put his hand out to congratulate Fernández. He knew he lost the fight.

Fernández jabbed and ran for ten rounds, and he never let Argüello turn on his punches. By the end of the fight, referee Arthur Mercante had it even at 5-5, Sam Irom scored it 5-4-1 for Fernández, while Artie Aidala (6-4) also scored it in favor of the majority-decision victor Fernández.

"Against Fernández there was nothing at stake. Great fighters have down days. It meant more to Vilomar than it did to Alexis," said boxing writer Ed Schuyler Jr. "It was just a nontitle bout. There was a day when you could lose and it wouldn't hurt your reputation. It didn't hurt Argüello."

The lightly regarded Fernández, meanwhile, ran into his dressing room, yelling, "I did it! I did it! I beat Alexis Argüello!" A despondent Argüello made excuses for his performance, and any talk about a matchup with Durán quickly dissolved at the sound of the final bell.

"What could I do?" he asked. "The guy just wouldn't stand and fight with me. He challenged me to a foot race, that's what he did. He won the race. If he wanted to fight I would have won. Running is not fighting. Not in my book, anyway." Away from the ring, Argüello was settling in with his third wife, Loretto Martinez; Roman had threatened to stop managing him if he didn't seek a divorce from Barreto. Argüello heeded his advice.

Years later looking back on the bout, Argüello provided a more objective assessment: "Against Fernández I became overconfident. I was in New York and I wasn't concentrating. I was shopping with my third wife."

Manager Dr. Roman commented on his fighter's lackluster performance when he said, "Vilomar was fast moving. Alexis trained and was in good condition. But he had a different style and Fernández was a lot better than he had expected. Alexis had to change during the fight, but he didn't. Nobody trains the exact same way for each boxer. The way he moved and was throwing punches . . . he told me, 'He didn't even put me back.' But that is not the way to explain a fight because nobody put you back. It is a matter of how many punches you give or receive. I think sometimes he pretended that he didn't receive as many punches, but he had."

Ironically, former foe Alfredo Escalera had outshone Argüello that evening. He became a title contender again in the 130-pound division as he dispatched rugged Larry Stanton in three rounds.

Having survived a roller-coaster ride of marriages, messy divorces, and brief retirements over the previous two years, Argüello finally began to settle into his role as champion, and the boxing world started to view him as the "Gentleman of the Ring," to complement his nickname "Flaco Explosivo" or "Explosive Thin Man," which he had earned back in Nicaragua.

Following a disciplined regimen without disruption was a tenet of Argüello's career and legacy. The Fernández fight was merely a blip, but it disgusted the champ. Boxing historian Lee Groves understood the ramifications of the bout: "That fight got a lot of play. It was the fight that essentially killed the Duran bout. Duran said, 'Screw it. I'm not waiting for him.' The purpose of Argüello fighting that bout was to establish a ranking at 135. They got the safest guy, who was a fringe contender. They knew Vilomar would be a nice 'B' side at the Garden. Get the Dominicans in and Argüello's crowd in, and let Argüello knock him out. I am convinced Duran would have made it one more fight at 135."

Promoter Don King continued to gain leverage as the world's most influential promoter as he infused cards around the world with his loquacious personality and intimidation tactics. The fall after the Fernández loss, the *New York Times* reported that Argüello had signed a two-year promotional deal with Madison Square Garden's Teddy Brenner on October 1, 1978. Brenner gave King permission to promote Argüello's next bout with Arturo León, but then Brenner and King became embroiled in an ongoing controversy. Since negotiations for an October 27 bout disintegrated, King negotiated a November title matchup with Arturo León.

Argüello met León (19-13-2) on November 10, 1978, at Caesars Palace in Las Vegas. Critics looked at the weight issue as the decisive factor. Those who labeled León, who weighed in at 128¼ pounds, a mere diversion for the 130-pound champ were sorely mistaken. The startling ebb and flow of León's record proved deceiving. In fact, a late 1977 split-decision win over Bobby Chacón, who later would win another crown over Rafael "Bazooka" Limón, boosted him to the WBC super featherweight (now the junior lightweight) title match. The win catapulted León up six spots from No. 12 to No. 6 in the rankings. Meanwhile, rumors surfaced concerning Argüello's difficult struggle and loss of strength while making the 130-pound limit. The match would warm up the headliner between Larry Holmes and Spaniard Alfredo Evangelista for Holmes's WBC heavyweight crown.

In his third defense of his super featherweight crown, Argüello waited for referee Davey Pearl to go over the rules. Understanding the magnitude of the situation and that he wasn't close to optimal shape, Argüello hastily attacked León early. In previous bouts, the often patient and exacting Argüello moved laterally and bided his time; now he ambushed and threw punches. A nonchalant León walked into heavy hooks and a straight right that would have felled many 130-pounders. Alexis punched to hurt in that first round and looked to end the bout. To his chagrin, the underdog León survived to see another round.

Stylistically, not much changed over the next two rounds. While Argüello hit, León both took big punches that Argüello was able to "sit on" and slowly showed a willingness to fight back. The turning point came with thirty seconds remaining in the third round. León weathered a brutal flurry, landed his own right lead, and then tagged a punched-out Argüello with a clean left hook. The image of a concerned Argüello pawing at the first of two cuts as the round ended gave León fans hope. The fast start had Argüello clinging early to a big lead and forging exhaustively through the middle rounds. While broadcaster Howard Cosell ruminated on the Mexican fighter's fortitude, León staged a comeback. He neutralized Argüello's reach and visibly frustrated the champ with his defiance. Meanwhile, a sharp Argüello occasionally transformed into a sloppy, lunging fighter. Anytime Argüello rushed his punches, however, it was a cause for concern. Halfway through the fight, Argüello's camp was tending to a cut over his left eye and the blackening under his right eye.

At the outset of the sixth round, León felt the champ's power again. This time an arcing left hook sent León down immediately, without hesitation or stumble. León planted his arm for leverage and was up by the count of six. More dejected than hurt, León recovered and moved away from Argüello. The champ landed consecutive left hooks to the body and clipped León again as he headed for the ropes. But León was not one to panic, and he grabbed Argüello's right glove to buy time. Despite the crafty move, Argüello wiggled free, rushed in with abandon, and bullied the smaller fighter.

Over the next three rounds, Argüello continued to breathe heavily, press the action, and stay in control. With the exception of a few impressive flurries, Argüello didn't take any risks until the twelfth round when he jarred León with a long, straight right. The energized Nicaraguan found his second wind and followed León around for the rest of the round. Another punishing right hand put him back in charge. Despite the frustrations, the spirited Argüello never wavered from the task. As the fight headed into the late rounds, Argüello stirred a rambunctious crowd with a barrage of body shots with seconds left in the thirteenth; yet, both combatants were too weary to mount a full-fledged attack in the final three minutes. Awarding the win was an easy decision for the three judges, who all went for the champ: 146–139, 146–139, and 145–140. Still, León didn't lose any fans in what many considered an admirable performance. Argüello looked ahead.

Two months later a return bout with Escalera was confirmed through the press outlets. The championship bout would be held in Rimini, Italy. Instead of getting to Italy early, Argüello trained in Mexico City, where he stayed to catch a glimpse of Pope John Paul II.

The return bout with Escalera spearheaded Argüello into 1979, a year that proved pivotal in Argüello's growth. Anointed the Explosive Thin Man and Gentleman of the Ring, Argüello now spent his time cruising on Miami yachts and mixing with the country club crowd. After a failed marriage to Patricia Barreto, Argüello had moved on and married his third wife, Loretto Martinez, whom he met in Miami in 1978. Martinez's grandfather had been a lieutenant in Anastasio Somoza's army. According to friends and family, Loretto had provided Argüello with the stability and support he needed. Often, she followed him to training sessions and vigilantly watched his diet. While Argüello, now 62-5, had excelled since winning the WBC junior lightweight crown, his nemesis Alfredo Escalera had experienced surprising setbacks against inferior competition. The Puerto Rican challenger had gone 2-1 in the year since their initial meeting.

After several battles over the fight venue almost completely severed negotiations, the rematch found a home at Rimini's Sports Palace. Independent matchmaker Teddy Brenner sold the bout's promotional rights to Bob Arum and Top Rank. Argüello was prepared to defend his title against Alfredo Escalera (42-9-2) on February 4, 1979. The rivalry had the potential to capture the fight fans' imagination much as had previous rivalries, such as the middleweight trilogy between Tony Zale and Rocky Graziano or the legendary featherweight battles between Sandy Saddler and Willie Pep.

When Don King was involved in the proceedings, there was always an undercurrent of mistrust. Before the return bout, Paul Ruiz, Escalera's manager, felt that King tried to undermine him in order to sign for the rematch and instead opted for working with Brenner.

"One night in New York at a Cuban restaurant, I was with Garden President Sonny Werblin and Teddy Brenner. I told Sonny, 'I don't have a contract with Don King [for a rematch with Argüello].' Then King walked in and Teddy was a SOB [son of a bitch]. He stood up and walked out. After he did that, Sonny fired him," said Ruiz. "He didn't give a shit. Teddy called me and said, 'I need this fight.' So I gave him the fight, and we made it on CBS [Columbia Broadcasting System]. I never had to sign anything with him. Not one contract."

King and Brenner eventually were mired in lengthy legal proceedings after the fact, but the fight was signed. Although Argüello, who had parted ways with trainer Al Silvani in the interim, came in three-quarters of a pound lighter than Escalera did in the rematch, the weight—or anything else for that matter—would not make a difference. When the two men entered the ring, a brawl was imminent. It was just a matter of seeing what level of punishment each man would be able to withstand. The Italian referee Angelo Poletti wouldn't interfere as often as the referee from the first bout, Arthur Mercante, had, but Poletti had to be aware of Escalera's backhanded tendency, which invited criticism during the 1978 matchup. Moreover, this time, the men were indoors—the first meeting took place on a canvas constructed under a tin roof—and there was no place to hide in the suffocating sixteen-foot ring.

Unlike the turbulent period leading up to their first encounter, Argüello now felt more at ease. No longer was he contemplating an early retirement; instead, he was feeling more comfortable with the perks of being a champion. Argüello was solidifying a legacy inside and outside of the ring that would be difficult to match: Inside the ring, he was nearly flawless; outside the ring, fans, reporters, and opponents all flocked to him. His ability to master English helped him transform from a Latin icon to a worldwide superstar.

Unfortunately, his ferocious ring reputation preceded him. Sometimes it worked against him.

"In Italy, we couldn't spar with anyone, there were no boxers," remembered Dr. Eduardo Roman, his trusted manager. "Then he got Guillermo, his older brother, and his friends to spar with him. He used to spar with Orlando [his brother], but he used to say, 'Please, Alexis, don't hit me hard. If you are going to hit me hard, then I am not going to spar with you.' When he was sparring, Alexis wouldn't try to knock out anybody, but he used to throw hard punches. Sometimes his sparring partners would complain. They just threw up their hands and said, 'Stop it, please!' Alexis was a very highly disciplined person. He wanted to learn everything and he wanted to be the best."

Thus, Argüello also expected a lot from his trainers. While Don Kahn remained by his side throughout his entire career, the fighter had to acclimate to several different trainers in the corner. By this time, Argüello felt comfortable relying on the team of legendary Mexican trainer Cuyo Hernández, Pambelé, and Kahn because each man contributed something unique to his career. Undoubtedly, Hernández was the strongest personality of the three men, but if he needed advice outside the ring, Argüello turned to Kahn.

"Cuyo Hernández was the head trainer, the main guy in the corner. But he didn't get very close to Alexis. If he had to tell Alexis something, he might come to me and say, 'You know him better, tell him this.' But Alexis liked him because he was a 'figure' in the corner. Roman liked having a 'name' trainer in the middle of the ring to better influence judges or decisions," said Kahn.

"Cuyo would stay on the outside and always call on us to tell Alexis something. And he told me, 'Never call the fighter a champ.' He was a quiet man, never joked or played around. The kind of guy who doesn't wait for your reaction."

As for the particulars, the Escalera camp wanted to get an edge, so the group spent a month acclimating the fighter to the weather, culture, and time difference. As Escalera's manager, Paul Ruiz wanted to ensure that his fighter was prepared for all of the mishaps that occur before a fight. For example, in the first fight they had had to weave through six miles of traffic in Puerto Rico simply to reach the stadium.

At the sound of the opening bell, Argüello unleashed a furious attack. Instead of establishing a jab and staying on the outside, the champ opened by just throwing combinations. Yet, he appeared dried-up and gaunt compared with the loose and fluid challenger. By the second round, Alfredo Escalera, "The Snake Man," or "El Salsero," suffered few lingering effects from the epic first battle. First, Escalera lashed Argüello with a superior right cross that buckled Argüello's legs. Then he capitalized on the shot by following up with a short uppercut that Argüello couldn't defend. Whether preconceived or done impulsively, Escalera's uppercut showed that he had learned from his past mistakes. As he adapted, Escalera also forced Argüello to fight while backing up, which was one of the champ's few weaknesses. By getting inside Argüello's long arms, he landed three or four major uppercuts that bounced off the champ's face. It was clear that Escalera had won the round convincingly with an assortment of jabs, uppercuts, and right crosses.

Another element that might have alarmed Argüello's corner early on was Escalera was not taking any risks. Escalera was more aware of his defense as he held his hands higher and reined in his wild punches for sharper pinpoint offerings. As the fourth round got under way, the strategic battle slowly evolved into the war that defined these bouts. The consistent geyser of blood that was sliced open on Escalera's face in that first fight opened again in the fourth round. The incision under Escalera's right eye was the result of an Argüello left hook. The men traded power punches early, and while Argüello initiated the attack, Escalera finished with an awkwardly thrown uppercut that led into a long straight right and a short left hook. After a ten-second lull in the frantic pace, Argüello landed what appeared to be an ordinary left hook, but it sent Escalera down immediately. The challenger rose and took the mandatory eight count from referee Poletti. Argüello went after Escalera. While a litany of left hooks missed the target, a straight right landed squarely. Escalera showed his toughness as he survived the round.

Escalera was down again in the fifth round from another, more damaging, left hook, and he angrily threw his fists in frustration as he got up from another crunching left hook. Referee Poletti administered the second standing eight count in as many rounds. Escalera didn't have a quality corner to staunch his cut between rounds, and Argüello didn't need to land a punch before the cut seeped blood. Less than a minute after the second knockdown occurred, Poletti halted the action again, this time with Escalera still throwing punches. Concerned that the vicious three-punch combination that Argüello threw would lead to the end of Escalera, Poletti stepped in at 1:27 for one last eight count.

Blotches of blood crowded Escalera's face, but he still seemed aware and ready to return fire at any minute. The fight had not yet mirrored the brutality of the first meeting, but there were distinct parallels; that is, as the fight continued, Argüello got stronger. When Escalera impeded Argüello's progress by landing a rangy right hand and then controlled the infighting during the last thirty seconds of the round, the quiet crowd gloriously stirred at the brief comeback. Few men would have withstood the punishment that the champ doled out; even fewer would have had the strength to fight back. Escalera finished the round by landing three straight uppercuts and winning the hearts of the fans.

Again, Ruiz felt the sprints that they had practiced during Escalera's training would make the difference. He felt they would help break the lengthy fifteen-round fight into negotiable parts.

"The only difference [in the rematch] was that I had him moving a lot more. Alexis came in thinking, 'I've got to knock him out.' He was throwing one punch and looking for that knockout. So I had [Alfredo] moving side to side. The Italians were really cheering for Alfredo. The arena was packed and everyone was going crazy. They were like two roosters looking to maim each other," said Ruiz. "I always told Alfredo that we could break those 15-rounders with what we called 'sprints,' every five rounds. That was the plan because he had such great wind. During fights he would come on suddenly: 'Boom, boom and boom.'"

Escalera's sprint was not evident in the next round. Punches came in moderation in the sixth, as the story of the round was Escalera's condition. Another cut surfaced, this one under his left eye. At one point, Poletti halted the action to send the bloodied Escalera to his corner. The Snake Man slithered back into the fight in the seventh and punctuated the round with a brilliant right hand that shocked the champ. Argüello calmly took a step back, only to receive two more left hooks. Argüello covered up, and the Snake smothered him. The round ended with Escalera smiling. As they headed to the corner, Escalera playfully gave Argüello a headlock and two bops to the face. Although he opened a nasty cut on the corner of Argüello's right eye, Escalera's infectious smile wouldn't last.

Argüello, too, was battered. With swelling under his left eye and a severe cut on his right, his internal clock had to be ticking. It was time to get Escalera out of there. To add to the concern, Argüello's wife Loretto had exited between rounds, finding the punishment overwhelming. The champ pawed at his eye throughout the eighth round, clearly frustrated that Escalera walked through his stinging jab. If getting back to the jab was the key, Argüello demonstrated its effectiveness in the ninth and tenth rounds as he struck, jabbed, and moved at will. He mixed a jarring left hook that rocked an incoming Escalera, then missed a right hand that would have ended the fight at the close of the tenth.

The riveting ebb and flow of the rematch had already surpassed the first go-round as the men came out for the twelfth round. In fact, the tide turned in Escalera's favor one last time. Although he was blinded in the left eye, he not only landed a huge right and several uppercuts, but he also clearly won the round. He walked to his corner with his head held high.

"In the twelfth we knew the fight was close," Ruiz recalled. "I told him, 'We're getting closer. Keep moving.' But he never told me about the problem with his eye. Then in the next round, Alexis comes in with the picture-perfect shot. Alfredo never saw it coming. We just had bad luck. When he came back to corner. I said, 'No more.'"

Few Italian fans could believe what they were witnessing. Sequels weren't supposed to live up to the hype. Then, the fight was over, as quickly as the tide had seemingly turned. Victim of a stunning hook a minute into the thirteenth round, Escalera lost control of his faculties on the way down. He was able to prevent major injury by using his hands to cushion his fall and to protect his head. But the punch, a standing left hook, had caught Escalera by surprise. He was up by the count of five, tried to his maintain balance, and then helplessly fell into the ring post, landing in his handlers' arms. "I stuck my upper body and held on to Alfredo," Ruiz recalled. "That was enough for me. I did not want Alfredo to go on anymore. Alexis went down on his knees and held up his arms thanking God for the stoppage of a war he thought would never end."

"Well, the second fight was not easy. In the second round, Alexis had closed both of Escalera's eyes," said trainer Don Kahn. "But Escalera kept punching from all angles. In the twelfth round, I told him no more straight punches and to 'start throwing the hook! You have to throw that hook and catch him and that will be it.' Then he caught him on the chin and that was it."

As the handlers cradled Escalera, his deformed face was nearly unrecognizable with the swelling and cuts. The fighters embraced, shared the moment, and moved on. After twenty-six rounds of torture, both men realized they had been part of something special. Years later, the two combatants would become close friends.

"After that Escalera fight in Italy I had to make a flight, so we had to leave directly after the fight," Argüello recalled from a hotel in Managua. "The Mexican Dr. Horacio Ramírez Mercado had to do the plastic surgery right on the train with no Novocain. I was shaking all over, but I didn't feel a thing because they ripped off this piece above my eye right here. See this [pointing to it], it's like a flap. Didn't feel a thing. He gave me nineteen stitches that night."

Kahn remembered it a bit differently: "He got fourteen stitches on the train from Rimini to Valencia by Dr. Horacio Ramírez Mercado from Mexico. He had to sew him up on the train. That was a bloody time in that train. Everyone was carrying on in there. It moved so much it was a hammock. Every time Alexis felt the needle through his skin, he was yelling."

Roman had become so accustomed to using Mercado's services that he refused to allow any other doctor to stitch up his fighter. "Dr. Horacio Ramírez Mercado used to give him the stitches. He did it so when he received another punch, Alexis would never bleed again," said Roman. "That was a very good thing for him. One day Mercado left and we had to get a plastic surgeon in Miami to do the stitches, and Mercado said, 'No, I will come to Miami and do them.' He never got another opening or anything."

After this fight the fractured relations between Argüello's matchmakers King and Brenner provided the impetus for a much-publicized trial two years later between Brenner and the World Boxing Council president José Sulaimán. The WBC mandated that Argüello had to face the winner of the April 9 junior-lightweight elimination bout between Bobby Chacón and Bazooka Limón.

Several issues outside of the ring had taken center stage. After signing a two-year contract with the Garden's Teddy Brenner, Argüello was informed that the WBC had suspended the matchmaker on May 2, 1979, for "violating the organization's rules." Brenner believed that his rift with King and his refusal to adhere to José Sulaimán's every whim were the real causes of the suspension. More important, though, Argüello had to deal with increasing tension between the Contras (counterrevolutionaries) and the Sandinista National Liberation Front (FSLN) in Nicaragua. At the time, his younger brother Eduardo was fighting for the Sandinistas, and reportedly Argüello had donated money to the cause. His family's welfare weighed on his mind as he prepared for Limón, who earned the opportunity to fight for the title with a technical draw against Chacón.

Prior to his next title defense in New York, Argüello went to train in Mexico, where he owned a home. Loretto and his son A. J. accompanied him and had moved out of Managua two months prior to the Limón bout, but his parents and sister stayed in Managua. It was spring 1979 and the war was in its final stages in Nicaragua. Argüello would not return home for more than a decade.

Two weeks before his title defense, Argüello received the news that his brother Eduardo had died fighting for the FSLN on June 17, 1979, only a month before the Sandinistas broke free from Anastasio Somoza's rule. To make matters worse, Eduardo's body had been burned and dumped on a pile of tires. His father, Guillermo, had refused to believe that Eduardo was gone and wandered the streets for days, looking for his son. Not only had the Sandinistas derailed Somoza's abusive regime, which was defined by graft, power, and cronyism, but the Contra guerrillas also showed the United States, which had supported the Somozans with artillery, tanks, and planes, that they would not be bullied into submission. Somoza had stoked the fire for revolution on two occasions. First, he had used humanitarian aid money for his own benefit after the 1972 earthquake; then, he had ordered the assassination of the newspaper *La Prensa*'s editor Pedro Joaquín Chamorro on January 10, 1978. The people had carried Chamorro's body through the streets of Managua, where stone-throwing protests and riots ensued. Those who recall the tumultuous time remember that Somoza had ignited a fervor he was unable to defuse. Thus, in his mind, his only recourse was to decimate the country.

"I didn't know how much things would be changed," Argüello told a *Sports Illustrated* reporter years later, "so I just took ordinary luggage when I left home six weeks before the fight. The full-scale civil war had started when I was in Mexico training for Bazooka Limón, and when I got to Miami after the fight, Dr. [Eduardo] Roman, my manager, said there was a big problem getting back into Nicaragua, so I stayed for a while in Miami."

The only constant that remained for Argüello was his opponent, and he had no time to analyze the turbulent situation at home. He told a reporter: "I still have property back home, and according to the last phone call I made, everything is all right." Argüello responded to a question about his return to Nicaragua: "It all depends. If the country is on fire, I don't go back."

Rafael "Bazooka" Limón—Argüello's opponent and No. 1 in the world rankings—looked as if he had walked right out of a cartoon. His slow, telegraphed right hooks released from awkward angles; his bushy afro that bounced carelessly; and his stalking style were all part of the allure of the crafty but courageous southpaw from Mexico City. Limón (43-8-2, thirty knockouts) had faced Bobby Chacón in April 1979 before meeting Argüello at Madison Square Garden's Felt Forum on July 8. The bout marked the first Sunday afternoon bout ever held at the fight haven. Argüello was defending his WBC junior lightweight belt for the fifth time at the Garden and was favored to beat the twenty-five-year-old challenger. While both men weighed within a pound of the 130-pound limit, Argüello had a three-inch reach advantage, which was slight when compared to what he had enjoyed against his previous foes.

The fight had become a political event. Of the 1,547 in attendance, few could miss the huge Sandinista flag that followed Argüello down the aisle or the Sandinista robe draped over his frame. The men in Argüello's camp made a clear statement about their loyalties, as the flag was situated in front of the TV camera. Argüello's legal representative, William Ramirez, had orchestrated the plan to bring the flag into the ring. However, some considered the move clear posturing since the Sandinistas had already solidified their position, and President Anastasio Somoza was backpedaling significantly. On each side of the political spectrum, however, people voiced their opinions.

"In 1979, I lost connection with Alexis because I was with the Frente [Sandinista], and they took all of his belongings," Nicaraguan journalist Edgar Tijerino said in 2011. "I think that bringing the flag to the ring was an idea from Dr. Roman to Alexis because they knew the FSLN was winning, and there is a video where Roman was giving a flag to Alexis. Rather than a gesture, it was an analytical thing because of the political things that were happening in the country."

Roman, a conservative with no party affiliation, reasoned, "I'll tell you why they brought that flag into the ringside, because Nicaragua didn't want a dictatorship anymore. A doctor friend of mine asked me if he could bring it on his shoulder and I accepted that. But you have to understand that all Nicaraguans wanted to get rid of the dictatorship. They passed the flag on TV, but it was only because people protested against the dictatorship." Alexis loved his country. We felt that if we didn't have the right government, we had to be part of the opposition.

The boxing journalists in the United States did not completely grasp the magnitude or ramifications of the war between the Contras and the Sandinistas. In fact, few media members were concerned about what was occurring in Nicaragua at the time. Throughout Argüello's career, he did a commendable job of keeping the sport separate from his politics.

"I covered the Bazooka Limón fight, which was the fight where they carried the [Sandinista] flag into the ring," said boxing journalist Steve Farhood. "So in a way it was more of a political event than a prizefight. As I remember it was the start of a civil war in Nicaragua. But we didn't know anything about what was going on in Nicaragua. So the flag wasn't as much of an element in the U.S. He came in with the flag, but we didn't know much. We thought he was making a patriotic statement for his country. We vaguely knew, but no one understood the depth of what was occurring there."

Despite the lack of stability in his country, Argüello focused on the ring. Pushing everything else to the background was his specialty. Limón was an awkward fighter, whose petulant nature and persistence either aroused or infuriated his opponents. To Argüello, he represented a festering sore that refused to go away. To the Mexicans that crammed the Garden that evening, though, he represented something much different.

"Mexicans loved their boxers more than their, well, families," joked Dr. Roman. "Bazooka was supposed to have bazookas in both hands, but that was only according to Mexicans. Bazooka kept trying to push up his [Argüello's] Adam's apple. Alexis used to make some bad things happen to fighters when they did bad things to him. Alexis knew how to do that so no one would see."

Ring journalist Christopher Coats anointed Limón as "an accomplished dirty fighter with a God-given talent, honed to perfection from diligent practice, at thumbing, butting, and hitting on the break, and he is not at all squeamish about aiming a solid punch at the inside seam of an opponent's trunks. Other fighters occasionally try these tactics, but the 'Bazooka Man' really puts his heart into it."

That evening, Limón didn't disappoint. Whether it was jumping in with hooks and jabs or burrowing in headfirst, Limón showed early in the first round that he wouldn't be a tailor-made foe for the disciplined Argüello. In fact, the first round was not without controversy. Midway through the round, after taking a left hook and a sharp battering, the beleaguered Limón stopped punching, dabbed his right eye with his glove, and pleaded with referee Tony Perez that he was intentionally headbutted. Instead of attacking, Argüello gave him a reprieve and waited for Perez to force the action. The referee later notified broadcaster Howard Cosell and ringside scribes that there was no butt. Bothered by the cut, Limon stalked Argüello, only to run into straight rights. The crowd roared for the underdog Limón as the round ended.

Neither man was razor sharp, but Limón gained momentum when he brushed off the persistent Argüello with a busy straight left at the end of the second round. Although it didn't damage the champ, it woke him to Limón's strength. If Limón earned Argüello's respect during the second, he became overzealous in the next round. With fifteen seconds remaining in the third round, Argüello broke through the jab and caught Limón coming in with a crushing left hook coupled with a compact right hand. Limón stumbled across the ring and clinched to survive.

Argüello walked through those lead lefts and continued to control the rounds with his ferocity and precision. Limón's nonchalance was a factor again in the fifth as he stopped mid-fight to complain about another headbutt. Referee Tony Perez missed the clash and ruled it a punch. However, Argüello wasn't as cordial this time around, as he sliced a right cross along the bridge of Limón's nose. Suddenly, another cut opened as blood seeped from underneath Limón's left eye. Yet, Limón pushed on and won the round by opening a cut of his own over Argüello's right eye. While both fighters jabbed away, the fans cheered the magnificent brawl.

"There was a mass of blood," said AP writer Schuyler. "Bazooka was a dirty fighter known for using his head, and Alexis knew it. He just got his head in first. He would stand up and, boy, he could punch. But he never panicked. I think it hurt him when they moved the bouts from fifteen to twelve rounds because those five rounds were his territory."

Targeting the cut, Argüello forced Limón to play the matador. As in his previous title bouts, Argüello adapted to the style of his opponent; therefore, if Limón wanted to play dirty, Argüello would oblige. No longer standing in front of the champ, Limón, drenched in his own blood, showed glimpses of his punching power but not enough to win rounds. Instead, the crowd watched the gradual attrition of the Mexican challenger.

Although the ring doctor let the fight continue in the later rounds, Limón's cornermen couldn't staunch his bleeding. It poured down his yellow trunks, blinded him completely, and only worsened with four rounds to go. In the eleventh round, Argüello penetrated the mask of blood with two rights to reopen the cut. Referee Tony Perez stepped in to stop the fight at 1:40 of the round. Argüello was comfortably ahead on all three cards at the time of the stoppage.

The brutality of the fight wouldn't deter Limón from continuing to face the top fighters across Latin America. After Limón, however, the defenses only got tougher for Argüello.

"Bazooka Limón was pushing up my Adam's apple," Argüello recalled. "He was squeezing out of desperation. A wounded animal had to find something to do. I thought he was a dirty fighter. He was just trying to survive."

Argüello added: "It's natural that I wasn't punching as well as I have in the past. I had to work hard to get down. I'll tell you one thing, when I get out of this division, I'll be happy. Then I'll eat three meals a day, and I won't have to starve myself."

Limón responded to the criticism: "I was hit harder down in Mexico on my way up the ladder."

Eleven days later on July 19, the Sandinistas, led by the nine-member National Directorate, declared victory. The rallying cry—"Somoza left!"—could be heard throughout the country. Somoza would not leave empty-handed, however, and he scooped up the remains of his father, Anastasio Somoza Garcia, and carried them to Miami. Nicaraguan minister of the interior and one of the nine members the National Directorate, Tomás Borge, illustrated the resilience of the vanguard group when he said, "We were like ants, like a hammer blow; we were the stubborn ones, the ones born with iron wills."

When the dictator Somoza fled to Miami, the Sandinistas took over the country. With all their hubris and idealism, ironically, the Sandinistas went after Argüello and drove an immovable wedge between themselves and the embodiment of the country's hopes and dreams. In their mind, Argüello was not a part of this revolution, even though Eduardo, his younger brother, had died fighting for it. Instead, the rebel group expropriated Argüello's belongings and kicked his family to the street. As the news of their actions spread, Argüello's life outside the ring began to unravel.

"After we carried the flag in for the Limón fight, everything happened negatively," said Kahn. "He couldn't go back, he was so angry. I told him, 'There's nothing you can do. If you go back, they will take your life. You're still in your prime and you can make that money back. You have a long life to live. Don't worry about them.'"

There were rumors that Dr. Roman had Gen. Omar Torrijos fly Argüello's family members to Panama as soon as the Sandinistas threatened them. Years later after reuniting with them, Argüello, who had donated $4,000 to the Sandinista cause when he trained in Mexico, would look back on the FSLN's decadence and thievery with an open mind. When they expropriated everything he owned, Argüello recalled, "I wasn't here [in Nicaragua]. The poor people were the kids of the block. I understood. I didn't have to forgive. You can't avoid something like that."

However, as a twenty-seven-year-old world champ in 1979, he had been not as diplomatic. The plan for Roman to bring the flag and then hand it to Argüello after the bout in the corner had backfired.

"Revolutionary leaders saw this as a piece of opportunism organized by Roman," said Tijerino, who denounced the confiscation of Argüello's belongings on his radio program. "Nobody knows if Alexis had the Sandinista flag in his heart. As for Eduardo, his brother who was killed—in a big family, there are many ways of thinking. If the father of Carlos Fonseca [the greatest hero of the revolution, who was killed in the mountains in 1976] came to Managua, he would be put in jail.

"When the revolutionaries were victorious they had to control the country. There had to be a starting point. The majority of lands, farms, and houses belonged to Somozans and had been obtained illegally. Individual cases of confiscation could not be discussed. There were a lot of errors. For me, the case of Alexis was one such [example]."

When the "new kids on the block"—the Sandinistas—forced his family out on the streets and seized all his belongings, Argüello experienced a wound so deep that it would be decades before he could recover from it. He observed, "My opinion is that I don't like the Communist people. I am a Catholic. I still love my country, but I will not go back. At first I supported the Sandinistas. But nobody knew for sure what they were going to do. After the Revolution they wanted to take away my house. I owned it, I paid all the taxes. Then they did away with all pro boxing and all professional sports. This is the Communist way. I am very happy in America. Here I can work and make sure my son gets a good education and that my family lives well."

A Country Lost

Anyone who gives up his nationality is an asshole.
—ALEXIS ARGÜELLO

The less risk we ran of actually getting killed, the more we feared death.
—OMAR CABEZAS, FIRE FROM THE MOUNTAIN:
THE MAKING OF A SANDINISTA

Decades before Argüello was fighting bullies in his Monseñor Lezcano neighborhood, another Nicaraguan rebel was busy etching his own legacy. By the 1920s, images of a rebel named Augusto César Sandino began to ignite nationalistic sentiment. With his signature ten-gallon hat, black leather boots, cigar nestled between his fingers, light complexion, and boyish stare, Sandino became to the Nicaraguan peasants what Ernesto "Che" Guevara later signified for communist Cuba—a glimmer of hope amid perpetual blight. Sandino led a guerrilla campaign in the 1920s against both the U.S. forces occupying his country and rampant Nicaragua cronyism. In 1927 Sandino upset the Nicaraguan National Guard, which was led by Anastasio Somoza, when he refused to sign the Tratado del Espino Negro, a cease-fire pact created with U.S. support. On May 4, 1927, Sandino initiated the movement later known as Sandinismo, and it fought the "war of liberators to end the war of oppressors." Inspired by the prospect of ousting the U.S. Marines from his homeland, Sandino and twenty-nine fighters ignited a rebellion that began on the outskirts of the turbulent nation's city of Las Segovias. Sandino and members of the Army for the Defense of National Sovereignty refused to accept the agreement that Gen. José Moncada signed with Juan Bautista Sacasa that called for both sides to disarm. Instead, Sandino battled the U.S. contingent for seven years, fostering a reputation and passion that would provide the impetus for the Sandinista Revolution of the late 1970s.

In the foreword for *Fire From the Mountain: The Making of a Sandinista*, Carlos Fuentes wrote: "The Marines could not defeat Sandino in Nicaragua because they could not defeat the hills, the insects, the shadows, the loneliness, the trees, or the fires of Nicaragua."

After forcing the Marines out by 1933 and establishing his iconic status, Sandino's next step was to assist in a cease-fire with then President Sacasa. However, as Sandino left the Presidential Palace after the initial meeting that evening on February 21, 1934, Somoza's men accosted and promptly executed Sandino. The National Guard, which had been left behind after the earlier Sandino battles with the Marines, refused to stop there and began widespread executions. The first of many Somoza regimes came to power three years later.

During the 1970s, President Anastasio "Tachito" Somoza Debayle manipulated the eighteen-year-old boxing phenom Argüello. Tachito represented the last of the Somoza rulers in Nicaragua, and as many witnessed during his two terms, he was as brutal as his father, Anastasio Somoza Garcia, had been.

Embracing the fight against Tachito's regime was Daniel Ortega, who would later serve as Nicaragua's president in 1985–1990 and 2007–2011 and just began a third term in January 2012. José Daniel "Danielito" Ortega Saavedra was born to Daniel Ortega Cerda and Lydia Saavedra Rivas on November 11, 1945, in the city of La Libertad, a cattle-raising department of Chontales.

Ortega became the face of the Sandinista movement, which in July 1979, through dogged persistence, finally ousted Somoza. However, like Somoza, Ortega would also play a key role in Argüello's future.

In 1975, Somoza asked his deputy René Molina, who also helped support a local baseball team, to call the newly crowned champion Alexis Argüello and arrange a photo opportunity during a parade in Estelí, a mountainous region sixty-five miles south of the capital. Argüello felt that he owed a debt of gratitude to the town of Estelí and Molina, for the way its people had treated him and his family when they stayed there after the 1972 earthquake. He did not, however, consider the possible repercussions. While he was with Somoza, it was not clear to Argüello that Somoza was seeking positive publicity and using the boxer to gain political leverage. For Argüello, he did not hesitate; he was doing a favor and giving back to the people of Estelí. Later, the government also appointed Argüello an honorary lieutenant of the National Guard.

"All the presidents wanted to get close to him," said manager Dr. Eduardo Roman. "Somoza didn't try to help Alexis in a real way. He invited Alexis to a presentation with 100,000 people, and Alexis went to the presentation. [Alexis] went without telling me. I forbade him to attend political things like that. When I saw that I went to him the next day and told him, 'You are not the champ of the Somozistas. You are the champ of all Nicaragua!' Alexis was a friend of everybody and didn't show any political opinions."

There was also concern amid the Sandinista ranks that Argüello was being managed by another Somoza supporter, the president of the light and power company and Somoza's brother-in-law, Luis Manuel Debayle. Argüello quickly dismissed this notion.

"I was never managed by Luis Manuel Debayle. When Dr. Roman was paying me out of his own pocket, he was working for the power company," said Argüello. "Somebody said: 'Why not have the power company sponsor him, like companies sponsor teams?' Same thing. So I wore a T-shirt with the name of the power company. But Dr. Roman paid me and was my manager. Debayle was just president of the company. Does that make me a Somozista?"

Realistically, Ortega and Argüello did not realize how much Somoza similarly influenced their lives. The politically naive Argüello, then twenty-three years old, was more concerned with people's perception of him. One of his strengths and flaws was that he always wanted to please people, a quality that left him vulnerable for personal attacks. After Argüello won the featherweight title from Rubén Olivares in 1974, he accepted Molina's invitation for a ceremony in his honor but did not comprehend the political implications. Back then, leaders often sought allegiance from celebrity athletes. Argüello could not foresee the severe repercussions.

"That incident that happened with Somoza was very innocent. He was a genius in the ring, but out of the ring, Alexis was very naive and clean. He didn't have a sense of manipulation or ulterior motives or the education to help eliminate the naïveté. In that situation, just like many others from the lowest to the highest rungs of society, they had a sympathy for Alexis, and, more importantly, politicians wanted to take advantage of his fame and popularity for their own motives," said former member of the Nicaraguan Boxing Commission Sergio Quintero. "Alexis had no idea what was going on in the backdoor dealings; he didn't decide to do it. He didn't even think about it. When he became popular, everyone wanted a piece of him. He was the first real figure to bring Nicaraguans to . . . a world stage."

Whether it was dictator Manuel Noriega in Panama or the drug kingpin Pablo Escobar in Colombia, the leaders' fascination with world-class athletes created reluctant connections. The truth was that Argüello did not know any better; he did not grow up in a politicized household.

"All the political parties tried to use Alexis," said Roman. "It's obvious. For example he was once invited by a deputy of the mayor to ride on a horse. But he's a simple soul and doesn't understand about those things. He said, 'Yes,' and the next day there is a picture in the paper saying that the food the horse was eating was more expensive than anything Alexis ate in his life [to that point]."

Both the manipulation of the government and the malicious acts of the press infuriated Argüello. Instead of celebrating his newfound fame, now he had to be conscious of everything he did in the public forum. He could never have envisioned the consequences of one appearance and how it would galvanize his life and career four years later.

In Nicaragua, few, if any, people believed that Argüello deserved persona non grata status or to be exiled when the Somoza regime was toppled. Yet, during that time of much upheaval and confusion, they could not protest the new government's decision.

"There was a lot of anger and sadness when Alexis was exiled," said Quintero. "The reason why people looked at him as anti-Sandinista was because of when he went in the horse parade as he rode alongside Somoza. Because of that image, when the revolution triumphed, the FSLN looked at him as a sympathizer."

Sports and political journalist Edgar Tijerino, who had been a close friend of Argüello's, lost touch with the boxer after he was exiled. Their relationship was permanently scarred, as each man was forced to take sides. "Molina, a congressman, brainwashed Alexis with the horse. It wasn't a personal decision taken by Alexis," Tijerino acknowledged.

Although Argüello denied the allegations vehemently, the Sandinistas, coming off their celebration in 1979, claimed that the world champ was a proponent of the Somoza regime. First, they banned professional boxing in the country and then went after Argüello directly.

Looking back on what he considered the deceit and manipulation of the FSLN vanguard group, Argüello noted, "That's part of life. But I think you have to realize that there's different times and reasons for everything. They confiscate my belongings because they said I was a lieutenant of the Somoza Army, which was major bullshit.

"A lieutenant was supposed to get paid, but I never got paid, but they confiscate my belongings because they thought I was a part of the Somoza regime, which I wasn't. I accepted that when the Sandinistas were in power, there were a lot of guys who didn't want me to come back to Nicaragua for many reasons. I lost a lot of things in this country, but they were physical. Emotionally, I don't care about that because I came to this world naked with nothing, and through my effort and my determination I became somebody."

As a result of the allegations, the Sandinista brass spread Argüello's wealth. Reports confirmed that they seized two houses, including a gated mansion in Las Colinas, Managua; his BMW and Mercedes; a motor home; his gym; a boat; his chicken business; and his bank account. Argüello surmised that the Sandinistas stole more than a $1 million from him. He would later find out that Soviet envoys were driving his cars and living in his house. Argüello knew he could regain the material things, but as noted earlier, he despised Ortega and the movement for the way they treated his family, forcing his mother and sister out of their home and on to the streets. To add to the fractured relationship between the Argüellos and the Sandinistas, Alexis Argüello was barred from returning to the country to attend his mother's funeral years later. Decades after the wounds had healed, Argüello, then mayor of Managua, looked back on the turbulent period diplomatically. "My brother Eduardo was killed while he was fighting for the Sandinistas. Well, it was part of the development of a country," he said. "It's what a country has to go through in order to develop a good society. I don't blame them. It was a war."

Although his supposed position as a Somoza sympathizer had a polarizing effect on Argüello in his native country, the members of the boxing fraternity in the United States refused to turn their collective backs on him.

"I don't think we focused on the war, it was mostly boxing. But when we heard he had lost everything, we felt it was pathetic and unfair," said Steve Farhood. "To flip a coin and choose a side? I mean he was the most famous Nicaraguan in the world. He was the ultimate professional who gave 100 percent every time he stepped into the ring. So we looked at it as grossly unfair to happen to Argüello, of all prizefighters."

ROUND 8

Defending a Title

Alexis was just too tough.

—Promoter/Manager Mickey Duff

Having developed a unique ability to block out any outside interferences, Argüello focused on the ring and his next title defense. The title bout against Bobby "Schoolboy" Chacón was confirmed for September 15 at the Inglewood Forum in California, but it was postponed when Chacón suffered an injury. Fraser lamented that the Torres bout represented a weak matchup. "I had a chance to use Argüello, but at the time Torres was not a big draw. After that fight, I went to Miami and signed Alexis to box Bobby Chacón. At the time, Alexis was being promoted by Don King, and King was not very happy with me. He thought we were interfering. I had to pay him a little side payment for that one."

While Argüello had dominated opponents unlike any featherweight in recent memory, he couldn't match the popularity of local boy Chacón. Born in Pacoima in the San Fernando Valley, Chacón was not even a year old when his father abandoned the family. In his dad's absence, the 5-foot-5 fighter struggled to find his true identity and spent his youth building a reputation as a street tough. He hid his frustrations behind daily fights at school and refused to comply with any rules at home, where he was the oldest of seven children. His recklessness in school often kept Chacón, an accomplished tailback, out of football games. Eventually Anthony Davis of future University of Southern California fame would take over his spot on the high school squad.

"I was always smaller than the other kids," said Chacón. "I couldn't stand being pushed around. When one of the bigger kids tried, it meant a fight."

Chacón eventually took his anger and skills to Johnny Flores's Boxing Gym in Pacoima, where he worked with future trainer, Joe Ponce. Chacón earned the monikers "Little Muhammad Ali" and "Schoolboy" because of his decision to take college classes in physical education.

Bobby Chacón, a maturing twenty-seven-year-old, was a West Coast legend years before he faced Argüello. The boyish smile and cowboy swagger helped to amplify his reputation and to make him a staple at the Inglewood Forum. Schoolboy Chacón was the kid from the streets who made it big. Inside the ring, Chacón invited violence at every turn, as did Argüello. And Chacón had never faced a man so technically sound and skilled as the 5-foot-10 WBC super featherweight champ Argüello. The contest between the two, however, lacked the usual prefight theatrics.

"There was no animosity between the two guys. It was tough to get mad at Argüello. He wasn't a guy to pop off," said promoter Don Chargin. "Bobby was just being Bobby, a happy kid. You never knew what he was going to say. He was always with everybody, one of the most popular guys there."

The match's uncertainty irritated Argüello. Before the fight, those associated with the bout went through many aggravating machinations, mostly coming from Chacón's camp. On September 26, Argüello learned that Chacón again could not fight, and when Don Fraser, the Forum promoter, could not find a suitable replacement, the card was canceled. Having left the Biltmore Hotel in late August after a fire, Argüello moved back and forth between Miami and Los Angeles as he waited for a new date. The California State Athletic Commission had suspended Chacón for pulling out of the September date, but by mid-October, he was back in the gym and awaiting confirmation of a November bout with Argüello. Reports circulated on October 10 that the fight would finally take place at the Inglewood Forum on November 16. By that point, people felt Chacón had "as much credibility as the Great Pumpkin," Los Angeles Times journalist Richard Hoffer said.

With the numerous postponements, the fight had lost its luster with the fans and suffered financially when it was pulled from ABC's Wide World of Sports. Argüello, who was already in form, comfortably moved with Loretto and his seven-year-old son, A. J., to Mexico City and into his regular preparation schedule. He did not allow the constant disruptions to interrupt his focus as he trained for the fight. Thoughts of the political situation in Nicaragua that had evolved over the past months, however, had left Argüello perplexed and hurt.

"I'll never go back [to Nicaragua], and my family will never join me here," Argüello told Hoffer. "I talked to my mother and told her I'd like to see her here. She told me she'll send a picture. That's the only way I'll ever see her again. She won't come here and I won't go there."

Argüello did bring his mother to Miami, but she quickly turned around and headed home. Her choice left Argüello distraught. He could not cope with the fact that his own mother would choose to live in a country where the leaders were so venomous toward his family. He confided in Dr. Roman, his father figure, regarding his mother's decision to leave.

"He took his mother to the U.S. after the Sandinista problem. But his mother decided she wanted to go back," remembered manager Dr. Roman. "He complained to me when his mother wanted to go back. He asked me, 'Why did she leave?' I told him that he had his mother-in-law living in a nice area, and she had to live in an area of black people. There was nothing wrong with black people, but they didn't speak Spanish, so it was hard for her. Alexis said, 'Do you want me to kill myself?' I said, 'You are not supposed to give that kind of answer.' He tried to deal with what happened when his mother left."

Meanwhile, as Argüello cleaned out the 130-pound weight class, the subject often turned to the lightweight, or 135-pound, division. Argüello's constant battle with an unnatural and painful weight class had become a much-publicized source of irritation for the Nicaraguan. Only five other fighters had reached the pinnacle of three titles in as many weight classes.

"Winning a third title would be nice," he said. "I intend to do that some day."

Promoter Don Fraser had been aware of the issues and excuses that boxers come up with prior to a title fight; however, the exhaustion he suffered in arranging the inevitable Argüello-Chacón battle tested his faith in the sport. "It took me two years, two postponements, and two nervous breakdowns just to get Argüello and Chacón in the same town and same ring in the same year," an exasperated Fraser said.

After being fined $5,000 for the postponements, Chacón went through the motions at the Main Street Gym in Los Angeles. Argüello picked up where he left off.

"Alexis was a beautiful fighter," said Don Chargin. "He was getting good experience on the West Coast boxing circuit. But Alexis always had a master plan for his career. He would take it one step at a time. When it came to boxing, he was a pretty bright guy. He knew what he wanted to do and then he would go out and do it."

As Chacón finally entered the Inglewood Forum on November 16, 1979, the crowd gave him a lengthy ovation. It identified with Chacón, the local kid. Both Argüello (59-5, fifty-one knockouts) and Chacón (42-4-1, thirty-seven knockouts) weighed less than a pound under the 130-pound limit. Nearly 11,200 fans filled the Forum for a gate of $165,137. Argüello would receive

$110,000, while Chacón settled for $35,000. ESPN aired the live broadcast, which was a coup because the upstart station had only recently launched its first program two months earlier. Referee John Thomas read the boxing rules before the opening bell rang, and the crowd waited calmly as each man prepared for battle. While Chacón rocked comfortably on the balls of his feet, Argüello pulled in his gaunt cheeks with an anxious stare. Their eyes never met.

Similar to other David versus Goliath battles, the smaller opponent, Chacón, circled while Argüello stood his ground. The smaller fighter buzzed in, and Argüello swatted him away with hapless jabs. Chacón continued dancing as the chant of "Bobby, Bobby" rose from the crowd. A right cross by Argüello midway through the round elicited the only response in an otherwise dull first round.

In bouts against smaller, more compact men, Chacón was a killer. Former opponents Danny "Little Red" López or Bazooka Limón knew about the strength of the 130-pound spark plug. But Argüello, no longer playing the passive elder's role, figured out that he could throw and land his powerful counter left hook at any moment. Perfectly coordinated with Chacón's height, Argüello unleashed the hook over Chacón's lazy jab. Bang! Argüello hooked off his jab and then jammed Chacón again with another short hook. Schoolboy had no remedy for this punch. The Nicaraguan, usually a slow starter, was not finished, catching Chacón in the corner and landing a fusillade of body shots and quick uppercuts. A straight right would be Chacón's kryptonite and opened up the barrage of blows from his opponent. Yet, Argüello missed as many as he landed during the brief confrontation.

Before the second round ended, Argüello spun Chacón, landing four consecutive hooks to the body followed by one last short uppercut. The rally left a bitter taste in the Schoolboy's mouth. Argüello's early intensity and sharpness proved a bad omen for the California native. Usually it took seven rounds before Argüello composed himself.

If body language revealed the mental place of a fighter, Chacón was already beaten. Still the Schoolboy wasn't an antsy Vilomar Fernández (who moved constantly and refused to engage in battle) and didn't run from confrontation. Yet, through the third round, he kept walking directly into Argüello's vicious short hooks. Each one was a sharp reminder to think twice before he entered the Nicaraguan's space. Somehow, Chacón stole the round with speed, movement, and an accumulation of punches.

Somewhere between the second and third round, Argüello's intensity waned while something stirred in Chacón, who exhibited a fearlessness not evident in previous rounds. Midway through the third round, Chacón missed a hook only to come back and nail Argüello flush with a right cross. He found a minor flaw in Argüello's guard, and his revival reminded staunch boxing fans of Chacón when he was in his prime, an expert boxer. Despite getting nearly paralyzed from Argüello's hook to his ribs, Chacón forged ahead. The San Fernando Valley natives stood and applauded.

As the tide shifted in the third and fourth round, Chacón outgunned Argüello for the first time in the fight. Few men were brave enough to stand in front of the champ and trade, but the aging Chacón showed Argüello that he could beat him at his own game of warfare and mental strategy.

It was one thing to outbox Argüello and another to outslug him. Although Argüello was not privy to the judges' scorecards, he was behind significantly on each one as the fighters started the sixth round. Midway through the sixth, Argüello was back to cutting off the ring, sticking the jab, and finally throwing his straight right. During a vicious one-sided exchange, Argüello shoved Chacón to the ropes and landed short but crisp uppercuts that took their toll during the twelve-punch barrage. In an atypical move, Argüello slashed Chacón with a right-left combination, clearly after the bell. A disgruntled Chacón and camp members protested the foul, but Argüello soothed the situation at center ring with an extended glove.

With his contingent avidly following every blow, Chacón tumbled into the ropes after an Argüello left hook in Round 7. Referee Thomas started the count. Chacón rose from a squatting position at five, went back down at six, and was up by the eight count. Chacón did not escape to buy time, but he got caught again in the corner and absorbed several sharp left hooks. Blood flowed freely from a two-inch gash about Chacón's right eye.

Referee Thomas halted the action to bring in Dr. Roger Thill. A determined Chacón made it through the round, but he never threw another punch. Thomas called the fight while Chacón sat on the stool between rounds. All of the skills and ring qualities that had made Chacón so irresistible had now dissipated; it didn't take a world-class fighter such as Argüello to reveal these truths.

Directly after the bout and successfully defending his title for a sixth time at 130 pounds, Argüello talked about moving up five pounds to the 135-pound weight class. Then he sang Chacón's praises: "Chacón is a good fighter. He is a real intelligent guy. He knew what he had to do out there. He has a really good style. He fought his hardest. I told everyone it was going to be a tough fight and it was."

Chacón conceded the peril of fighting Argüello. "The guy's dangerous all the time. I saw him sitting back, just waiting. I knew he'd come out sooner or later," Chacón said. "Well, he's the champ, all right. I guess he showed why.

"I had the right strategy. A few punches were bound to get in, and the ones that did were good ones. I have nothing to be ashamed of. It was the cut that did me in."

Years later Argüello recalled, "With Bobby Chacón, he knew it after the fight. His manager Jackie McCoy told him, 'I have to stop it.' I would've killed him. He knew that I was the best. In that time, there wasn't a man who could control me."

Every fighter had to deal with the tedium of waiting for Argüello to come out of his shell, as he would wait patiently for the right moment, never rushing or wasting any punches. Two months later, Argüello had the fortune of being matched up with another slugger, the undefeated Ruben Castillo (46-0, twenty-four knockouts). The fight, which would be shown on ABC (except in Phoenix and Tuscon, Arizona, where it was blacked out), was scheduled for January 20, 1980, in the Tucson Community Center. The ring was smaller, only 17½ feet instead of the typical 20 feet. Promoter Don King promoted the bout, which would be Argüello's seventh defense of his super featherweight title. A natural 126-pounder, Castillo was originally scheduled to meet Little Red López for the WBC featherweight title, but he moved into the slot with Argüello when the latter's matchup with WBA super featherweight champ Sammy Serrano fell through.

Anyone who understood the sport knew that Castillo only had one way to beat the man: He had to stick and move all night long. For many fighters it would have been an impossible task. A Bakersfield, California, native, Castillo was a ripe twenty-two-year-old when he faced the great super featherweight champ. Argüello, at age twenty-seven, was reaching his peak in the 130-pound division as his stalking yet controlled style had taken down the top contenders in the world. In his sixty-eighth fight, the 130-pound Argüello had already faced Hall of Fame–caliber opposition. Castillo, at 129¾ pounds and trained by Beto Martinez, was the third-ranked featherweight in the world and was moving up to face Argüello. The Bakersfield fighter liked to bring a rooster to the ring because an opponent once referred to him as "chicken." Despite his unusual antics, Castillo felt he had the recipe to beat Argüello, vowing to "move, move, move" and never allow the powerful Nicaraguan to sit on his punches.

Argüello, who was trained by Cuyo Hernández, was emaciated from his battle to make weight. During sparring sessions at Beto's Gym (later the South Tucson Civic Center), Argüello's agent, Bill Miller, brought in local bantamweight Mike

Moreno so that Argüello could practice against ample speed and movement, two ingredients that unsettled him. Ironically, Moreno was Castillo's stablemate. It was an oddity in boxing circles to "cross lines [work as a stablemate and then cross over to work with the opponent]." Argüello also worked with flyweight Pulga Torres, who also simulated Castillo's speed as he moved in and out of the champion's range.

"It depends what Argüello wanted to do at the time," Head of Arizona Boxing Commission, Gerald Maltz remembered. "When he was training for Castillo, he sparred with Moreno. He wanted someone fast in his sparring session. He wanted to just touch or make contact with the other guy. So he would land the punch, but he wouldn't try to hurt or knock out his opponent. He wanted to make contact and contend with his speed. He was focusing on timing and being able to hit, but he always pulled his punches. When he hit the heavy bag, it was with such a thud that I got chills. You could only imagine what it was like when he hit a person."

Maltz added: "At the time, he was struggling to make 130 pounds. But the minute he walked into the gym, he was completely focused."

Castillo trained at the same gym. When he entered to train from 2 p.m. to 5 p.m., Argüello, who trained from 11 a.m. to 2 p.m., was leaving. When they crossed paths, Castillo saw firsthand how much Argüello was struggling to make the weight.

"The only time I saw him ever pissed off was because he couldn't eat," said Castillo. "When he came into the locker room, he asked his wife Loretto for an apple and she said, 'No puede (you cannot).' And he got so pissed off. But he couldn't take off the weight. At five foot nine, there was nowhere for him to take the weight off."

Maltz and his wife Katherine developed a lasting friendship with Argüello. They invited him to spend time at their home, dined at local restaurants together, and engaged him in intellectual dialogue. Argüello even took classes at Maltz's yoga studio. During the brief period, Argüello made an impression on the family.

"We had many intelligent conversations with Alexis," said Katherine. "Intelligent and detached says it all. He had a broadband intellect that of course I didn't know was unusual because I'd never been around any other boxer. He was unique and exhibited a sensitivity which was in my recollection unusual for his profession. He had this all-encompassing sensitivity. He had a tremendous amount of compassion for people and their suffering. He had a broad-based sensitivity to life in general. I was fortunate to meet someone so dedicated, but exhibiting such interest in life."

Crowds gathered to watch the historic event. Argüello was the headliner in the first title fight ever held in Phoenix. Don King Productions, in association with Phoenix Sports, Inc., promoted the high-profile card. Castillo entered the bout on Super Bowl Sunday as a 5–2 underdog, but he had never faced anyone with Argüello's power or experience. Despite the scheduling conflict, the fight was a natural sell.

"The fight in Arizona was the first title fight in Phoenix. It was a big deal because it was on Super Bowl Sunday," said Gerald Maltz. "But we were on the Mexican border, so we had a market for the live gate that went 150 miles into Mexico. As the boxing commissioner, I licensed Argüello, licensed fighters, and handled the weigh-in. I went with guys to watch him work out.

"Nearly 5,000 to 6,000 people showed up. Those were the days when you would sell a fight to the TV for TV rights. Then the promoter would sell the undercard to a local promoter. When they were looking for a venue, Tucson was a good proximity to the Mexico border and the indigenous population."

The actual figures from the bout amounted to a real coup for the Tucson sports scene. A crowd of 4,415 people jammed the Tucson Community Center and paid $57,450 for the ABC-TV televised bout. Argüello earned a $100,000 payday; Castillo, the challenger, took in $35,000.

Referee Octavio Meyran, who would make headlines as the middleman in the Durán-Leonard No Mas bout in November, watched the men closely during that feeling-out round. From the outset, a handler urged the 5-foot-6 Castillo to "stick and move," a style that, when used effectively, befuddled Argüello. Speed and power were a toxic combination against the champ. Often, Argüello showed his hand early when it came to styles. If he threw combinations and cut off the ring in that first round, he was serious about taking his man out early. However, if he pawed his weak jab and slowly circled his opponent, then the champ was willing to take the time to measure his opponent. Thus, his lack of combinations during that first round tipped his opponent off to his strategy.

"The crowd was evenly divided," recalled Maltz. "Alexis was a big star, and I would say that more than half knew him more than [they did] Castillo. Castillo was a local guy who was well known by boxing aficionados. For the broadcast audience, Alexis was the TV star. But because of his dignity and accomplishments, Alexis was broader known than Castillo, and the people came out to see him."

Castillo showed "pop" in his punch with a straight left hand in Round 3, followed by a lead hook that awoke Argüello. The methodical Argüello watched as Castillo slipped punches through his nearly impenetrable guard. Argüello appeared awkward, and his body language communicated a visible frustration that belied his usual calm disposition in the ring.

A natural counterpuncher, Castillo dictated the flow of the fight, and Argüello quickly lost rounds on the scorecard. Castillo had assessed his opponent's strengths and weaknesses, and he knew exactly where to look for openings.

"I knew he wasn't quick and I was a counterpuncher, so after you hit him, he would go to grab his trunks," said Castillo. "Once he did that I was all over him. Then he would back up and regroup. But the problem was that one punch could ruin your whole day. My goal was to stay away from him, but he was too long and rangy. I thought I was out of range, and he hits me with a jab to my mouth. He had arms for days."

While masterfully picking off punches with his right glove and also landing his extended straight right, Argüello had his best round in the fourth. Buoyed by the West Coast contingent, Castillo countered Argüello with a furious combo, jumping in with the left and then turning Argüello's head with a straight right. But Argüello was unflappable. When he got nailed with a right lead in the sixth, and three punches to end the seventh, Argüello walked through the punches, headed back to the corner, and thought about his next strategical move. In Argüello's mind, a chess match had begun, but an anxious Castillo felt that he was eight rounds from dethroning a warrior.

The men exchanged punches to start the eighth, and a round later the pro-Castillo crowd was screaming again after a running right hand and left hook bounced off the side of Argüello's face. Referee Octavio Meyran issued his second warning of the fight to Argüello for throwing low blows. However, the edict did not deter the champ from being aggressive. After landing a pawing left and a huge right hand in the early portion of the tenth, Argüello trapped Castillo in the corner with consecutive jabs.

Those who had observed him closely during the prefight sparring sessions began to see a pattern develop. "In the early rounds of the fight, he was doing all of the things that he'd done during sparring," said Maltz. "Then, when he punched with his full power, it was totally awesome."

Although Castillo searched for solace in the tenth, he thrived on his own version of rope-a-dope in Round 11. "I thought going into that eleventh round, 'I am going to beat a legend.' I knew I had twice the hand speed," said Castillo.

"I started thinking, 'This fucker had me against the ropes and he wasn't hitting me hard.' I wanted to go toe to toe with him. But he was just reeling me in. And then, pow! That was it."

Buttressed by the ropes in the eleventh, Castillo fought valiantly from a seated position. Castillo tried his best to avert the punches as Argüello gained confidence. The end started with several hooks off jabs that left the bouncing Castillo flat-footed. Then, Argüello unleashed a fifteen- to twenty-punch barrage in the next thirty seconds as Castillo tried desperately to minimize the impact of the destructive body shots.

Castillo slivered to the left along the ropes, but he could not elude the Nicaraguan. One last huge right and a compact left and Castillo was closer to helpless. Then Argüello quickly deposited him on the canvas after a left hook to his body and a brisk hook to his head. The warrior sank to the canvas, exhausted. Castillo fell through the ropes at the count of five and gathered himself at eight, but when Referee Meyran counted to nine and the fighter was still flailing, the fight was called at 2:03 of the eleventh round. Argüello had defended his title for the seventh time. Two of the three judges—Juan Guerra and Richard Rizo—had the champion ahead at the time of the stoppage, while all three had the challenger winning heading into that pivotal tenth round.

"As I was winning rounds, the only thing I was thinking was that I could overcome Alexis," said Castillo, who moved back down to 126 after the fight. "I figured he would fall apart because of the weight issue. I was banking on him getting weak. Then in the eleventh round, he hits me with a body shot and a hook, and I thought I saw the ropes, I went over to them and grabbed air. I felt like he hit me with a rock. I'd never been hit that hard."

After the fight, Argüello hugged Don King, smiled, and then slipped from his grasp. Broadcaster Howard Cosell waited for Argüello after the fight.

"I'm proud to talk to you," Argüello told Cosell. "I have fights where I learn every day; my trainer explained to me that I must demonstrate what I learned from that time. I have natural power, and I have to weigh the opportunity. When I found it, I hit it. My trainer told me, 'You hurt him, you have to go close to him to hurt him more.' That's why I have to pay attention to my trainer."

Cosell stepped in to show Argüello a tape of his knockout. As he reviewed the tape, Argüello said, "[Castillo's] a very good boxer. He's too young, a good boxer. He has to learn like I learned. I learn everyday and I am proud. He knows. His corner worked very good. They told him how to move, because it's a problem to come very close to me.

"I am going to fight more in junior lightweight. If I can fight at lightweight, I will do the best I can. I promise to my country and my friend because I consider you my friend, I will do the best I can. I want to thank Ruben Castillo because I know he is a very good fighter, and his corner is very intelligent."

Castillo sat dejectedly as he talked about leaving the division to face opponents his own size. He made it clear that he had been hoping to face Danny López, and not Argüello, but that he had to take the payday. Later he went back to Bakersfield and faced the newspaper headlines, "Castillo and the Rams Get KO'd."

"I was very confident," Castillo told Howard Cosell. "I was working my game plan, but I started coming in and leaving myself open and got caught on the end of his shots. He's a very strong fighter. I want a chance to return as a featherweight. The junior-lightweight is much taller and I want to stay with my height. He hits hard with both hands, and I think he will be the lightweight champ as well. I never saw him go to the body very much in the tapes, so he surprised me when he started going to the body."

Next, promoter Don King arranged for Argüello to fight on the Vegas undercard of the WBC heavyweight tilt between Larry Holmes and Bad Leroy Jones on March 31. That evening, Argüello came in at 131½ pounds, the most he had weighed since the loss to Vilomar Fernández. Argüello couldn't get his next opponent, Newark's 131-pound Gerald Hayes out by the allotted ten rounds in an over-the-weight bout. Reports noted that Hayes merely wanted to survive. After the dull bout, the scores read: Dalby Shirley, 98–92; Lou Tabat, 98–92; and Dave Moretti, 97–93.

After earning a unanimous decision over Hayes, Argüello set his sights on cleaning out the rest of the division and moving to higher ground, the 135-pound lightweight division, but he wanted to do it on his terms. Argüello felt he had earned the right to move into the division without a tune-up bout. Many felt he was on a crash course with Roberto Durán, if only the Panamanian could stay in the division long enough to allow the fight to happen.

"I cannot stay at 130 pounds, it is too difficult for me to make," Argüello explained to a reporter. "My manager wants to arrange for me to fight for the title."

Argüello next defended his WBC super featherweight title against Filipino southpaw Rolando Navarette (34-6-3) on April 27, 1980. Ranked fifth by the WBC, the 130-pound Navarette was a clear underdog when he went to San Juan to face the reigning champ, who had struggled to make weight. On the King-promoted card, Argüello made his first appearance at the Hiram Bithorn

Stadium and appeared on the same fight card as WBC super bantamweight champ Wilfredo Gómez. A year earlier, after Gómez had doused an over-matched Nelson Cruz Tamariz, he had called out Argüello: "[Danny] López is nothing. I want Alexis Argüello." Critics debated whether the youthful knockout artist was big enough to handle Argüello, especially since the Nicaraguan was always eight to ten pounds heavier than Gómez was.

Regarding the Navarette fight, Argüello said, "I went to Puerto Rico to promote the fight. They treated me like a champ the moment I stepped on the island."

Despite being a formidable challenger who was determined to put up a better showing than his Filipino counterpart Rey Tam had, Navarette was already in trouble and pawing at a cut by the third round. The cut on Navarette's left eyebrow was a result of Argüello's left hook and right uppercut that jammed the challenger. Still Navarette fought on and even landed some heavy blows; however, it was to no avail. In the fourth, Argüello used movement to escape harm and his counterpunching to offset Navarette's recklessness. As Navarette's blood flowed, there was cause for concern when Argüello targeted and sliced his opponent's other eye in the fourth.

Referee Roberto Ramirez brought in the ringside doctor, Dr. Amaury Capella, and less than a minute later the fight was called before the fifth round opened. There was no controversy or outrage over the stoppage as Argüello was ahead by two and three points on all three cards.

"That guy [Navarette] was trying not to confront me in order to survive. He would hit me and then get into clinches," said Argüello. "He tried not to put them into action. He tried to survive in a personal way. It was no contest. I was too much for him."

There had been rumors regarding a possible unification bout with Puerto Rico's Samuel Serrano, but those talks quickly dissolved when Argüello announced his move up to the lightweight division. Unless provoked or forced, few fighters openly campaigned for a bout with the devastating puncher Argüello. In fact, in a 1980 *Ring* magazine article, Christopher Coats wrote, "Serrano would be wiser to seek root canal without novocaine than to confront Argüello." Manager Jackie McCoy quickly nixed a possible bout this time with his fighter Frankie Baltazar.

Two elements factored into Argüello's decision to leave the super featherweight division: He had grown out of the weight class and had ravaged the division's competition. Ironically, the long-awaited match between Latin icons Argüello and Roberto Durán had to be postponed because Durán not only had abandoned the lightweights for the welterweight division but also had beaten Sugar Ray Leonard that June to become world champ.

Everyone in the fight game who had salivated over the Argüello-Durán combustible matchup were discouraged. Now Argüello needed to establish himself in a division where Durán had set a precedent that few believed would ever be equaled.

As Argüello recalled, "[Durán] tried to make me look like a moron, an asshole. [He had] an idea of putting Argüello and Durán in the ring. Don King had invited me to a fight at Caesars Palace, and I was in line of a hotel lobby when Durán came up to me and started pushing me. He said, 'Sign the contract, you son-of-a-bitch, you son of a gun,' and all kinds of dirty words. I stopped him because he was pushing me, and I said, 'Don't touch me again because I am going to kick your ass.' I told him because I didn't want him to lose my respect. I was pissed off, so I walked a little down and he chases me. He said, 'Alexis, just hype it up, sign a contract. Maybe we can make some money.' I told him, 'I don't want you to lose my respect, because I respect you. I don't like you to push me.' That was it, he understood that I don't like those kind of games. I am [the] guy who climbs into the ring and does his best. I know it would have been a helluva match, Argüello and Durán. But I don't like anyone to push me, and that was my message to him. If I have to sign a contract, I have to sign a contract, but not in the street. In the street we don't have the right to do certain things. But as a pro with rules, I'll do it.

"No, I don't regret that we didn't face each other. It would have been a collision between two trains. But I couldn't see an outcome where we could jump in the ring. It was a boxer being a short guy, and a boxer-technician. It would have been more than a brawl. But since we didn't do it, it is better not to talk about it and leave it like that. It was all promotional stuff back then, nothing was announced. We were both moving divisions. Even though Don King was talking about it, it never happened."

When asked about the outcome, Argüello, who said his best weight class was 135 pounds, hemmed and hawed: "That's a good question. I don't want to disrespect a great fighter. What I can tell you is that it would have been a great clash. It would have been a collision where we both don't know . . . I could say that I would have won and he could say he could beat me. Actually, we cannot talk about these things, and I respect him as a fighter. He was a great fighter in the lightweight division and as a welterweight. But we can not speculate at this point, it is not necessary to lose my respect for a great champ like Durán."

It was impossible to avoid the temptation to imagine the "collision course" as boxing fans and experts around the world salivated over the possibilities. Unfortunately, Argüello lived in the shadow of the maniacal Durán. In a 1978 *International Boxing* magazine article, Argüello pondered the appeal of the bout, but he warned, "I can knock out anybody I hit and I know I can hit Durán." To many, Argüello did everything right, from the way he learned English to his gentlemanly demeanor to his class in the ring. Conversely, during his boxing career, Durán never learned English, berated opponents, embarrassed sparring partners, was crude and obscene in public, and showed little respect for press members. Yet, he managed to galvanize audiences in a way that eluded Argüello.

"There was a tendency to compare him to Durán," said boxing journalist Steve Farhood, who noted that Carlos Monzon and Roberto Durán were the top Latin fighters of the decade owing to their television exposure. "They were both from Central America, and they were close in weight. It would go down as one of the five greatest matchups that never happened. We missed out. Here was Durán who was emotional and fiery and then you had Argüello who was cool, detached and methodical. The tremendous contrasts made the matchup more appealing. Durán relied on speed and aggression while Argüello used technique and range. We dreamed about that matchup."

Chargin promoted Durán's fights on two occasions and also noticed a clear distinction between the fighters. He said, "At the point before the uprising in Nicaragua, Alexis was the idol of the whole country. He and Dennis Martinez were 'it.' When his fights were over, he always wanted to get back to his country because of the way they treated him. As engaging as he was and always smiling, Alexis was all business when he worked out in the gyms. Durán wanted to kill you before the fight, in the gym, everything. It's funny. Durán fought for me twice, and he didn't make a hit on either card."

Comparatively, Durán cultivated his following in the United States with his magnificent bouts at Madison Square Garden. Although Argüello downplayed "the matchup that never was," the boxing community debated the possibilities for years to come.

"Durán and Argüello were both gods in the Latin community. But they were completely different in and out of the ring," said Florida promoter Ramiro Ortiz. "Durán was admired for his brutality; Argüello was admired for his brutality and gentleman aspect. They each had a charm to them. Durán's charm was that he was a great fighter and could be brutal in and out of the ring; Argüello was very conscious of his image outside the ring; Durán was not."

During his championship reign, Argüello went 11-1 and defended his 130-pound title eight times. Critics were curious to see how Argüello's punching power would affect bigger bodies at 135 pounds. Although twenty-eight-year-old Argüello had not officially abandoned the WBC crown, his decision to fight an over-the-weight bout clearly indicated his intentions. The bout promised to be a showdown of paradoxical styles. Cornelius Boza-Edwards (27-1, twenty-two knockouts), a Ugandan residing in England, was another in a line of south-paw opponents for Argüello. Boza-Edwards had caught the eye of the loquacious managers Mickey Duff and Terry Lawless, and at age twenty-four, the fighter was slowly making a reputation as a versatile boxer who could box and punch.

Argüello walked into the Superstar Theater in the Resorts International Hotel Casino in Atlantic City, New Jersey, on August 9, 1980, with a record of sixty-three wins, five losses, and fifty-three knockouts. Seventeen hundred people paying between $15 and $25 filled the small arena that afternoon for the ten-round bout, which would be the headliner on ABC's *Wide World of Sports*. Argüello came in a half pound over the lightweight limit, while Boza-Edwards was 134½ pounds. Before the fight, manager Duff tried to rouse Argüello by telling him his fighter would "kick his ass." Argüello calmly told him they would talk after the fight.

Dr. Eduardo Roman recalled, "Mickey Duff came to him. They tried to influence . . . Alexis. So don't even talk or look at him. They are scared, that's why they are doing it. They tried to make him think he was inferior to their fighter. It was a psychological weapon that I never tried to use. Alexis used to forget about hate. He never hated. He realized he was a professional and they were professionals too. I used to tell him, 'He wants to kill you,' and he said, 'Yes, but he won't be able to do it.' That was the truth."

From the opening bell, Boza-Edwards used his muscular frame to try and bully the Explosive Thin Man. This bullying tactic had never worked in the featherweight division because no one could exert his physical presence over Argüello. After shoving Argüello in that first round, Boza-Edwards received a lightning jab and a straight right that backed him up.

There were few, if any, signs that Argüello was unable to adapt to the jump in weight class. But in Round 3, Boza-Edwards patiently waited and landed a crushing straight left through Argüello's guard. The shot visibly stunned Argüello, and he couldn't recuperate. As the round closed out, Boza-Edwards slipped an Argüello offering, then worked in a short right hook to complement his straight left, the bread and butter for all southpaws against an orthodox fighter. This round awoke the casino crowd, which saw that a real fight had begun.

Both men rushed out to brawl in the opening minute of the fourth. A Boza-Edwards right hook highlighted the flurry, but a counter right by Argüello caused Boza-Edwards to stumble across the ring. Argüello stayed on top of him and threw uncharacteristic wild hooks to get rid of the Ugandan. But Boza-Edwards survived the storm.

While Argüello needed distance to land those shots, Boza-Edwards used his short, powerful arms and crunching hooks to get inside on the taller fighter. Halfway through the fight, Argüello realized that he had rarely met such physically strong, capable challengers at 130 pounds. Boza-Edwards controlled the action in the middle rounds by sticking and moving. His movement and jabs aggravated Argüello, who now only had four rounds to catch the southpaw.

Realizing he was behind, Argüello picked up the pace in the seventh. Implored by his corner to throw more than one shot at a time, Argüello stormed out, throwing punches. Early on, a straight right wobbled Boza-Edwards, but the Ugandan returned with a fiery left hook that again forcefully jammed Argüello's head back. Argüello landed two big rights in a fifteen-second barrage that overwhelmed the southpaw. Then, with forty-five seconds remaining, Argüello again knocked Boza-Edwards off balance and set up a glorious left to the body, left to the head, and a crushing right hook. Argüello wasn't finished. He stalked Boza-Edwards and administered one more left and a straight right that nearly ended the bout. However, an untimely slip by Argüello allowed Boza-Edwards some precious time to regain his senses. The round ended with Argüello landing a beautiful straight right. In fact, Argüello hit Boza-Edwards so hard that he had stomach problems during the bout.

The domination continued in the eighth as Argüello knocked out Boza-Edwards's mouthpiece with a straight right. Boza-Edwards showed a resiliency that belied Argüello's past opponents. In the post-fight press conference, Argüello would tell reporters, "I hit him so hard my hands hurt, but he would not go down." Not only did he take Argüello's biggest punches, but he swiftly walked through them and gained the Nicaraguan's respect. Yet, with 1:27 left in the round, Argüello had Boza-Edwards in trouble again. Four straight hooks had Boza-Edwards staring aimlessly at the canvas, but he refused to go down. He was beaten and took a big hook to the stomach. Bravely, Boza-Edwards clinched and threw punches to end the round.

Between rounds, Boza-Edwards's manager, Mickey Duff, decided to save his fighter and asked referee Tony Perez to end the fight. Argüello was ahead on two of the three cards at the time of the stoppage; only judge Richard Murry had it even. Argüello later told a reporter that Boza-Edwards was the toughest opponent he'd faced. The garrulous manager, Duff, was silenced.

"At the weigh-in, Duff said Boza-Edwards would knock the shit out of me," said Argüello. "I told him to talk to me after the show. At the end of the fight, he knew. Then Duff came over and said, 'Alexis, you're the best.' He grabbed my head and said, 'You're too tough.'"

In Boza-Edwards, Argüello had faced a different kind of southpaw: "I was really proud of my effort today because he surprised me, gave me a lot of trouble. I had only ten days to train against southpaw sparring partners. Boza-Edwards was different. He upset my timing and counterpunching. Most southpaws attack all the time."

A humbled Duff explained his hesitation to send out his charge for more punishment. "Corny was in shape," he said, "but not the 100-rounds-of-sparring shape you need for an Argüello."

One journalist applauded Duff for his compassion. Said Steve Farhood, "My memory of that Boza-Edwards fight was how it ended. Mickey Duff knew he had a good young fighter. Boza-Edwards outboxed Argüello over the first half of the fight, and then Argüello just turned it up a notch. As soon as he did that, Duff pulled his fighter out. It was a brilliant move. It was like Duff acknowledged Argüello's greatness. He wanted his fighter to get that experience, but he didn't let him get hurt. Boza went on to have a big career, but what might have happened if Duff allowed Argüello to stretch him?"

Few had expected Argüello to have such a difficult time with Boza-Edwards, but his foray into the 135-pounders would get more difficult yet. On August 26, only weeks after the Boza-Edwards bout, Argüello officially announced his move to the lightweight decision and vacated the WBC super featherweight crown. That November, *Ring* magazine catapulted Argüello to No. 3 behind Aaron "The Hawk" Pryor and Hilmer Kenty, the WBA champ. The WBC champ Roberto Durán had vacated the division the previous June.

On November 14, 1980, WBA world bantamweight champ Julian Solís and challenger Jeff Chandler headlined at the Jai-Alai Fronton Stadium in Miami, Florida. Argüello (64-5) faced Mexico's José Luis Ramirez (67-2), a southpaw, at 135 pounds.

Locals were familiar with Argüello, who had made a name for himself at the famed Miami Fifth Street Gym.

"I remember one time he was sparring with Ike Hooks, who was a good local fighter, and a great 'gym' fighter. He gave everyone a hard time," former lightweight contender Frankie Otero. "But Argüello throws a jab, and then this short left hook, and it sounded like he hit Ike with a baseball bat. And he dropped him. Actually, I think the punch sent him through the ropes. Alexis was very reserved and respectful in the gym. He didn't mingle or show off, but he just wanted to get down to business, and that was how most boxers were at the Fifth Street Gym."

Few took notice of the nontitle affair. Argüello's bout with Ramirez was hardly a blip in the sports pages. Compared with the established Argüello, Ramirez was an understated lightweight who had fought most of his career outside of the United States against fringe opponents. Conversely, Argüello, an established star, was making his second foray into the lightweight division.

In the Jai-Alai Fronton stadium, Argüello had all of the pieces set for a reunion of sorts. At this point, what did he have to prove? Having won and successfully defended two titles, along with positioning himself as one of the top-five fighters in the world, Argüello demanded respect. By November 1980, he had faced the Sandinista regime with dignity, refusing to act out against its socialist party. Now, the displaced Cubans who had left their country during Fidel Castro's regime looked at Argüello as a heroic figure. Argüello was paradoxical in many ways, and his ability to internalize the disdain he held for a party that his younger brother Eduardo died fighting for was extraordinary.

Often, Argüello waxed philosophically on the subject. "'Cause I know how to be something in a world . . . I know how to make it, how to make a living. I am trying to prove to my people that no matter what they take from you, they can't take my love for my country. They can't take the respect that I have for my people. They can take everything from me . . . [but] not my pride, my nationality."

When Argüello, at 135 ½ pounds, stepped in to face Ramirez, who weighed in at 135 pounds, on November 14, 1980, the former champ was well aware that his new division had no pushovers. Sammy Marshall copromoted the bout with Chris Dundee and Tuto Zabala. The height and reach measurements favored Argüello against the smaller, squat Ramirez.

"This was supposed to be a tune-up for Alexis," said Florida-based promoter Walter Alvarez. "Nobody took him that seriously."

All of the flaws and errors that previous opponents had made against Argüello, Ramirez instinctively understood how to avoid. Frugal with his punches and economical with his movement, Ramirez didn't waste his time forcing his way through Argüello's guard, and he didn't recklessly bull ahead when he couldn't puncture it. Ramirez's remedy was a timed double jab, intelligence, and power that stemmed from accuracy.

Not especially quick or powerful, Ramirez stabbed Argüello with a straight left and a stinging jab early and often. Ramirez hailed from Sonora, Mexico, but he didn't employ the tactics that defined the typical Mexican brawler. While Mexican prospect Pipino Cuevas punched to kill and Rubén Olivares was a whirlwind of energy constantly throwing punches, Ramirez could shift gears when he needed and masterfully used his 5-foot-6 frame to elude danger at any given moment.

So when Argüello landed a sneaky right hand in the second round and looked to attack, Ramirez effortlessly visualized the next punch and moved away. The pace shifted in the third as Ramirez's short left bounced Argüello's head back with the best punch of the fight. The Mexican lightweight won the round and even opened a cut over Argüello's left eye, which clearly concerned the Nicaraguan. In fact, the cut was in the corner of the eyelid, which pressured trainer Al Silvani to staunch the bleeding to avert any blood seeping into his fighter's eye.

Both Argüello and Ramirez fought recklessly to start the fifth round, with Ramirez winning the bulk of the infighting. His short right hook proved problematic for the straight-up Argüello. Also, Argüello saved his right hand as if he'd hurt it and wildly missed shots, moves that were out of character. Ramirez, who was trailing on points after the fifth round, broke any rhythm or routine that had become commonplace for Argüello.

The telltale round of the fight was the sixth, when Argüello felt that the fight was slipping away from him. Having won the first half of the round, the aggressive Argüello followed Ramirez around the ring, throwing punches. Then he walked directly into a pulverizing left hand. For the first time since a flash knockdown against José Torres in 1976, a punch sent him to the canvas.

"[When Alexis got knocked down] it was as if the whole arena said 'Holy shit' as a chorus," Alvarez recalled.

Argüello also had another problem.

"He broke his knuckle hitting the speed bag a week and a half before the bout. I asked Roman to call the fight off, but he didn't want to stop the fight," said Don Kahn. "So they wanted to give him a shot of cortisone, but I asked, 'What will happen when it wears off during the fight?' When that happened he couldn't use his right hand, and I told him, 'You still have to throw it, so they don't see that you are hurt.'"

The shock of seeing Argüello getting off the canvas only cemented the sentiment that critics felt he had become overly ambitious in moving to this perilous weight class. Argüello rose immediately and referee William Connors gave him the mandatory eight count. Ramirez went after Argüello with a flinging left, but the round ended. A dejected Argüello headed back to the corner.

"He wasn't hurt," Kahn recalled. "Still he kept coming back to the corner and saying, 'Negro, my hand hurts.' I told him that he had to use it one way or the other or I would tell them to stop the fight."

Argüello's corner worked on his left eye as well as a cut that had opened on the bridge of his nose. The fighter had been knocked down before. The punch wasn't a flash knockdown against a power puncher but a well-timed punch from a skillful boxer-puncher. Yet, few fighters understood how to cope with adversity as Argüello did.

Glimpses of the old Argüello surfaced in the form of a five-punch combination in the seventh that was punctuated by lefts to the body and then the head. But Argüello was sent stumbling again from another left hook toward the end of the round. Argüello rallied in the last two rounds, igniting a barrage to close out the ninth. However, the tenth was a back-and-forth affair as neither fighter had a decisive edge, and the last seconds of the fight ticked off with the understanding that Ramirez had fought the better fight. As soon as the fight ended, Argüello walked over to raise Ramirez's hand in victory. The judges didn't see it that way. James Kenon scored it, 98–95, for Ramirez; while Sam Biller and Bill Connors scored the fight for Argüello, who earned a split-decision victory. Although the pro-Argüello crowd cheered, knowledgeable fans understood who won the bout.

"José Luis Ramirez hit me with a left hook," said Argüello. "He was a guy that never fought the way I wanted."

"I think he won that fight," said Dr. Roman. "When you expect somebody to dance marvelously, then you see them dance as a normal dancer then you think that he is not the person you thought he was. In this case with Alexis, you were expecting him to make a spectacular fight and he did not make that fight. He made a good fight. Sometimes you don't get the result you are looking for. In the case of José Luis Ramirez, he was better than we thought he was."

When it came to assessing Argüello's performance, few believed the champ fought a winning fight. "Everybody knew he got a favorable decision," said Alvarez. "It wasn't highway robbery, but it was a hometown decision. But Argüello was a huge draw, and he was good for boxing. I am never opposed to giving a hometown decision with guys who are good for the sport."

More important than Argüello's victory was the signing of his agent, Bill Miller. A previous director of Don King Boxing, Miller would immediately leave his imprint on Argüello's career.

"I was director of Don King Boxing, and we did a three-fight promotion with Roman. So we got to work with him directly. When the promotional deal was up, Roman asked if I would like to handle his fighter," said Miller. "We never signed anything officially. It was just another one of those deals where he said, 'Will you handle my fighter?' Some managers do everything. They line up fighters, line up bouts, and put together a team. Roman wasn't that type of manager. He wasn't a boxing guy, but he respected my judgment."

Argüello Joins Boxing's Elite

I shall defend it with my heart and my blood, the same way Jim Watt did.
—ALEXIS ARGÜELLO AFTER WINNING THIRD TITLE

After easily dispatching Robert Vasquez in Miami in February 1981, Argüello positioned himself for a shot at the lightweight title held by Scotsman Jim Watt. For this defense against Argüello, thirty-two-year-old Watt would earn £350,000 ($780,000) and a chance to compound his legacy by defeating the former super featherweight champ in London's Wembley Stadium. Argüello settled for $280,000.

Despite the Scotsman's persistence and recent bloodbath victory over Sean O'Grady, Argüello had little to fear from Watt. Few boxing insiders felt the Scottish southpaw had exhibited the strength, speed, or fortitude to challenge the legendary Nicaraguan. He had not beaten one opponent on Argüello's level, and the betting odds reflected their disparate boxing styles. Having feasted on two divisions, Argüello had outboxed and outhustled nearly every fighter placed in front of him. Going into the championship bout, the lightweight challenger had won sixty-six of his seventy-one bouts.

"The Argüello fight materialized because Watt beat Howard Davis Jr. No one expected him to beat Davis, who had just come out of the Olympics with Sugar Ray Leonard," said Don Chargin, who copromoted the bout. "But Watt gave him a thumping for fifteen rounds. Then Watt's stock really went up. We put that fight in Scotland, and his stock really went up when he beat Howard. A lot of people were looking for Howard Davis and Alexis Argüello. After Watt beat Davis (and then knocked out Sean O'Grady), the mandatory was Alexis. It went to a purse bid. The Watt people weren't anxious to meet Alexis. They had to fight him. At the time, Rogelio Robles, Mickey Duff, and myself promoted the bout. Over there, Watt was very popular. So a lot of fans believed he could beat Alexis. Alexis was favored."

Although Dr. Eduardo Roman and Argüello both resided in Miami at the time, outside distractions still had become a staple in Argüello's life. Months prior, boxing had been banned completely in Nicaragua, and anyone who refused compliance was subjected to a jail sentence or a hefty fine. When Argüello was not dealing with family problems, a conflict with the Sandinistas over TV rights had surfaced. Ironically, members of the Sandinista directorate, angry and resentful at Argüello, still managed to see all his fights.

"The time he fought Watt, they had stopped the fight from being shown in Nicaragua because Daniel Ortega didn't want it to be seen. So we didn't make a deal," Chargin recalled. "So a guy comes up to us a half hour before the fight and tells us he has to show the fight in Nicaragua. Well, Mickey Duff, who was a shrewd guy, was afraid he wouldn't get paid, so he was hesitant. The guy shows him a briefcase full of cash, and it was allowed to be televised. Alexis was so happy when he found out about it."

Nicaraguan journalist Edgar Tijerino supported the story. He said, "His fights were still shown by television. The Sandinistas paid for all the fights in Nicaragua. They even paid $80,000 to see his bout with Watt. Even with the problems they had with Alexis, they still paid for each fight."

The championship bout on June 20, 1981, would highlight the *Sports Saturday* boxing program televised on CBS. Unlike most championship bouts, there was no prefight animosity. Instead, a cheerful Argüello approached Watt to ask about his family, and the usually raucous English audience respected the challenger.

"But there was no [animosity] with Alexis. Days before the fight we met and he came up to me, put out his hand and said, 'Please to meet you, how's your family?' It was so strange," Watt recalled. "All of the other American fighters were just the opposite. There was no ill feeling. It was our job. It was my job to keep my title and his job to take it from me. I had enormous respect for him."

Career-wise, pundits contemplated Argüello's place in boxing lore as he searched for that treasured third world title. The Argüello camp did balk at the 16-foot ring and insisted on it being changed to a 20-foot ring. Promoters Harry Levine and Mickey Duff compromised with Argüello's people and found a ring that met their standards.

Another storyline that developed was the longtime relationship between trainer Cuyo Hernández and Argüello. For this bout, Hernández insisted that Argüello improve his lateral movement and mobility in order to best Watt. In fact, in a story repeated to Mexican journalists on many occasions, he went to great lengths to help Argüello accomplish this change. Hernández adopted the temperament and motivational tools that Alexis wanted out of a trainer. Although Argüello enjoyed his time in Mexico working with Hernández, it would be their last big fight together. Later on, Hernández questioned the trajectory of Argüello's career, and they parted ways.

While Hernández used a fear tactic to improve his fighter's mobility, Watt began his roadwork for the bout that winter and ended his training above the Royal Oak Pub in London's East End. Duff tried his best to ruffle the feathers of the Argüello camp as he was accused of often orchestrating midnight pulls of the fire alarm and other strange occurrences.

Argüello was the clear favorite, as Vegas had him at 3–1, while London favored him at 7–4 odds. Argüello entered the ring at 134½ pounds, while Watt weighed 134¾ pounds. Nearly seven thousand fans packed the Wembley Arena that Saturday evening.

Fighters commonly watch hours of taped bouts to gauge their opponents' strengths and weaknesses. Back in 1981, fight tapes weren't as accessible as they are today. Having watched a few fights prior to the showdown, Watt labeled Argüello a mechanical fighter who could be outsmarted. Then, in the ring, reality set in. Through the first three rounds, Watt cautiously jabbed as he circled away from the aggressive Argüello. Neither man looked to engage, but Argüello attempted to initiate the action and, in the second round, caught Watt with a straight right hand.

The bout lacked the fluidity or the tension that accompanied most of Argüello's matches. Watt was too slow and unwilling to initiate confrontation, and if it weren't for Argüello's short, compact hooks to the body, there would have been little threat of meaningful contact. Overall, the fight didn't reflect a championship-caliber matchup. Laborious and dull and rarely stirring the crowd, the fight only picked up intensity occasionally as the rounds progressed.

Argüello relied on an uppercut in the fourth and battered Watt in the fifth. In that fifth round, Argüello pounced on his durable opponent with a left hook that sent the Scot reeling.

"My game plan was to use my southpaw style to frustrate him. I wasn't a flashy fighter and I didn't put my punches together. I was a right-handed southpaw so I wanted to frustrate him with my jab," said Watt. "But nothing would rattle him. Halfway through the fight I knew that I was struggling. I knew the title would change hands, and I couldn't do anything to change that."

Watt wasn't as awkward or elusive as Argüello's other southpaw opponents, so no one was surprised when Argüello sent him down with a left hook to the jaw in the seventh round. Watt was bleeding from his nose, a cut that was never staunched effectively throughout the bout.

"When he hit me I was moving away. My legs didn't collapse, and I wasn't on the floor for any length of time," Watt recalled. "It was a good punch, but I came right back up and I didn't need much time to recover."

If Watt sensed that he was being shut out, he only showed outright concern as he became more aggressive in the eighth round. Another cut opened on Watt's right cheekbone in the late rounds, which prompted referee Arthur Mércante to visit the corner. The combatants traded to start the twelfth, but the release of emotions was not indicative of the previous eleven rounds. A pattern continued until the end, with Argüello punching, though not at the intense pace of a man searching for a knockout, as Watt covered up.

A "Jim Watt, Jim Watt!" cheer echoed throughout Wembley during the fight. In the final thirty seconds of the fight, Argüello tried to end the bout, but Watt staved off the rally. Argüello took an easy and boring unanimous decision: 147–137, 147–143, and 147–143. A downtrodden Watt buried his head in a blood-spotted towel.

"I have a car business, and if I had to do an estimate on my face, I would probably treat it as a write off," Watt lamented. "I reckon he won by five rounds. I've been under a great deal of pressure ever since I became world champ. Now it's all over I feel a great relief."

Argüello had won his third world championship, placing himself in the same category as legendary division jumpers Henry Armstrong, Tony Canzoneri, Barney Ross, Bob Fitzsimmons, and contemporary Wilfred Benítez. Argüello broke down and cried as he spoke with a member from the Nicaraguan press. With the bitter taste of the Sandinistas forcing him into exile still fresh, Argüello forged ahead. Staying true to his "Gentleman of the Ring" moniker, Argüello praised his opponent.

"Watt was a great champion. He fought like a man of 22, not like the 32 that he is," said the new champ. On winning the title, he added: "I shall defend it with my heart and with my blood, the same way as [Watt] did."

Ironically, Watt's former challenger Howard Davis Jr. was already looking toward a showdown with Argüello when he said, "I'd like to meet Argüello. He would be easy, he just comes right at you."

Sean O'Grady, who nearly faced Argüello before becoming an accomplished broadcaster, assessed Argüello's greatness: "The difference between analyzing

Alexis from the ring and the booth was so much more than just conversations. In every fight you have to have total body commitment. It appeared that Argüello would fight in waves. Once he saw an opening or a weakness, he would zero in. He was impeccable like that. Trainers don't see when a fighter is getting ready to get knocked out. But Alexis saw the sign. He was as perspicacious as anyone at understanding when a fighter was ready to go."

Not only had Argüello won his third title, but also he had won over the people inside and outside the sport with his class and dignity. Argüello had stayed balanced in and out of the ring, and the boxing world, especially the writers, appreciated his honesty and compassion.

"With Alexis, you have a choice," says Jimmy Jacobs, the manager of Wilfred Benítez, the WBC junior middleweight champion. "You can go in the middle rounds or you can go a little slower, when he boxes you to death over the distance, as he did Jim Watt."

A possible collision course with young box office smash Ray "Boom Boom" Mancini surfaced exactly a month later when the exciting young fighter decisively beat José Luis Ramirez over twelve rounds in Mancini's home state of Ohio. The win opened up negotiations for a showdown with Argüello.

Mancini said he had learned from Argüello's loss to Ramirez the previous November. "The José Luis Ramirez fight really gave me the confidence to believe that I could beat Alexis. I had watched that fight, and José Luis Ramirez really beat Alexis. José Luis was not that quick or strong, but that whole fight he was a step ahead of Alexis. So I said to myself, 'I was catching him at the right time.' I was stronger, faster, and younger," said Mancini. "It was exactly the right time for me. I don't think my manager Dave Wolf really pushed for that fight. It just came up that if I beat Ramirez then I was next in line to face Alexis. The fight presented itself in the natural order. Ramirez fought well with Alexis, so I knew it was the fight for me."

While Mancini still had much to prove to the boxing public, Argüello had solidified his position among the all-time greats. *Ring* magazine ran a panel discussion on the best Latin fighters of all time and placed Argüello fifth behind Argentine middleweight Carlos Monzon, welterweight phenom Kid Gavilán, new 147-pound champ Roberto Durán, and Cuba's "Kid Chocolate" or the "Cuban Bon Bon." Argüello was among select company. That September, *Ring* placed the newly crowned WBC champ atop his division looking down at Argüello's WBA counterpart Sean O'Grady, Detroit resident Hilmer Kenty, and the man who many considered the most dangerous fighter in the sport, Aaron "The Hawk" Pryor.

While many fighters looked to wind down after winning a world title, Argüello signed to fight the whirlwind Italian-American Ray Mancini only four months later in October. In fact, Mancini was the hot prospect who, at 20-0 with fourteen knockouts, had the power and effective intensity to give Argüello problems.

"Every day for two months [I trained for the Mancini fight]. I trained every day. I never stopped training," said Argüello. "If the fight was on Saturday, I went to sleep early after the fight, and on Monday I was back in the gym. I don't recall having to rest for one or two days after the fight."

Always in perpetual motion, Mancini was coming off an impressive win over the veteran Ramirez. Mancini won the lightly regarded North American Boxing Federation (NABF) lightweight title with a unanimous decision over the Mexican stalwart. With his sharp Italian features, movie star looks, and fierce love for his father, Mancini's story was similar to that of the 1975 film *Rocky*, and his passion made for great drama. Now Boom Boom would face Argüello for the WBC version of the 135-pound belt. Winning a world title for his father, a former boxer, worked as motivation for the young fighter.

Mancini followed Argüello's career religiously before he began to move up the ranks. Mancini said, "When I watched his early fights I was impressed by his composure. He would go across the ring and shake the other guy's hand, and I had never seen that before, except for the old-timers. They were gentlemen back then. He never got rattled, never. He always believed that he could weather the storm."

"In our day it was such a responsibility to come across as a good sportsman. Actually, Don King told us a couple of times to hype things up, but I looked at it as a mistake," recalled Argüello about the Mancini title fight in Atlantic City. "Hype is not good because you are selling good shows for television audiences. When you have a mismatch, it's bad. I fought for promoters Teddy Brenner at the Garden and George Parnassus in Los Angeles. For them to hire you, you have to do the right thing. When I fought for ABC, CBS, they were something special and they meant something. In those days, it was to look as good as you can, technically and physically."

Argüello had peaked at an optimal time. With the advent of weekly programs on USA Network and Entertainment and Sports Programming Network (ESPN), along with the weekend bouts shown regularly on ABC, CBS, and National Broadcasting Company (NBC), Argüello reaped the benefits. While prime-time bouts garnered purses close to $1 million, the paydays for the weekend networks ranged from $100,000 to $600,000. Cable television had become a viable threat to broadcast television. Media darlings such as Sugar Ray Leonard were making too much for subscription TV; thus, Home Box Office (HBO) had begun to televise their fights. Argüello, though, still lacked TV star power. Ironically, even after fifteen years of boxing professionally, Argüello had to take a backseat to the TV star Mancini.

The resilient Mancini never backed down from Argüello and won over the fans with his engaging style. Mancini was a Damon Runyon character, tugging at the heartstrings of all boxing fans. He fought for approval, he fought for acceptance, and most of all he fought for pride. Everything that he did was for his father and hero, Lenny Mancini. It was a storyline that Argüello could indirectly relate to because as a teenager growing up in Managua he had fought for his parents' security. Although Argüello didn't experience the same father-son bond reflected in Ray and Lenny's relationship, he understood the emotional drain of fighting for something other than oneself.

Boom Boom II inherited all his dreams from his father. Lenny Mancini, the original "Boom Boom," was a young lightweight prospect in the 1940s who was preparing to rematch Sammy Angott for the lightweight title when he was drafted to fight in World War II. After earning a Purple Heart at the Battle of the Bulge, the elder Mancini was too damaged from the war to return as the same fighter he once was. His title hopes had vanished.

"I told the recruiters I'd go in a day after the Angott fight," Lenny Mancini told reporters years later. "I offered to donate all my purses to the Army Relief Fund. The draft board said, 'We don't want your money, we want you.' Almost broke my heart."

Young Ray had become the "Pride of Youngstown," a gritty blue-collar steel town. Employing a fearless and, at times, self-destructive style, Mancini provided hope for a town that had been ravaged in the late 1970s from a layoff of five thousand steel workers. Mancini understood what he symbolized every time he walked into the ring, as his heightening popularity merged well with the small-town charm. The fight promotions emphasized the father-son tribute and Mancini's obsession to fulfill his father's missed opportunity. Heightening the drama of the October title fight with Argüello, Lenny had undergone a double-bypass coronary operation in mid-September. The touching storyline also proved lucrative for the champ, as Argüello was set to make his biggest purse of $450,000.

"My dad told me to take the shot because you didn't know if you'd get another one," said Ray Mancini. "I learned from him that in order to be the best, you had to beat the best. My father knew something about fighters, maybe not as much as me, but he had watched tapes of Alexis and knew he was a great fighter. We saw tapes and thought his style was perfect for me. Of course, Alexis also felt the same about how my style fit his."

Mancini's inexperience also had boxing people buzzing: Did Mancini's people rush their young star before he was ready? Although Argüello rarely revealed his true emotions, he must have felt some reservation about the attention Mancini was receiving in only his twentieth bout, while Argüello had fought his whole life for this level of recognition.

"It's easy to look back on that fight in retrospect and say they threw Mancini to the wolves against a top-three pound-for-pound fighter. But the truth was that Mancini earned that fight," said journalist Steve Farhood. "He was the type of fighter who peaked early with that aggressive, ambush style. His manager, one of the best this sport has seen, knew this. He knew that if it didn't work out for Ray, then it wasn't the end of the world. Mancini helped to justify this by fighting him well for 13 rounds. And to be fair, although it sounds silly, Argüello was the epitome of a fifteen-round fighter. He always started off slow, preserved energy and came on strong late. We learned that with Rubén Olivares who was outboxing him. . . ."

Prior to the showdown, Mancini's manager Dave Wolf questioned the WBC-appointed officials. Specifically he contested the choice of Nicaraguan judge José Mayorga and criticized the choice of referee Tony Perez, citing Perez's supposed reluctance to let fighters fight on the inside. Both the judge and the ref would work the fight.

Days before the fight, both fighters worked out in New York City. Ironically, their paths crossed, but the animosity that most fighters use to sustain themselves was not evident.

"We had a press conference in New York. While we were getting ready, I went running in Central Park one day with my trainer. I was running along and I see Alexis coming the other way with someone. He looks over and says, 'Hey Ray, how are you doing?'

"I said, 'What the hell? I'm fighting this guy.' I just lost it," Mancini recalled. "But it was a business. I learned that from him. Whenever you fight a guy, there's always going to be tension, but not with him. I ran by him thinking, That's the guy I'm fighting, and he's waving to me and asked how my day was. But that was just him. He was a wonderful human being."

Thousands of devoted Youngstown fans made the trip to Bally's Park Place in Atlantic City, New Jersey, on October 3 to see the bout, which was televised nationally on CBS's *Sports Saturday* program. Argüello, now 67-5 with fifty-eight

BOXEO

ARIZONA'S FIRST WORLD TITLE FIGHT

TUCSON COMMUNITY CENTER

SUN. JAN. 20

FIRST BOUT 11:00 A.M.
MAIN EVENT 1:00 P.M.

NO TV!!   (15 ROUNDS)   NO TV!!

W.B.C. SUPER FEATHERWEIGHT CHAMPIONSHIP

(PESO SUPER PLUMA DE CONSEJO MUNDIAL DE BOXEO)

ALEXIS ARGUELLO

NICARAGUA – CAMPEON DEL MUNDO
ENTRENADOR: CUYO HERNANDEZ

VS.

RUBEN CASTILLO

TUCSON - INVICTO EN 44 PELEAS
MGRS. BETO MARTINEZ & RAUL GARZA —

10 ROUNDS FEATHERWEIGHTS

NICO **PEREZ**   VS.   ANGEL **SALINAS**

TUCSON — CAMPEON NORTEAMERICANO   PHOENIX — HOMBRE MUY DURO

TAMBIÉN REAPARECEN: JOSE "CUEVANO" CABA ★ MARIO TINEO ★ CLAYTON ROSS ★ JOSE TORRES ★ RANDY CLOVER ★ BOBBY KREUGER

PRICES - $25 Ringside $15 Reserved - $10 Gen. Adm. On Sale Now at T.C.C. Outlets	STEVE EISNER, Promoter BRUCE TRAMPLER, Matchmaker with DON KING PRODUCTIONS	W.B.C. (Jose Sulaiman, Presidente) ARIZ. ATHLETIC COMMISSION (Al Munoz, Gerald Maltz, Richard Davis, Johnny Montano)

This fight poster from 1980 pits Alexis against formidable lightweight challenger, Rubén Castillo. *COURTESY OF GERALD MALTZ*

One of Argüello's fiercest rivals, Mauricio Buitrago, tapes the hands of one of his prizefighters in a Nicaraguan gym. *PHOTO BY THE AUTHOR*

Aaron and Alexis share the dais as they promote the Miami extravaganza before their first big showdown. *COURTESY OF WALTER ALVAREZ*

Walter Alvarez of the Miami Boxing Commission talks about the upcoming mega-fight between Alexis Argüello and Aaron Pryor. *COURTESY OF WALTER ALVAREZ*

Always supremely focused during training sessions, Alexis turns his attention to the speed bag. *COURTESY OF WALTER "BUTCH" FLANSBURG*

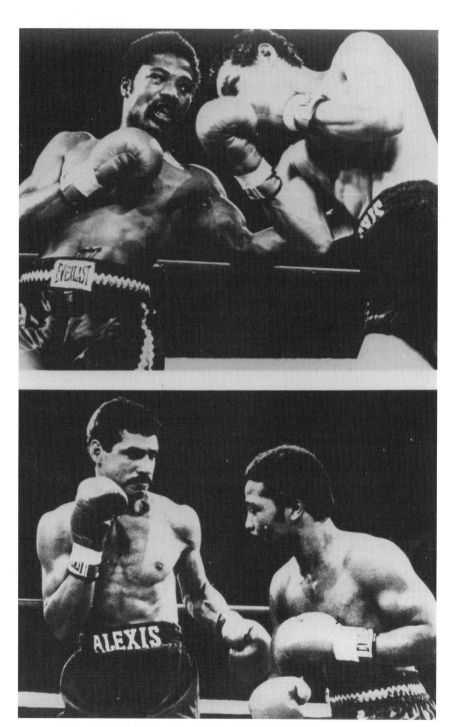

Alexis and Aaron in the trenches, trying to land that one big shot.
COURTESY OF WALTER ALVAREZ

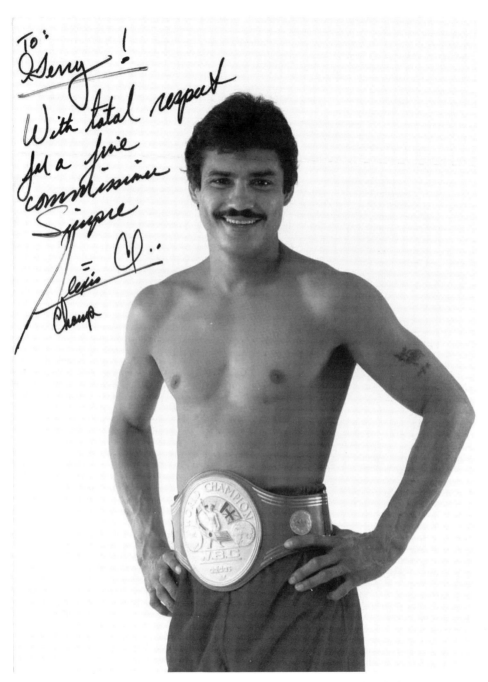

Three-time champ Alexis Argüello poses with his WBC championship belt.
COURTESY OF GERALD MALTZ

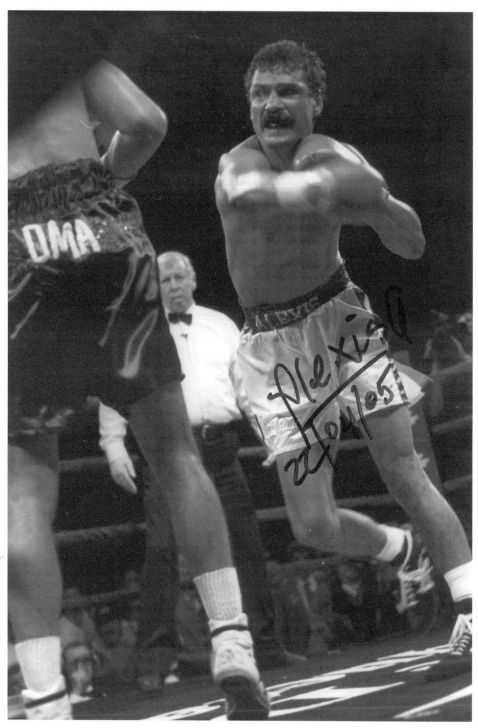

Nearing the end of his career, Alexis keeps coming forward and plugging away.
COURTESY OF WALTER "BUTCH" FLANSBURG

Alexis Argüello clowns around with the great Muhammad Ali.
COURTESY OF WALTER "BUTCH" FLANSBURG

Eduardo Roman and Dr. Henry Castillo were close friends and confidantes of Alexis's until he passed away in 2009. *PHOTO BY THE AUTHOR*

The controversial statue built in Alexis's honor drew more criticism than praise.
PHOTO BY THE AUTHOR

This is Alexis Argüello's childhood home in the Barrio Monseñor Lezcano.
PHOTO BY THE AUTHOR

knockouts, stepped into the ring at a taut 135 pounds, while Mancini appeared focused at a half-pound under the limit. Commentators Gil Clancy, Sean O'Grady, and Tim Ryan worked on the broadcast of the fight for CBS. The WBC would get its 1.5 percent of the purse after the fight.

Referee Tony Perez stood between the combatants, and neither fighter looked up. Argüello towered over the 5-foot-4, twenty-year-old Mancini and would take advantage of a seven-inch reach advantage.

"The training camp was great. I felt great going into that fight. But like I always tell people, even though you feel confident there's always a negative energy that enters little by little," Mancini recalled. "You have to find a way to combat that. Sure, I felt strong, liked what I saw, but there was a little part of you that will say, 'The guy hits so hard' or 'That right hand. . . .' Those are the types of things you have to combat. So it becomes a battle of wills with yourself."

Argüello measured his smaller opponent throughout the first round with a soft jab, and he realized that he could work that powerful left hook each time Mancini threw a right hand and left himself exposed. Mancini was content to slow down and fight more of a tactical fight early on, but he had not landed anything substantial through the early rounds. Despite his cautious style, Mancini walked into a straight right and two left hooks in that second round.

"No one could prepare you for how hard he hit," Mancini recalled. "You know he hits hard with that right hand, but he hit just as hard with that jab. I made him miss 1,000 right hands, but then he got me with 1,001. And he jammed you like a ramrod. Geez! Those are the types of things you have to combat."

Had Ray Mancini shown too much respect to Argüello? The Youngstown fans may have asked. Only in the third round did Mancini show glimpses of keeping up with the torrid pace that had figured into his previous twenty fights. Although Argüello had perfectly timed his left jab to hinder Mancini's path, the challenger awoke from an earlier slumber to attack and ended his round with a jolting straight right hand. To heighten the drama, CBS perfectly juxtaposed shots of Lenny Mancini in the bottom corner of the picture throughout the broadcast.

A jab, then a short left hook had been the potent combination that staunched Mancini's caustic ambushes. Argüello's plan rendered the smaller man virtually harmless as he neutralized Mancini's straightforward style through the early rounds. Still, Mancini did not become discouraged.

"Over the first five rounds, I felt good. But I was giving him too much room," Mancini recalled. "I needed to shorten the distance, and I didn't do that early enough. I would go in and out on him. I think that fooled him a little, because he thought that I would come out and jump on him early. I would land a flurry and then move away, and I think that threw him off. I felt good [about] how we were carrying out the game plan."

Then, midway through the fifth round, Mancini broke through the shield to land a soft right, compounded by a severe left hook. In the last thirty seconds of Round 5, a calculated fight had turned into a brawl. Had Mancini located a chink in Argüello's armor?

"I learned that he had to reset before he threw a punch. I used side-to-side movement, jumped in and out, making him reset. But little by little he started to dissect me," said Mancini. "He sets little traps for you and then comes back later on to make sure he caught you. Boom, then he turns it over on you. We knew he got stronger in the later rounds, but we felt confident that I would be just as strong. So we felt we had an advantage."

A slit on Mancini's nose and a puffy left eye were the only two indications that a fight had broken out as the fighters came out for the sixth round. After carelessly missing three jabs, Mancini watched helplessly as Argüello leveled himself and landed a shuttering right hand on his jaw. But Boom Boom answered with a punch that he would have been hesitant to throw five rounds earlier. In the final minute of the round, his Youngstown spirit was encapsulated in a sharp combination as Mancini made Argüello appear old and frustrated for the first time.

Throughout the last three or four rounds, Mancini realized that success relied on suffocating the champ. In the seventh, Mancini jammed Argüello, now on unstable legs, to the ropes, and he backed off in the eighth as he allowed Argüello to dictate the entire round. Slowed by rangy uppercuts, Mancini lacked the spunk of the previous round. Much to the consternation of the pro-Mancini crowd, Argüello returned to the jab. In two consecutive scenarios, Mancini's head swiveled from an Argüello hook and then a left uppercut.

Argüello pawed at his eye during the closing seconds of Round 9, his concern coming from an accidental thumbing from Mancini. His thumb caught Argüello as Mancini inadvertently slashed it along his face. However, as Argüello lowered his guard and motioned for a response from Mancini, the challenger refused to take advantage and walked toward Argüello as if to apologize. Argüello darted out of the corner in the tenth round. The bruise darkened under Argüello's eye while Mancini's running nosebleed was no longer visible. Mancini, a notorious bleeder, developed a cut that opened under his left eyebrow. Both fighters succumbed to the frantic pace of the fight and slowed considerably in that round. With only five rounds remaining, conditioning would play a major factor.

"Alexis was always starting slow," said Don Kahn, who was in the corner for this bout. "He would take his time on his own. Mancini was a young, strong kid. I told Alexis, 'This kid is younger than you. Put your punches together with power. You power will beat his speed.'"

The tactical Argüello emerged in that next round to find that Mancini had unknowingly fallen into his trap. To offset Mancini's movement, Argüello patiently waited for an opening to release the one right hand that would reverse the tenor of the bout. As in the early rounds, Mancini, either from exhaustion or concern, sat on the outside and absorbed fierce jabs and hooks. Each punch stunted the young fighter's progress, and with seconds left in the twelfth round, Argüello landed a picture-perfect right hand that forced the courageous challenger to one knee. Struggling to regain his equilibrium, Mancini bounced up and sleepwalked over to his corner as seconds ticked away. Referee Tony Perez didn't call it a knockdown and tried to reverse Mancini's course back to the middle of the ring, but the bell sounded to end the round. As Mancini was being worked on in the corner, blood crusted on his lips. A cut had formed on the inside of his mouth, in all likelihood from Argüello's vicious right hand.

Mancini had no choice but to become the matador. Although he survived the punch, he had tasted Argüello's power too often to fight back with the same passion. Now he was trapped in Argüello's close confines, where the only escape was a lucky punch.

At one point, manager Dave Wolf nearly stopped the fight, but the towel never came into the ring. Those observers who questioned the decision to match the young prospect against Argüello could point to these final two rounds as the illustrations of their fears. Except Argüello, few champions were as dangerous in the final rounds as they were in the early rounds.

Argüello's final barrage started with a right hook to the ribs that left Mancini paralyzed. Then a dazed Mancini was defenseless to an incisive left hook that sent him reeling to his left. Argüello, who was very critical of Perez's hesitance, looked to the referee for guidance, hoping to save the young fighter. As Perez tried to intervene between the fighters, one last straight right jarred Mancini's head back in a frightening manner. The fighter finally fell backward, and the fans turned from the violence, haunted by Mancini's head swivel. Perez cradled him and called the fight as soon as Mancini got to his feet. The stoppage was called at 1:46 of the fourteenth round.

Retrospectively, Mancini attempted to assess his late-round deficiencies. "At the end of the twelfth round, I got knocked down and was still dazed going into that thirteenth round. I needed to regroup. Before heading into the thirteenth, my trainer told me to move, and stay away. If you notice, in the fourteenth round, I jumped right on him. I was banging him, pushing him back, and making him retreat," said Mancini, describing his first professional loss. "I was hitting him with combinations, then he sees an opening and he hits me with that left hook. I was stunned. Like I said, he knew when to turn it on. I think it was a left hook, right uppercut, another left uppercut, and the right hand before Perez jumped in."

"From the beginning, I had the best condition of my life because I knew it . . . Mancini in the future is going to be one of the best fighters of all time," Argüello said in the post-fight interview. "I expected a tough fight, and that was it."

Argüello continued: "The right hand to the belly, the solar plexus, was the number one punch because Mancini is strong in the head. But my trainer told me to do it because you slowed him down. Around the seventh round is when I started to do it [go to the body]. Beautiful, he was doing beautiful [early on]. But the main thing that I have is my condition and my resistance. He is a ten-round fighter and I am a fifteen-round fighter."

As the broadcaster Tim Ryan finished his interview, Argüello embraced Mancini and squeezed his cheeks as a father might do to a son.

"First ten rounds, he gave me hell," said Argüello. "During the first round, I knew it would be a tough fight. After those first ten rounds, my trainer was real nervous. I told him, 'You will see him go down.' I had too much fight.

"He was undefeated. Even his look was hurting me. He was a tough kid. But I knew that after he passed ten rounds, I had him in my pocket. When I went back to my corner, my trainer was concerned, but I told him, 'I got him. Don't worry about it.'"

Upon review, many felt that Argüello had become too cautious, and two of the three judges concurred as they had Mancini ahead going into the thirteenth round. The hook that Argüello threw in the thirteenth round pirouetted the smaller Mancini, but he did not go down. A round later, Argüello put all of Mancini's dreams on hold.

"I hit him [and he fell to his knee like this]. The referee Tony Perez wanted me to finish and kill the guy. . . . 'Fuck you. I don't want to kill him,' I told Perez. 'If the guy gets hurt, that's on your conscience,' I said."

The eloquent Argüello did nothing to taint his Gentleman of the Ring reputation as he looked into the stands at the elder Mancini and cried out, "I'm sorry. I'm sorry." Later they embraced, and Argüello told Mancini, the son, "I love your father. That's the most beautiful thing you have. . . . I promise, if I can do something for you, let me know, please, okay?"

Mancini responded, "I feel good. I feel great. I am disappointed because I wanted to finish one way or another on my feet. I am not disappointed in my performance. I feel very good about what I did. I want to apologize to the people of Youngstown."

Later Mancini added: "I realized that I belonged after that fight. That's what it told me about myself. I belonged to fight the best in the world. I learned patience and composure."

Argüello closed the interview by saying, "I think it was my conditioning and experience that helped me. . . . In fact I know it."

Boxer-turned-broadcaster Sean O'Grady called the fight and never forgot the aggression and passion of the fourteen-round affair. He said, "When Argüello hit Mancini—and Mancini showed so much heart and determination—Mancini was ahead. And then, Alexis nailed him. Mancini showed such heart and determination to get back up. Then, how Alexis told him after the fight about how important his father was. You saw how Alexis saw beyond boxing—he saw the human side. You learn about people by boxing. You learn that the eyes are the windows to the soul. You look into your opponent's soul. Both [of] those fighters wore their hearts on their sleeves. It was the best fight I ever called. It had all of the elements of what boxing is."

"When Argüello fought Mancini, the late manager Dave Wolf felt that Argüello was so gracious after he knocked out his fighter," said Muhammad Ali's biographer Thomas Hauser. "The way that he said, 'I love your father' was not staged. It was real."

Mancini listened to Argüello's kind words of advice and would go on to win the WBA lightweight crown in a one-round shootout with Arturo Frias seven months later. He finally gave his father the one thing that had eluded both of them, a championship belt for the Mancini household.

"It was a great time for all of us," said a proud Mancini. "Everyone was so proud. My dad told me after the Argüello fight not to worry about it, and I would win a world title one day. I was hurt that I couldn't win it for him. I never thought I would get another chance. I was so despondent. My trainer said, 'Do your job, get back in the gyms, and you'll be back there again.' I felt confident. After I fought Alexis, I knew I had what it took within me."

When negotiating for that fight, Argüello's agent Bill Miller questioned the decision to make the bout when he said, "We knew Mancini was a big draw. CBS wanted him badly. I told Mort Sharnik from CBS, 'He's your meal ticket. Do you want to ruin him?' We didn't ruin him, but we burst the bubble."

Nine days after he stopped Mancini, Argüello traveled to Caracas, Venezuela, to provide the Spanish commentary for the bout between Sammy Serrano and Leonel Hernández, for the WBA super featherweight crown. As Argüello walked through the lobby that evening, he ran into a familiar face, close friend and respected Nicaraguan sports journalist Edgar Tijerino with Sandinista representative Sammy Santos. Ever since the Sandinistas had confiscated Argüello's property and finances, Tijerino and Argüello had been estranged and at odds. Tijerino's article, titled "From Idol to Puppet," only served to widen the chasm between the old friends. For many, it was an unlikely and unsavory break, and some blamed the revolution for the fractured friendship. Many Nicaraguans once hoped that the beloved journalist and athlete would enjoy a friendship into their golden years, but politics reared its ugly head and prevented it.

It was Tijerino who had originated the nickname Flaco Explosivo, or "Explosive Thin Man," during Argüello's championship bout with Rubén Olivares and who had monitored the fighter's growth from his pro debut to the government's exile order. The attachment between the two men was still fresh. War had nearly dissolved that friendship, but in the Hilton's lobby that evening they embraced like old friends. Argüello apparently held no ill will toward Tijerino, even though he was representing the Sandinista Party.

Through his daily radio show, Tijerino protested the decision to commandeer Argüello's funds and property; however, he also claimed that one of the other nine members of the National Directorate—not Daniel Ortega—had ordered the confiscation in 1979. Indeed, Ortega had asked Tijerino to act as a mediator between Argüello and the party.

"When you start a revolution, you appreciate the revolution more than anything, even your family, because you are there for a reason," said Tijerino, who also covered sports for the newspaper *Barricada Internacional*. "Only someone who was part of the revolution can understand that feeling. What happened, and what they did to Alexis, was a failure of the revolution. Alexis was a victim.

"I thought they were going to give all the belongings back. I was sent because of my friendship with Alexis. It wasn't justice, but it was all they could do. I thought that he would accept it but wouldn't return to Nicaragua. He was advised by Dr. Roman that he would run into problems if he came back."

"They send these persons to ask me to come back to my country," Argüello told a reporter. "Then they tell me the reason they invite me—because they have the birthday of the revolution. They're going to make, like, a party. Teófilo Stevenson is coming from Cuba, they say. Muhammad Ali, Fidel Castro, communist people. They want to start making a new reputation for themselves. I told them, no." In the end, there was no reconciliation. Argüello never agreed to the terms. Further, only decades later would he consider forgiving the people who had taken so much from him.

"When the Sandinistas came to power, hundreds of thousands of people were thrown in jail. Some people were lucky enough to leave, and they left with their pride as well," said former judge and member of the Nicaraguan Boxing Commission Sergio Quintero. "[Anastasio] Somoza was a very open person, both physically and mentally. He also appreciated sports; on the contrary, Daniel Ortega was not a very nice person and a very closed person. When he was in control, they prohibited boxing. But Ortega realized later on that he had made a mistake of exiling Alexis and closing these sports heroes off when, in reality, they could help him with his own popularity."

Financially, whatever Argüello lost in his battle with the Sandinistas he gained back twofold from the love he received from the growing Hispanic population in Miami. No longer was he simply a boxing idol. He had become a political figure and a brother who stood against the communist regime.

"Locally all Cubans shared a common suffering," said Cuban author Enrique Encinosa. "I understood his stance totally. In Cuba they took everything. So what happened to us, happened to thousands of Nicas. He was seen as a humongous icon."

After the battle against Ray "Boom Boom" Mancini, Argüello signed to fight the hard-hitting Roberto Elizondo in Las Vegas. Elizondo, managed by the legendary Jackie McCoy, had quietly blossomed from a prospect to a talented boxer. Argüello had had the opportunity to face Elizondo earlier, but he had opted for the bout with Ray Mancini. For twenty-five-year-old Elizondo, the dream to face Argüello came to him one day in 1974.

"[When Alexis fought Rubén Olivares] I was jumping up and down in my living room," Elizondo recalled. "Rubén Olivares was my idol. I wanted to beat Alexis so bad because he beat my idol. I was 15 years old and I pointed to Alexis and said, 'I will get into the ring with you and knock you out.' I never thought I would actually get the chance."

So when Elizondo initially heard about the first date for the showdown with Argüello, he was determined not to miss what he saw as the chance of a lifetime.

After suffering through an intense but effective training camp where he knocked out sparring partners, his manager broke the news that the fight was postponed until after Argüello fought Mancini. Although Elizondo was dejected about having to start over again, he had five weeks to build that same momentum during training. After intially training at the Westminster Gym in Los Angeles, Elizondo moved to work with the trainer Jimmy Montoya at the Olympic Auditorium Gym. There Elizondo could face better sparring partners who were similar in size, style, and reach to Argüello.

Still, Jackie McCoy faced the same question that fans asked Mancini's manager, Dave Wolf: Why put a young kid in the ring against a proven legend? Boxing people questioned McCoy's decision to allow such a great young talent as Elizondo to confront the great champion.

Don Chargin recalled, "We had the chance to set up Elizondo to fight Alexis. Jackie McCoy managed Elizondo and he told me, 'I don't want that fight. But I know that for a world title bout you have to let the fighter in on it because—as a fighter myself—he might not get another chance.' When we sat down with Elizondo in the office, he looked at us and said, 'This has been a dream of mine since I was six years old, please don't turn it down.' We had to do it."

Elizondo supported Chargin's claim, saying, "Maybe I could have become a world champion if I fought one of those guys like Sean O'Grady or Hilmer Kenty. But to tell you the truth, the thing that I am known for is fighting Alexis. That is the only thing people want to talk about. They all say, 'Did you really get in the ring with Alexis Argüello?' If I would have fought somebody else, there wouldn't be a story. People think that Jackie McCoy pushed me into this fight, but he didn't."

While Elizondo tried to recover from the fluctuating training schedules and develop a routine, Argüello chose to train in the familiar Tucson, Arizona camps where he had been embraced by the boxing people and the local fans.

"[Alexis] was a newcomer, but he was accepted right away," said IBF boxing judge and Tucson resident Joe Garcia, who developed a friendship with the fighter. "He was intense in his training, but [away from the ring] he was a guy who would look you right in the eye, very gentlemanly, and assertive. Unlike a lot of guys who had their minds somewhere else, Alexis listened intently to what you were saying."

Unfortunately, when Argüello returned to train, he was not well received by everyone. Local police officers egregiously interrupted Argüello's stay in Tucson,

Arizona. Prior to the fight, Argüello, new trainer Eddie Futch, and a *New York Times* reporter were in the Estevan gym training for the bout when two local police officers barged in and forced Argüello outside before he could change. The officers erroneously claimed that Argüello's presence had threatened the status of amateur boxers.

"When Alexis was expelled by those two cops it was because they were concerned about the status of the amateur fighters, which I can't understand because it was a public facility," said Gerald Maltz, the Phoenix boxing commissioner and Argüello's longtime friend. "No one has ever shown me anything that explains why they did that. But Alexis was very classy about it. I took him to another gym called the South Tucson Boxing Gym and Alexis kept training like nothing happened. Later, he wrote an apology letter to the mayor—which was my idea—where he apologized if he offended anyone in Tucson. Then, the mayor wrote another apology to Alexis for the stupidity of the police force. Both letters were published in the local newspaper. Not only was the action stupid, but it was done while a *New York Times* reporter was there.

"There was absolutely no basis for the expulsion. I was called at my office and I got there after everything happened. I asked the police chief, 'What could have possessed them?' He supported his officers. At the end of the day, his apology to the mayor came out and Alexis's class and dignity prevailed. He was very cool about it."

Few fighters would have exhibited such grace. Argüello shrugged off the disrespect and agreed with Futch's sentiment that he had been "kicked out of better places." While the local police chief stood by his officers, Argüello returned to his intense preparation. He had faced discrimination a decade earlier when Los Angeles police officers detained and harassed him over a bogus immigration issue.

By the time the champ made his grand entrance alongside manager Eduardo Roman and corner Don Kahn, Argüello had already been delayed momentarily by a minor glove issue. Elizondo, a big body puncher from Corpus Christi, Texas, was already in the ring throwing punches. Elizondo only had one loss in twenty-three fights, with eighteen wins by knockout. His stats were impressive, but did they matter against a guy like Argüello? While Elizondo was relatively unknown, his punching power galvanized the boxing community. Coming in at 135 even, Argüello looked sharp and focused. Elizondo was on the cusp of being either a full-fledged star or a one-hit wonder. For a young fighter, going up against Argüello was a litmus test for greatness. The prefight hype excited the cocksure younger fighter.

"Elizondo was telling me, 'I will kick your ass, Alexis.' I was telling him, 'Don't scream at me. Let's see what will happen tonight,'" said Argüello. "His trainer was upset and said to Elizondo, 'Show respect,' and 'Don't lose respect.'"

With Sugar Ray Leonard and Argüello's wife Loretto at ringside, Argüello had the attention of the boxing world. Loretto had become the first of his three wives to show Argüello the support and love he needed; she understood the sacrifices and demands of the fight game.

"Loretto was a nice lady whose father was a close friend of Somoza," said Roman. "They met in Nicaragua, and she always tried to help him and behave well with him. Some of his other wives didn't behave well with him."

Azteca Promotions used West Coast matchmaker Don Chargin for the world title fight. A crowd of 1,489 paid $34,900 for the bout, which was broadcast on CBS Sports with Tim Ryan, Sugar Ray Leonard, and Gil Clancy as commentators. With sixteen straight title wins, Argüello was heading for a record of his own.

Referee Joey Curtis stood between the two combatants. Argüello wore a detached stare as if his mind was elsewhere, possibly distracted by the prefight hoopla regarding the gloves. Regardless, he charged out at the opening bell. Forgoing any probing period, Argüello used the uppercut early and often, and he punctuated the first round with a straight right and left to the body. Meanwhile, a tense Elizondo acted as if he was fighting an international star.

"When I walked into the ring, everything came back to me. I couldn't believe I was in with such a great fighter," Elizondo recalled. "I wasn't scared, but when the fight started and he hit me with a jab, it was exactly like what Boom Boom Mancini said—'a hammer.' It knocked me off balance. In my mind I asked myself, 'Is this really what you wanted?'"

A sharp Argüello pinpointed a cut on Elizondo's nose throughout the early rounds. Elizondo came alive in Round 3 and landed a right hand that stirred the champ. Having recalled the sweat and suffering of the two training camps, Elizondo passionately dug hooks into the man who had dethroned his idol. Gaining confidence as the seconds ticked off, Elizondo began to walk Argüello down and cleanly landed counter left hooks and straight rights. As he smothered Argüello, the champ refused to pull his right hand from his armor, as if he was waiting for the perfect moment.

For one moment, Elizondo was in charge.

"In the third round I hit him hard with lefts and rights. All the judges gave me the round," Elizondo said. "When I got back to the corner, Jackie starts yelling and cussing at me, 'I don't care who this motherfucker is. You can beat this motherfucker. Forget about who he is! Get out there.'"

Heeding his manager's advice, Elizondo stayed aggressive, but his bravado landed him on the canvas in the fourth round, compliments of the latter of two straight rights. Elizondo got to his feet quickly, took an eight count, and absorbed more punishment before the bell sounded.

Elizondo recalled, "Argüello hits me with a left hook and knocks me down and I go back to the corner and tell Jackie, 'All I did was make this guy mad, Jackie.'"

From that round on, Elizondo was never the same fighter. Through the sixth round, Argüello continued to lull the rookie with lazy jabs or a short uppercut in order to set up the vaunted right hand. Argüello landed a huge right to start the sixth, but he saved his magnum opus for the seventh. In the final round, Argüello started with a vicious flurry, and Elizondo no longer wanted to engage. Argüello let loose a hook to the body, then an extended long right that caught Elizondo on his neck. The challenger went down.

Once Elizondo got back on his feet, Argüello finished him off with a right uppercut to the solar plexus and a short left. An uppercut with twelve seconds remaining was the punch that separated Elizondo from his senses; the hook was simply an added benefit.

In the corner, Elizondo rose, thought about his options, sat down on the inside rope, and then decided he'd had enough. Referee Joey Curtis called the bout; the official time was 3:07 of the seventh round. Without a smile or a raised hand, a detached Argüello moved toward his fallen opponent, hugged him, and, serious as ever, walked back to his camp. He was winning by five points on all three scorecards when the fight ended. The champ also had cracked Elizondo's wisdom tooth and broken his jaw, which Elizondo only discovered two days later.

"After I knocked [Elizondo] out," said Argüello, "he vomited his mouthpiece out. After the fight, what could he say? He had nothing to say."

Argüello added, "[WBC president] José Sulaimán told me in my room [before the fight] that Elizondo would knock me out. After the fight I leaned over the ropes and yelled to Sulaimán, 'Hey, you have anyone else for me?'"

Chargin recalled a much closer bout: "Elizondo had made some big hits in California, so the fight was considered a contest. Elizondo was in there during those early rounds. Alexis told me after the fight, . . . 'If the fight didn't hurt Elizondo, then he will go a long way because he punches hard and moves well.'"

The win was another notch for Argüello, the most destructive force in all of boxing. "I knew this was a tough guy, when you have a champ . . . I need to concentrate because the opponents are tough and they all want to be champ," Argüello told a ringside reporter. "The punch that hurt was the punch to the body."

Then Argüello started talking about his favorite fighter. "Joe Louis said kill the body because the head will fall. Joe Louis and Sugar, I always look at the way they fight. I like to give 100 percent to the people, I love everybody! I love my fans! I love my job!"

When assessing his career years later, Argüello added, "When I fought with Rubén Castillo, he was a master fighter. I beat Rubén Castillo and Elizondo, then I was a master fighter; I could play with anyone I wanted."

Argüello's trainer Eddie Futch reiterated that it was nearly impossible for anyone to fight Argüello because "no matter what style his opponent employs, Alexis can come up with an effective strategy to counter and win."

Despite a bright future ahead of him, it was difficult to console Elizondo. Decades later, he lamented, "I got a broken wisdom tooth from that left hook. It was cracked all the way through the tooth. My jaw was hurting really bad too. I felt each punch and a pain went through my neck and down my back. Since I was in Las Vegas, I had to wait two or three days before I could see a dentist back in L.A. He said, 'The tooth is the least of your problems. You have a broken jaw, too.' It was wired shut for six weeks."

News reports already touted an imminent showdown with either the Mexican featherweight king Salvador Sánchez, who would have to move up to the 135–pound class, or the whirlwind dynamo Aaron Pryor, who was appropriately labeled "the man no one wanted to fight." Pryor thrived on a brilliant spontaneity in the ring and was the antithesis of the introspective Argüello. While Argüello spoke in a steady stream of aphorisms and regaled sportswriters as boxing's version of Aristotle, Pryor was raw and, at times, incomprehensible. Yet, it was these contradictions between the two men that made the possible match so intriguing.

Nearly three months after the quick seven-round stoppage of Elizondo, Argüello signed to defend his title against James "Bubba" Busceme. A Texas native, Busceme had won twenty-seven of his thirty contests but still failed to gain national recognition. West Coast promoter Don Chargin outbid other promoters and negotiated the bout with CBS. Although Chargin had received top billing to promote this show, the *Washington Post* reported that Argüello had paid $25,000 to Bob Arum for the rights to his next three title defenses. Arum and Don King had successfully cornered the market's greatest fighters.

Middleweight Marvin Hagler and Argüello were Arum's gems, while King had everyone else. Although few fighters disputed King's corrupt nature, nobody doubted his ability to negotiate title fights.

After feasting on durable opponents in the Fort Worth and Beaumont areas, twenty-nine-year-old Busceme and his manager Hugh Benbow secured a shot with Argüello. At the time, the confident Busceme, whose three knockout losses came against inferior opposition, felt undervalued. "The situation with my training was so ridiculous," Busceme lamented. "The cards were stacked against me. Before that fight, I didn't know a thing about Alexis Argüello. Boxing was just something I did periodically with my life. It was so crummy how boxing held me back for so long."

With the lightweight showdown against Busceme on the horizon, rumors circulated that Argüello, a 10–1 favorite, was nearing a possible matchup with welterweight champ Sugar Ray Leonard. Busceme's manager Hugh Benbow had kindled his own controversy by threatening to pull his fighter out of the bout if CBS did not enforce a local blackout of the title fight. Dueling television shows featured boxing's best pound-for-pound fighters. While Argüello headlined CBS's *Sports Saturday* card at 4:30 p.m., WBA light heavyweight champ Michael Spinks was the star attraction on ABC's *Wide World of Sports*.

On February 13, 1982, at the Beaumont Civic Center, Argüello came into the bout at the lightweight limit; Busceme entered at 134½ pounds. Top Rank copromoted the bout with Sports Associates Incorporated. As a CBS favorite, Argüello would earn $300,000, while the little-known Busceme would take home $100,000. Commentators Tim Ryan and Gil Clancy broadcast the bout, which was also telecast to Venezuela, Mexico, Peru, Italy, and Korea. Radio coverage to Nicaragua was refused.

"It sold out in two days," said Sports Associates president Lester Bedford, who at age twenty-six was the youngest man to promote a world title bout in the United States. "It did well over $300,000 [$358,000] at the live gate. It was still the biggest event there ever. It was Beaumont's Super Bowl. It was live on CBS.

"Even though Alexis was fighting the local guy, he treated people with such respect and grace that they couldn't help but love him. He ran six miles almost every day of his week in Beaumont. Almost at a sprint. Then he would go to his room and lay down. Other than for press conferences he stayed in bed. Rest was very important to him."

Fighting in front of 6,618 of his hometown fans, Busceme didn't disappoint early on. The Texas native decided to wage a battle of futility as he danced to his right while throwing his staple jab and straight left. Despite his lack of credentials,

Busceme didn't back down to the lightweight, and at times he perilously ventured in and out of Argüello's danger zone to score his straight left hand. By the end of the first round, the crowd validated their star with a rousing applause as he headed back to the corner.

Over the next two rounds, Argüello closed the gap and brilliantly cut off the ring, but he still hadn't exerted his power. For the first four rounds, Busceme refused to stray from his game plan: move, punch, and escape. No longer was he a prudent challenger in the midst of a legend; rather, he was a fearless boxer taking necessary risks. The measure of bravado would not last.

As in so many past performances, Argüello transformed from a cautious technician to an unrestrained beast in a matter of seconds. After absorbing Busceme's three-punch combination, which forced him to backpedal, the champ ricocheted a right hand off the southpaw's head. Busceme slowed, then walked into another right hand. However, the first punch represented the catalyst for a seismic shift in the bout.

"I held my own with Alexis," said Busceme (27-3). "In fact, one judge gave me the first five rounds. I just ran out of steam."

In the following three minutes, Argüello sought closure. He closed space, increased the acceleration of his dormant right hand, and stalked Busceme. First, he landed a left hook that took the life out of Busceme. Then Argüello landed a right hand that spun the challenger and sent him reeling to his corner as if he were a drunk leaving a local tavern. Before allowing any real damage, referee Octavio Meyran stepped in after the corrosive punch and hugged Busceme at 2:35 of the sixth round.

"It was the left hook that hurt me in that fight," Busceme recalled. "And then he drove me back with that right hand three steps in the other direction. It drove me back three steps to my corner, and then I turned around to fight again and the referee stopped it. I can at least always say, 'He didn't knock me down.' He hit me hard though."

All three judges had Argüello ahead by one point at the time of the stoppage. A day later, Busceme was celebrating his thirtieth birthday at a local restaurant and ran into the lightweight champ.

"Alexis was the greatest guy," said Busceme. "I wouldn't have wanted to fight a better person or bigger fighter. I remember the morning after. My wife and I were coming in the restaurant, and we finally sat down. Fifteen minutes later Alexis walks in with his wife and comes over with this cake. It was a nice gesture. It was the nicest thing that happened to me for months."

Busceme continued: "My experience fighting for the championship of the world was excellent, but I couldn't enjoy it. I was so mentally incapacitated. Once they finally got the fight, that was the end of it. They didn't worry about getting me prepared and that was the end of it."

In the post-fight press conference, Argüello's normally tight-lipped agent Bill Miller hinted at a possible showdown with Salvador Sánchez. "All our options with a specific promoter are now exhausted," he said, "and we can now offer our services to the highest bidder. Salvador Sánchez would be a big money fight for Alexis. Sánchez wants to move up a weight division or two, and certainly is a big attraction. Don King is currently promoting Sánchez, so we'd have to deal with him. He also promotes the defenses of junior welterweight champs Aaron Pryor and Saoul Mamby if we want to go for a fourth title. But there may be other alternatives such as Andy Ganigan, or perhaps a unification of the division with Art Frias. We'll just have to wait and see."

After Leonard disposed of Bruce Finch in a welterweight clash two days after the Busceme bout, his manager Mike Trainer all but extinguished talks of a Leonard-Argüello bout and turned his attention to Milton McCrory, the undefeated mainstay of Kronk Gym. When questioned about the possible showdown with the lightweight champ, Leonard responded, "The Argüello fight is still in negotiations. Something may materialize in the fall." Those familiar with the world champ knew he was merely being coy, and there was no real substance behind the statement.

Before an eventual showdown with Pryor, Argüello prepared to travel to Las Vegas and defend his title against No. 1 challenger Andy Ganigan. For this fight, Argüello would take home $400,000 to Ganigan's $130,000 purse. Originally, the showdown had been set for April 3, but a viral infection forced Argüello to postpone. Now both men settled on a May 22 date at the Aladdin Hotel. The boxing world, however, was more concerned with the next Argüello opponent. WBA junior welterweight champ Aaron Pryor hinted at the eventual showdown with Argüello when he said, "Every time I get close, there's a black cloud."

Andy Ganigan, a Hawaiian southpaw appropriately nicknamed Hawaiian Punch, was a knockout artist, but he had lost three of his previous twelve bouts. Going into the fight, Argüello looked to extend his string of eighteen consecutive title fight victories and was well aware of Ganigan's recent two-round destruction of former champ Sean O'Grady. Record-wise, Ganigan (34-3) had registered thirty knockouts and had the ability to shock any opponent on any night.

Referee Carlos Padilla set the guidelines in the middle of the ring as the taut, supremely focused Argüello honed in on Ganigan. While Argüello rocked on his 134¾-pound frame, the heavier Ganigan had struggled mightily to make weight.

Not wasting any time, Ganigan went directly to Argüello's body from the opening bell. With the first round coming to an end, Ganigan expedited the feeling-out process by sending an off-balance Argüello to the canvas with a damaging straight left. Argüello's prefight concerns regarding Ganigan's quirky, smashmouth style were warranted. What Argüello had originally denounced as a "weird" style left him staring up from the canvas.

After physically overpowering Argüello in the first two minutes of the round, the Hawaiian contender forced Argüello to the ropes and dazed him with two lefts hooks, with the last one jolting Argüello's back before he hit the canvas. Argüello rose before referee Carlos Padilla began his count. Padilla administered the standing-eight count to a lucid Argüello. Still focused, Argüello refused to avert his eyes from Ganigan, who waited eagerly across the ring. Despite no lingering effects, Argüello had to quicken the pace for the last twenty seconds. The round ended with Argüello nodding at his opponent as he headed back to his corner. In the corner, the reserved trainer Eddie Futch implored his fighter not sit back and work as a counterpuncher when he said, "You got to take the lead!" Assistant trainer Don Kahn echoed the sentiment when he advised him to "take this guy out now, he's no piece of cake."

Argüello didn't heed his trainers' advice; instead, he was content to stay uncharacteristically passive during the first minute of the second round. Despite landing a sharp jab and right hand in the middle of the ring, Argüello was allowing Ganigan to have the same success that southpaw José Luis Ramirez had against him two years earlier. Then, halfway through the third round, Argüello woke to land his first significant punch, a right hand. He followed it with another straight right seconds later to send Ganigan to the canvas. Futch had stressed the set-up jab and the staple right hand, and the combination worked to perfection.

Like Argüello, Ganigan rose to his feet quickly and proceeded to throw wild, relentless offerings that only worked to Argüello's advantage. Argüello described the process of knocking down Ganigan as "waking a sleeping bear," and it played directly to Argüello's strengths. No longer backing up, Argüello stung the Hawaiian with a right to the neck that the cringing Ganigan acknowledged upon impact. Yet, with twenty seconds remaining in a round with a chaotic ebb and flow, Ganigan shook Argüello again with a left hook. Argüello's legs buckled, and Ganigan continued his unabated approach. Another left and right combination stymied Argüello, who covered up. The round ended with Ganigan being catapulted to the corner with a straight right. The crowd gave both men a well-deserved standing ovation as their cornermen weighed in.

The men fought more cautiously during the fourth round. Finally using his height to his advantage, Argüello began to sit on his punches as he deftly picked apart his shorter opponent with his staple left jab and pinpoint right. No longer was Argüello the timid fighter from the first two rounds. Now he incorporated a deadly uppercut to complement his straight right.

In the fifth round, a left jab stopped Ganigan in his tracks; in fact, the once brazen southpaw now confronted Argüello with trepidation. With thirty seconds remaining in the round, Argüello spun Ganigan's head 180 degrees with a straight right. After another right hand, Ganigan covered up; after a left jab, Ganigan retreated. Then, with the round winding down, Argüello attacked, leaving Ganigan in a heap on the canvas. With his head outside the ring apron and the round officially over, a bloody Ganigan spit his mouthpiece out as referee Padilla counted him out. As Padilla walked away to raise Argüello's hand, Ganigan lay motionless, still stuck under the ropes. He stayed on the canvas for several minutes. The knockout was recorded at 3:09 of the fifth round, and at the time of the stoppage the champ was leading on two of the three scorecards (39–37, 37–36), and the fight was even on the last one (37–all). The win marked Argüello's sixty-first knockout in seventy-six fights; Ganigan fell to 34-4.

"Thank God I was in good condition so that I woke up," said Argüello. "I was able to get up with my mind in a good place. Any fighter can be hit in the right spot at the right time. Sometimes it is lucky if you don't go to the floor in a 15-round bout."

Ganigan responded: "I thought maybe he was playing possum. So I played it cool and tried to box. If I fought him again I would be more aggressive. But that's why he's a great champion."

Although Argüello finished the heavy-handed Ganigan in classic style, he began to show a vulnerability, too. Even his children looked for answers.

"Hey, Dad, what were you doing on the floor?" his son A. J. inquired.

"I was down there looking for my pride," responded the elder Argüello.

Even the greatest fighters suffer lapses, but that early knockdown almost proved fatal for the Nicaraguan. That May, Salvador Sanchez eyed a showdown with Argüello and even called him out through the press.

"The reason I fight is to beat three champions: Danny López, Wilfredo Gómez, and Alexis Argüello," said Sánchez the WBC featherweight champ. "Two have been done." The fight between the great Mexican and Nicaraguan was not to be, however; twenty-three-year-old Sánchez died three months later in a car crash. The entire boxing community mourned the loss of a great champion.

In a matter of five years, Argüello had missed out on the two most significant paydays of his entire career—Sánchez and Durán. Roberto Durán had Sugar Ray Leonard. Leonard had Thomas "Hit Man" Hearns, and Hearns had Marvin Hagler to test their greatness. Each of those fighters had reached the million-dollar purse bracket. Without Sánchez or Durán to measure himself against, Argüello would have to wait for that career-defining payday. Meanwhile, in the newspapers, critics lamented that it may have been too late for Argüello to earn the worldwide recognition he deserved. He certainly would not earn it in his next bout. As Argüello closed out his dominance on the lightweight division, he had until July 31 to get ready for a young prospect named Kevin Rooney.

During that brief lull between bouts, promoters Dan Duva, Top Rank's Bob Arum, and Don King were competing for the rights for the Argüello-Pryor bout. Talks for a Leonard-Argüello bout dissipated after Leonard was diagnosed with a detached retina. Both Pryor and Argüello regretted Leonard's absence, which quickly negated a possible $8 million–$10 million payday. For a Pryor-Argüello bout, Duva proposed the Garden and offered $1 million–$2 million per fighter during the early negotiation period.

That July 5, a headline in the *New York Times* read, "Pryor Wins, Gets Argüello Next." Pryor had dismantled challenger Akio Kameda in what amounted to a tune-up for the WBA junior welterweight champ. Although Kameda went down five times during the six-round bout, Pryor also suffered a rare knockdown to a second-rate fighter in the first round. Highlighting a strange sequence, Pryor rolled over and jumped in Kameda's face, ready to continue fighting. At the time, Argüello was watching the bout from ringside.

"I was off balance," Pryor told a reporter. "If he hit me, he didn't sting me. When I fell, I looked at Argüello and got up right away."

As Pryor was busy talking to a reporter, Argüello slipped into the ring after the bout, and to many at ringside it appeared that his presence stymied the brazen fighter. *Los Angeles Times* journalist Richard Hoffer reported that as Pryor was detailing how great he was, Argüello smoothly entered the ring and agreed, "You certainly are."

Arum, who had won the bidding war, claimed to have finalized the contracts but not the venue. Each fighter was set to make between $1 million and $2 million.

Although Argüello was still the 135-pound champion, he needed a tune-up as well, especially before moving up a weight class and facing Pryor for his 140-pound title. Thus, Argüello turned his focus toward his fight with Kevin Rooney and prepared for his first encounter in the 140-pound division. Sportswriters posed the same question: Could Alexis bring his power up a weight class? Flirting with history, Argüello needed to get past Rooney and harden his resolve for the undefeated and mercurial Pryor.

A protégé of legendary trainer Cus D'Amato, Rooney would later gain acclaim as Mike Tyson's trainer during the fighter's initial destruction of the heavyweight division, but as a boxer, he lacked the talent to compete with the top-tier fighters in the welterweight division. Rooney (19-1 with seven knockouts) hailed from Staten Island, New York, and as a natural 147-pounder, he had to work to make the 140-pound limit.

On July 31, 1982, CBS broadcast the fight on the *Sports Saturday* showcase. Argüello had become a CBS staple and ventured to Bally's Park Place in Atlantic City for the bout. He needed a strong performance to impress Pryor, who sat ringside.

Commentators Tim Ryan, Gil Clancy, and Sugar Ray Leonard commented on Argüello's quick start. In the first round, Rooney foolishly brawled with Argüello. Rooney crowded him, threw body punches, and stayed in front of Argüello. However, in the second round, Argüello began to exert his dominance. With thirty seconds remaining in the round, Rooney carelessly walked into a straight right and then clumsily took two steps backward. Known as one of the best finishers in boxing, Argüello saw an opening and paralyzed Rooney with body shots. The brave challenger grimaced, but he moved forward.

Argüello feinted two jabs and then unleashed. The punch, a brilliant straight right, was thrown with such precision that it wiped away the boxer's memory. The explosive force emanated like a shotgun blast. Argüello had thrown harder punches, but he caught Rooney with the end of his fist, which delivered the brunt of the force. Rooney attempted to balance himself, but he appeared too disoriented to grasp the magnitude of the punch. Its power was reflected in Rooney's glazed look. Using the rope as his crutch, Rooney desperately attempted to rise, but he quickly fell again. After counting him out seven seconds after the bell to end the second round referee Larry Hazzard cautiously cradled Rooney's head as he tried to drape it along the bottom rope. In New Jersey, the bell can only save a fighter after the first round. Argüello walked over only to find a swarm of people hovering over the fighter, who lay there with his mouth open. A physician told Argüello that Rooney was OK. Still feeling the impact of the right hand, Rooney had to ask his wife in what round he had lost when they sat in the dressing room.

"It was a sensational right hand," said Harold Lederman, a judge in that bout. "Rooney threw a jab and Argüello shot that right hand directly over it. It was a helluva shot. He was moving up in weight when he did it. It was one heck of a good punch, and it was clear that Alexis took his punching power with him. There was a lot of concern for Kevin. He got hit with that right, and he fell hard. After that he was just out. But he came to. Kevin was a tough, gritty guy. He was OK. In that fight Alexis showed he could punch at that weight; the only question was his speed. He had an uncanny ability to throw his body into his punch."

The knockout was recorded at 3:07 of the second round. With the help of his handlers and with Argüello looking on, Rooney rose and soothed any lingering concerns. It was the most powerful one-punch knockout that Argüello registered in that division, and many considered it one of the best knockout punches of all time. But not everyone in the audience was impressed.

"Aaron don't stand still," replied Aaron Pryor, who was taking notes for the junior welterweight clash coming that fall. "That will be a key factor in the fight. I don't feel he can hit a moving target like he can a standing still target, which is what most of his opponents have been. They kind of stand in front of you and challenge you."

The punch had assuaged the doubts of most critics who covered the nationally televised bout. The self-deprecating Argüello, however, wasn't completely sold on his ability in the new weight class even after the quick knockout.

"I am not 100 percent sure I can handle 140," he said. "Next time I won't be fighting Kevin Rooney. I'll be fighting Aaron Pryor, who's the world's best champion."

Everyone wanted to see the 140-pound clash between Argüello and Pryor, but trying to find a venue proved a difficult task. Argüello's agent, Bill Miller, quickly became frustrated with what he considered a lack of respect for his fighter's worth, so he turned to his friends in Miami.

"That fight was an accident. In those days we used to go to promoter Chris Dundee's office on Saturday for coffee and donuts, and then head to the Fifth Street Gym. When we were there, Argüello's agent, Bill Miller, called and said that neither Atlantic City nor Las Vegas were willing to give Alexis what he deserved for the fight. Dundee responded, 'You tell them that if they don't pay up then I will just have to have it here.' Then, he hung up," Cuban boxing promoter and banker Ramiro Ortiz recalled.

"Fifteen minutes later Dundee received a call, and Bill Miller said, 'They told me to take the fight to Miami.' We talked for a while about the possibility and then [promoter] and president of Boxing of the Americas Inc. Walter Alvarez says, 'I can make it work.' He would get city leaders to pool their money together to get the ball rolling with the fighters and then get in touch with Bob Arum."

Often, when dealing with fights that turn into events, it is difficult to recall the specific details of the negotiations. Alvarez recalled a different scenario, saying he dealt with Argüello directly. Argüello had signed with Top Rank and Bob Arum and had established a strong friendship with Alvarez leading up to the bout.

Alvarez said, "Alexis called me and said, 'I want to fight in Miami.' So I called Top Rank, who I was doing work for, and I spoke to Bob Arum. I asked him, 'Why not do the fight in Miami? Alexis has a great following. There are a lot of Nicaraguans and a strong Hispanic constituency. Alexis owns a travel agency there, too.' Bob loved the idea but was worried that we were going to miss out on the casino revenue. I told him, 'I think we can overcome that.' So I began to assemble a syndicate of prominent people to chip in for the site fee. We were able to work out a deal; each guy would put up $100,000 and eventually would be paid back."

Alvarez then met Argüello at Top Rank's office in New York and obtained both his and Pryor's approval. Pryor told Alvarez, "I think I can do good on his turf." As soon as Alvarez received the word from Arum, he started organizing an exhaustive press tour to promote the bout. Deep down, Alvarez and everyone involved knew they were going to be part of something special.

"The promotion lived up to everything I expected. Aaron Pryor was a character and Alexis was also a character. Of course, they had totally different images: Aaron, the villain, and Alexis, the gentleman. But in reality both were villains," Alvarez joked. "Well, you know that boxers by nature are difficult to work with. That comes with the territory. But both of them got into the hype. They didn't mind the travel and loved the attention. It made them superstars. They were all over the TV, all over the newspapers. Parties every day. This became an event more than a fight. For all of Miami, it was all about the fight. They both loved it."

Prior to the press tour, Argüello was on the cusp of becoming the megastar that people expected. He had the skills, the good looks, and the gentlemanly demeanor, but he was still missing that one element that would help him reach that upper echelon.

"Sugar Ray Leonard was a great personality and educated," said Bill Miller. "Alexis was quiet and looked good, but he was not a great talker. The media was in love with great personalities. And Alexis was more of an introvert."

Securing the venue also proved to be a hassle. At the time, the Orange Bowl
was used for concerts and as the home field for the University of Miami Hurricanes
and Miami Dolphins football teams. Because the National Football League (NFL)
was experiencing a strike, the venue appeared available for a November date. A
high school football game was booked on that date, however, so Arum had to
ensure Alvarez and his investors had the $1.25 million to put down before talking
with Orange Bowl Stadium manager Walter Golby about contacting school officials
to release them from the November 12 date. Both Arum and Alvarez agreed that
the Orange Bowl's size made it appealing for such a monumental prizefight. After
negotiations, Top Rank set the date for November 12.

By August 11, the fight was confirmed in the press, and the fighters met in
the Starlight Room of the Waldorf-Astoria. The promoters billed it as "one of
the most memorable fights in our time." The fighters exchanged niceties as
Pryor noted that it was almost hard to "get psyched up" because of Argüello's
class. Argüello replied, "I wish the champ the best of luck." Prefight numbers
had already heralded the fight as a classic. The subscription company HBO paid
$1.8 million, the most ever for a live fight. Arum wanted to set up 100 to 125
sites for closed-captioned audiences. Ten days later, Arum had issued a statement to the press saying he was "99 percent" sure that the fight would be held
in Miami, Florida, at the Orange Bowl. Argüello announced that he would dedicate the bout to Henry Armstrong, who would sit ringside and was the only
other boxer who attempted to win four world titles in as many weight classes.

The roles of the incomparable Roberto Durán and Alexis Argüello had drastically changed during a three-year span. By September 1982, the forgotten
champ Durán had ended his relationship with promoter Don King and walked
over to Arum's offices, searching for compassion and an opponent. Ironically,
Durán later would sign to fight the walk-off bout against Jimmy Batten on the
undercard of the Argüello-Pryor bout.

Few could deny that Argüello was at the apex of the sport. Although he did
not have the same fluidity and speed that he had had in the late 1970s, Argüello
had every other quality that a prizefighter needed. Outside the ring, he became a
hero to all of the Cuban expatriates in Miami for his stance against the Sandinistas.
Inside the ring, he answered every challenge and proved that he could excel in
any weight class he chose. As Alvarez pointed out, "This [Miami] is Argüello country." When he wanted peace of mind, Argüello could take out his thirty-eight-
foot yacht, The Champ, from the Kings Bay Yacht Club in Florida. When he
desired balance, he looked to his wife Loretto Martinez and his boys, A. J., 11,

and newborn Roberto. Along with his two boys, Argüello also had a daughter, Dora, and son, Andrés, from his ex-wives, Silvia Urbina and Patricia Barreto. He also owned a travel agency and a construction company. Now, he wanted to cap his Hall of Fame career, and he looked to Aaron Pryor. The only drawback was that Argüello had the misfortune of meeting Pryor in the twilight of his career.

Many thought the heightened buildup for this fight was similar to that for the 1980 Montreal showdown between Roberto Durán and Sugar Ray Leonard. Personality-wise, Durán had blistered the naive Leonard. Pryor wanted to build anger toward Argüello in a similar fashion, but it wasn't an easy task. Nevertheless, Argüello embraced Durán's role as the seasoned veteran, while Pryor basked in Leonard's role as the quick-fisted, supremely confident champ. Comparisons aside, some boxing insiders refused to place the bouts in the same category.

"Durán vs. Leonard I was something special. It was too hard to ignore," said boxing judge Harold Lederman. "If they [Pryor and Argüello] had met earlier in Argüello's career, it may have been different. But to say the people were more interested in Argüello-Pryor would have been wrong. The Leonard fight was like Ali–[Joe]Frazier. Very rarely did you see a fight come along like that. Ray was something special, and Durán was fearless."

"In all the fights I have covered, I don't remember a more hostile environment for a fight," said sports broadcaster Barry Tompkins. "It was the entire week, you know, with the Sandinistas and the politics.

Despite coming from disparate backgrounds, both fighters felt underappreciated. No one gave Pryor, the WBA champ, his fair due, partly because they didn't trust him. Every time he completed an eye-popping performance in the ring, he made sure to match it with a foolish act outside the ring. Argüello was underappreciated because he had started his career in 1968, and only now was he being truly recognized.

"At the time, Alexis was not a big, big name," said Alvarez. "This fight catapulted him into greatness. Under Eduardo Roman, he trained fine. He was in his best possible shape. And Pryor, too, he was dead serious. They knew what was at stake. Both were very focused.

"But what made this promotion was that we needed both of them. It wasn't like a Manny Pacquiao fight where you just need him. This was about the fight, because neither Pryor nor Argüello were marquee names. Yet, when we matched them together, they were invincible. The fight was the gig."

Argüello trained in Palm Springs, California, at the Americana Canyon Hotel. The bar at the Canyon Hotel announced a new drink honoring Argüello called the "Triple Crown." Minor rumblings from Pryor's former manager Buddy LaRosa regarding a contract dispute proved to be a harmless distraction to the fight proceedings. Pryor agreed to pay a percentage to LaRosa, but the terms were not disclosed.

Meanwhile, Sugar Ray Leonard refused to allow the two fighters to soak up the spotlight. His star had clearly dimmed with retirement. He hemmed and hawed about his comeback prospects, thus making himself part of the extravaganza to take place that November. A week before the Argüello-Pryor bout, Leonard emerged amid speculation that he would campaign to fight the winner.

Bob Arum speculated on Leonard's intentions: "My feeling is that Ray will announce his retirement November 9, leaving open the option that he may come back, probably next June, at 140 pounds and fight the winner of Argüello-Pryor for the junior welterweight title."

He added: "The fight would have much greater value if Alexis Argüello wins. It would be the two ringmasters; a Latin versus an American and the two gentlemen of the fight game."

Argüello, however, had grown weary of Leonard's act. He said, "[Ray coming out of retirement] is a bad example. We're playing with our lives. If I was in his place, I'd quit. I don't care if I have to go into the street to work. He has a lot of money; what does he have to prove? A payday is good, but your vision, to be able to see, what is that worth?"

Pryor didn't share the same sentiment. After feeling slighted by Leonard after the Olympics, Pryor only wanted one thing, revenge. "I want him next," said Pryor. "I know he's going to fight again. It will definitely be me. He owes me something from 1976."

If Ray Leonard was the golden child of the 1976 Olympics, Pryor was the black sheep, or at least that's what he told himself. Pryor felt destined for stardom after amassing a 204-16 amateur record. He captured the 1975 National Golden Gloves at 132 pounds and decisioned Thomas Hearns in the 1976 final. At the 1976 Olympic trials, Pryor lost to Howard Davis Jr. in the lightweight division and fought as an alternate on the Olympic team that year. Pryor sat back and observed as those men he considered lesser fighters won gold medals. When he returned to Cincinnati after the Olympics, one person was waiting for him at the airport with a sign reading, "Aaron, You're Still My Hero." Upon seeing it, Pryor broke down. The pain festered within him. Pryor promised himself that his professional career would be different. All of those people who abandoned him on the way up would feel the brunt of his anger when he found glory on the next level. To Pryor, someone else was always to blame for his woes, and occasionally he was right.

That year on the Olympic team Leonard and Howard Davis Jr. were the standouts, while Pryor lived in their shadows. "Here I was," said Pryor. "I had beat Tommy Hearns in 1976 and Hilmer Kenty. I had 250 fights and lost 16. And what was I doing? I was a sparring partner for Howard Davis, that's what. He gave me $250 a week and treated me like dirt, gave me no time. He wouldn't even give me an undercard fight."

According to Pryor, neither Davis nor Leonard lobbied to get him a spot on their undercards. While Pryor toiled away as a nonentity, Leonard was being marketed and quickly becoming the marquee fighter people expected. Both Davis and Leonard would earn impressive debut paydays while Pryor settled for a $400 purse against Larry Smith. Pryor felt scorn for Leonard; he felt he had sold out on so many levels.

"In the amateurs, we went all over the world together," Pryor told a *New York Times* reporter prior to the March 1982 bout with Miguel Montilla. "We played cards for chewing gum on planes. I worked for him as a sparring partner for three years. Why did they fire me? Because Ray couldn't shuffle me.

"When I couldn't get a fight, he didn't help me. A lot of people didn't help me. I paid my own fare to work with him before he fought Wilfred Benítez [in November 1979], and I was making $100 to $200 a fight then. I didn't know he became an executive to his friends who knew him when Little Ray was on welfare. I didn't know you had to make an appointment to see him."

To Leonard's defense, Pryor had cultivated a reputation as being uncontrollable and irresponsible in and out of the ring. Pryor fought the first part of his career at 135 pounds, but he quickly realized that the lightweights wanted nothing to do with him. His bravado, reckless ambushes, and dexterity correlated with his label as the "odd man out." No one wanted to fight him, so he moved up a weight class.

Still, Pryor reveled in the role of the victim. Unfortunately, he became one in the ring when seemingly inferior competition knocked him down early in fights.

Flash knockdowns aside, no one in the fight game questioned Pryor's ability. Before facing Argüello, he had won his first thirty-one fights and ended all but three of them before the final bell. He had walked through an aging but favored Antonio "Kid Pambelé" Cervantes in four rounds on August 2, 1980, to win the WBA light welterweight crown. For a man often treated as an outcast in the fight game, the win meant redemption for the young fighter. The *New York*

Times's headline read, "Pryor Takes Title from Cervantes." According to the oft-victimized and jilted champ, the headline "Forgotten Fighter Silences Critics . . . and Olympians" would have been more appropriate. Contrary to his usual public demeanor, Pryor was gracious in victory and heralded Cervantes as a "great fighter."

CBS televised his November 21 defense against Gaétan Hart in Pryor's hometown of Cincinnati, Ohio. Pryor dedicated the fight to fallen fighter Ralph Racine. "I want Ralph Racine to see what I do to Hart," said a confident Pryor, "to pay him back for what he did to Racine." And Pryor stopped Hart in the sixth round.

Financially, Pryor was becoming a TV sensation because of his aggressive style, and he was earning $100,000 paydays by the time he fought his second title defense in mid-1981. In the ring, Pryor was more often than not an unstoppable force; but away from the ring, Pryor's Jekyll and Hyde disposition kept boxing insiders at a distance. To critics, the personality quirks were alarming.

They figured the real Pryor emerged thirty-seven days after the Hart fight. A small UPI blip summarized the tragedy: "Boxer Aaron Pryor Shot." His thirty-two-year-old girlfriend at the time, Theresa Adams, had shot Pryor, and the bullet grazed his abdomen and went directly through his forearm. The domestic dispute that landed him in the Cincinnati General Hospital revealed more about the fighter than any of his previous twenty-seven fights. Although the bullet only grazed Pryor, the story spurred those critics who were searching for flaws in the prickly fighter. He would spend the rest of his career answering questions about the wound.

Pryor, who sported his staple Santa Claus hat with his colorful gym suit, downplayed the squabble. "It was like a kid with matches," he said. "I was just joking around with the gun."

The light welterweight champ was out of commission from November until the end of June. When Pryor returned to defend his title for the second time on June 27, he forced an early stoppage of Guyana's Lennox Blackmoore (23-2), a capable fighter who had decisioned a young Claude Noel on two occasions. Pryor knocked Blackmoore down three times in the first two rounds to retain his title and scored his twentieth consecutive knockout. He earned $200,000 for his services.

CBS picked up Pryor's next bout. As he prepared for his third title defense, a twelve-round affair against third-ranked Dujuan "Mr. Excitement" Johnson (17-0, thirteen knockouts), one fact was clear: Cincinnati fans were not sold on their young champ. Pryor heard the whispers and used them as motivation. So when he had to pick himself off the canvas in that first round, the collective eyes began to roll. No longer was Pryor the whirlwind dynamo; now he was labeled an undisciplined, erratic champ who let his social life interfere with his focus. He was quickly branded as the antithesis of the classy Ray Leonard and later of the gentlemanly Argüello. Although he did knock Johnson out in seven rounds, the evident rust stained the performance.

The catchy "Hawk Time!" chant that his corner used to motivate him had quieted as Pryor mentally prepared for his fourth title defense against another lightly regarded challenger. According to reports, Pryor was disconsolate about the direction in which his career was headed and his lack of recognition. Instead of enjoying the limelight, the mercurial fighter felt detached and unloved by his hometown. Many attributed his lack of local appreciation to his on-again, off-again relationship with popular mogul and manager Buddy LaRosa. Others questioned his dedication to the sport. Meanwhile, Pryor asked himself on a daily basis, what do I have to do in order to be appreciated?

Pryor signed to make his fourth defense on NBC against Dominican stalwart Miguel Montilla (37-6-3), who was way past his prime. The fighters met at the Playboy Casino in Atlantic City on March 21, 1982. Although Pryor successfully defended his title, it was what he didn't do that stirred his critics. People had expected him to knock Montilla out early, but he didn't completely dominate the lesser fighter. He didn't satisfy an audience waiting anxiously for the start of "Hawk Time." Having to go ten rounds for only the second time in his career, Pryor ended up stopping Montilla in twelve rounds.

After the fight, Pryor showed nothing but respect for the seasoned challenger. "When I saw the size of his heart," said Pryor, "I said, 'The hell with knocking him out, I just want to win this fight.'"

As the showdown with Argüello got closer, twenty-six-year-old Pryor signed to fight the WBA's No. 1 and mandatory challenger Akio Kameda for his fifth title defense. The bout would be held in the Riverfront Coliseum in his home-town and shown on CBS Sports World. According to local newspapers, hundreds lined up to watch Pryor's training sessions, but nearly three days before the bout, the ticket sales were still low. By all accounts, fight fans looked past Kameda to Argüello. Arum suggested that they enlist Argüello to sit ringside and promote the encounter. As noted earlier, Pryor knocked Kameda down five times en route to a sixth-round knockout, and the early flash knockdown he suf-fered had little effect on the proceedings. Having Argüello sit ringside, moreover, only helped to increase the fans' interest for the coming showdown. A month later it was reported that Pryor would finally face a man on the same skill level, Argüello himself.

If only Alexis's magnificent skills in the ring could have offset his now capricious behavior outside the ropes. With fame and celebrity knocking at his door, Argüello's personal life became less stable. Although he didn't drink alcohol or take drugs, he revealed his penchant for women when he claimed, "My wife is married to me. I am not married to her." Ironically, his wife at the time, Loretto, was the one woman who had managed to keep Argüello grounded.

"Alexis told me that she was the woman who had more education, a good economic background, and was the granddaughter of a general," said journalist Edgar Tijerino. "She had a superior level to Alexis. She helped him because she managed his money, and it was the first time in his life that Roman wasn't managing his money between 1980 and 1983."

Yolanda Miller, the wife of Argüello's agent, Bill Miller, spent time with the Argüellos socially. She understood the contradictions.

"She [Loretto] loved him very much. She was a stabilizing force for Alexis," she said. "He had that strong macho Latin mentality. Girls were always around him, but if he came home and she wasn't there, he became very jealous. She was educated, very smart, and that created problems because she was able to think better than he did. He was street smart, but in other fields, he was not. She knew how to eat at the dinner table and he didn't. Yet, he could be so smart, and he could amaze you with some of the things he said."

Despite the similarities in their domestic lives and travails with women, Pryor and Argüello couldn't have been more disparate personalities inside and outside the ring.

Argüello carefully calculated his words; Pryor relished his unpredictability and impulsive ways. While Argüello never disparaged a friend, opponent, or manager in public, Pryor openly challenged people in his inner circle who affronted him. Often, boxers Sugar Ray Leonard, Howard Davis, and ex-manager Buddy LaRosa were the targets of his scorn. Argüello lived by the belief that he had to set an example for the kids who were his fans, while Pryor didn't openly consider such responsibilities. The public squabbles worked to diminish Pryor's reputation, deserved or not. Finally, Argüello constantly exclaimed that he loved people and strived to do anything to make them happy. Conversely, by making himself the victim, Pryor relayed the message that he was merely concerned with himself.

What Time Is It? Hawk Time!

I have never been hit by two punches at the same time.
—ALEXIS ARGÜELLO

The odds for the Argüello-Pryor matchup were stacked 2–1 in Argüello's favor. Close to fight time, Argüello envisioned winning a fourth crown as a "hell of an experience." Rarely was he so gregarious or exuberant, but the prospect stirred him. Meanwhile, Pryor could not elicit the resentment that he had had for past opponents.

"Argüello was such a gentleman that it wouldn't have mattered if Pryor tried to get into his head," said Steve Farhood. "He couldn't do it even if he tried. Argüello was favored, what did he have to fear? Also, Pryor didn't have the artillery to get under Argüello's skin. Argüello was impervious to that stuff."

There were rumblings that Argüello lacked the discipline and intensity that had defined his previous eighty-plus training camps. Close friends were concerned about the current atmosphere. For this fight, Dr. Eduardo Roman trusted veteran trainer Eddie Futch to monitor his fighter's progress. Former Mexican trainer Cuyo Hernández felt that Argüello had no chance to beat a strong and skilled 140-pound Pryor, so he had moved on. Despite the breakup, Argüello credited Hernández with shaping him and giving him a proper technique.

Argüello shared a training camp in Palm Springs, California, with lightweight champ and former knockout victim Ray "Boom Boom" Mancini, who was preparing for a November 13 title defense against Duk Koo Kim at Caesars Palace. He would take center stage in Las Vegas a day after the Argüello-Pryor showdown. Mancini recalled, "In the gym, he [Alexis] was all business. I was too. I have seen a lot of fighters that when they get older, they don't need to do things the same way as when he was younger. He was intense, but his workout was not as long. With experience, you don't need to be in the gym as long. He did his work and then got out. It was very interesting. I've learned as I train fighters that it's not how many hours you spend in the gym, but you kick ass and then get out. Do the job and then get out."

Mancini continued: "For me, I am old school. I believe that you have to cut off all the other stuff and don't play at all. You know, six weeks of nothing. Alexis could get away with it and do it. I don't know what changed after 1981. When I fought him, he was still making his mark. CBS introduced him to a worldwide audience. Everyone knew how great he was. Now he had a whole different fan base. After Pryor, well, maybe [the new fame] affected him more than people thought. At that point, he might have changed and become a different person. But I didn't know him personally."

Argüello's manager Dr. Eduardo Roman echoed the unflattering stories that filtered through boxing circles: "We knew that if he trained well and behaved well, he would always win. I sent him to Palm Springs to train. I sent him there because there were nice people, it was a rich area, but with a lot of nice people. I sent him there assuming that he would not get mixed up with anyone. I knew he was not getting up to run in the morning."

As such, Argüello's transgressions created disharmony among the camp members and interrupted an otherwise efficient camp. Although Argüello had reached a point in his career where no trainer could teach him anything new about the sport, he was no longer the invincible fighter that he once was. No one slacked against Aaron Pryor and got away with it. Few men were closer to each other during this time than the cornerman and lifelong friend Don Kahn and Argüello were. Kahn was the camp's Bundini Brown figure (Muhammad Ali's cornerman), and Roman kept him on because of that relationship.

"He and Loretto got along together at the beginning [of the camp for the first Pryor fight]. Then something happened," said Kahn. "Then he came to me and said that he wanted to go back home. I said, 'Champ, you can't come back home. There are promoters and managers who made nice promotions here.' But he still wanted to go back home. I told him it wasn't up to me. I told him that I would sit down with the entire team and make a decision, and if they decide you can go, you can go. So I sat down with Bill Miller and Eddie Futch, and we agreed to let him go. What could we do? Then he went back to Miami and everything went wrong."

In the weeks leading up to the fight, the camp moved back to Miami, where Argüello stayed at home and his team members stayed at a nearby hotel. Uncharacteristically, Argüello ran on his own, which he had never done before, and stayed detached from his team during training sessions. According to Kahn, he even struggled against his sparring partners.

"I told Eduardo Roman I should go home too. I didn't want to see him lose to Pryor, especially since he had the tools to beat him. His training was no good. And I said that 'at this rate he cannot beat anybody.' After he takes care of his problems, he can get into the proper shape to beat Pryor. It was something that he had never done before in his career."

Even close associates were cognizant of the mental breakdown that occurred during that camp. Said friend Gerald Maltz, "I went to Miami and I did not see Alexis before or after the fight. I [had] heard that there was so much pressure on him in that venue. I had a sense that he looked different, and that he didn't look as focused. I was told there were a lot of distractions in the training camp."

Conversely, Roman quashed any implications that his fighter had succumbed to the temptations that his ever-glowing celebrity appeal attracted. "When Alexis prepared for Pryor, he did not underestimate him. Alexis knew not to underestimate anybody," said Roman. "Things happen when you are a champion. Everybody says hello to you. Actors and actresses are waiting to say hello to you. Sylvester Stallone used to come to the bouts. Alexis was appreciated by a lot of actors."

When attending big-time boxing cards, fight fans typically skip the early bouts and show up one or two fights before the main event. But the newly appointed Miami Boxing Commission's members were inexperienced and needed all the time they could get in order to iron out their routine. All in all, only two of them had credible boxing experience.

"It was a Mickey Mouse atmosphere," said Ramiro Ortiz, who handled some of the local promotions of the fight. "I showed up for the first fight on the undercard. Walter [Alvarez] looked desperate. He said, 'Ramiro, I need a bell.' Out of coincidence I had a bell in my car that I used at the War Memorial Auditorium. I told him it was a bell I used at the small venue, the War Memorial. And he said, 'A bell is a bell. Go get it.' Then I read the *Sports Illustrated* story years later and it said, 'Even hearing the bell was a problem.'"

The bell was a minor issue compared to the problems that would surface later in the evening. Boxing people disputed the level of political overtures that evening. Some noted the pressure of the Sandinistas who were present, while others insisted that there was no tension among the various Hispanic factions. With the meteoric rise of HBO and the local blackouts, promoters Bob Arum and Walter Alvarez were more concerned about filling the seats. Ringside and low-end ticket sales were consistent, but Alvarez felt that the advent of HBO hurt his middle-range ticket sales.

To make matters worse, early in the process Pryor's camp, citing its opposition to apartheid, balked at the commission's decision to use a South African referee. The protest didn't stand, and respected referee Stanley Christodoulou was appointed referee.

"That just popped up about Stanley," said Alvarez. "But then it died. Pryor didn't know who Stanley Christodoulou was. That was upper management in Pryor's camp. Bottom line was that Pryor didn't give a shit."

Confusion reigned at the Orange Bowl in Miami, Florida, on November 12, 1982, when the Master of Ceremonies Hector Salazar couldn't silence the 23,800 fans and dozens of Pryor camp members flooded the ring. Earlier, in the dressing rooms, rumors had spread that a gun-toting man who was supposedly working for the Sandinistas had tried to break into Argüello's dressing room; he was immediately taken into custody. Journalist Bert Sugar reported that of the eleven inspectors who were supposed to monitor the dressing rooms and security sections, only six showed up at the fight. The one inspector assigned to Pryor's dressing room had been sent away before the fight.

For Argüello, the fight represented historic implications. Argüello was preparing to win his fourth title—Pryor's WBA World Light Welterweight belt— and eclipse other three-time champs such as Bob Fitzsimmons, Tony Canzoneri, Barney Ross, Henry Armstrong, and Wilfred Benítez. Promoter Bob Arum touted the bout as the "Battle of Champions," and the purists were calling it the classic boxer versus the brawler.

Most assumed that the brawler was Aaron Pryor. Those people who weren't familiar with Pryor at least knew he was a supremely talented fighter who could be equally outlandish, wild, and out of control. Thus, he was portrayed as the antithesis of the gentleman and classic stylist, Argüello. Pryor was a blur of emotion, a windmill dynamo who'd earned the reputation of being a contender no one wanted to face. Still, the boxing experts were not completely sold on the young phenom. Of twelve writers, boxers, and trainers polled by Ring magazine, only Steve Farhood and West Coast promoter Ahmed Bey picked Pryor by decision. Echoing the beliefs of most writers, Ring associate editor Randy Gordon said, "Anything Pryor can do, Argüello can do better."

At 31-0, with twenty-nine knockouts, the twenty-seven-year-old Pryor, or the Hawk, could throw more than a hundred punches per round. He often strutted around with a coterie of followers who would egg him on with their own post–Muhammad Ali call-and-response, "What time is it?" And the fighter and posse emphatically would respond, "Hawk Time!" The ringleader was the disruptive trainer Panama Lewis. It was impossible to control the ebullient Pryor before a fight, and associates believed he thrived on that energy and occasional disorder.

Conversely, the introspective Argüello looked within for guidance.

"[Alexis] was very different when he was going to a fight. He became very focused, tight, and quiet before a fight. It was difficult to approach him, especially the last week before a fight," said longtime friend Renzo Bagnariol. "He was always suffering and working hard to drop the weight. He was not a nice person, if you would, weeks before the fight. Then, his character would come back after the fight and he would be Alexis Argüello again."

The night of the fight, Pryor, with his posse in tow, sauntered out to disco music. With trainers Panama Lewis and Artie Curley leading the way, the Pryor camp and its hangers-on had waited for the Miami fireworks display to end and forced Argüello to sit and simmer inside the ring. After nearly a twenty-minute wait, the fight announcer was ready to begin. Argüello (72-5, sixty-two knock-outs) was already in his corner shaking out. In his previous twenty title fights, Argüello was 19-1 with three titles, and Pryor was defending his light welter-weight crown for the sixth time. While Argüello, ranked No. 2 by Ring maga-zine, had the height and reach to his advantage, Pryor had youth and speed on his side.

Gloria Estefan belted out the national anthem. Then Argüello stood enrap-tured as a Nicaraguan trio sang the Nicaraguan anthem. Pryor smiled and threw punches, while Argüello stood quiet and stoic.

"Pryor made himself into the bad guy," said Barry Tompkins, who broadcast the historic bout. "But it wasn't him, but the people around him. They were bad people, and it created a drama like no other fight. In fact, they weren't going to even let the fireworks show go on before the fight [because of the drama out-side the ring]. I remember the only light in the place was on me, and I hear this sound and they did shoot the fireworks. It scared the hell out of me."

Across the ring, Pryor attempted to stare down Argüello. Then, he put his glove out and pointed at his prey in an ominous foreboding of what was about to occur. Finally, after a thirty-minute delay, the fight began. In Round 1, Pryor didn't charge out as usual, but he did land the first shot, a straight right to Argüello's jaw. While Pryor raged from his crouched stance, Argüello stood upright and patient. They traded shots toward the midpoint of the round, and neither took a step back, foreshadowing the rest of the fight. Both fighters missed wild, knockout attempts. Pryor was backing up Argüello when he sliced him with an uppercut against the ropes and followed it with a straight right hand. Pryor continued the assault as he nailed Argüello with a short, jolting left hook and then banged the Nicaraguan with a right hand that temporarily lifted the former champ. Thirty seconds later, with jolting right hands Pryor caught Argüello lazily sitting on the ropes. It was too much punishment, too early for Argüello. At the bell, as they turned away and headed to the corners, Argüello was clearly dejected.

By Round 2, Argüello looked old. It didn't matter that he had a stringent defense; Pryor easily walked right through his guard. Despite Argüello's three-inch height advantage, Pryor was heady enough not to allow Argüello to create space on the inside. The Hawk smothered Argüello with his body and never stopped throwing punches. Argüello couldn't breathe. Becoming too analytical, Argüello thought about every punch he threw, a tactic that didn't work against an opponent like Pryor. Argüello landed a straight right, and Pryor, fighting like an uncanny veteran, fell into Argüello in order to avoid any more punishment. It was the first time that Argüello caught his attention; before that moment, the fight was all about Aaron Pryor.

Trainer Panama Lewis, who would become the focus of a post-fight controversy, excoriated his fighter before Round 3. "You're the boss. Be the boss!" he yelled at Aaron. A "mouse" had begun to form under Argüello's left eye. At the outset of the third, Pryor moved to his left and began to establish his jab. One flurry typified the fight: Pryor jabbed, blocked a counter, crouched, and came back up top with two shots. Argüello was helpless to the battering. Even when Argüello did land a single punch, he wasn't able to gain any momentum. It was the first Durán-Leonard fight all over again, with Pryor playing the Durán role to perfection.

Every punch Pryor landed took a year off of Argüello's boxing lifeline; yet, the Nicaraguan stood, absorbed the battering, and occasionally landed a punch. No longer was he the feared assassin. Even when Argüello did send Pryor between the ropes, Pryor danced his way out and kept his show intact. With thirty seconds left in Round 3, Argüello landed a left hook that sent Pryor swaying off balance—but he couldn't take advantage of the opening.

Trainer Eddie Futch told Argüello to "stop waiting and get on with it" as the fourth round started. Realizing the critical state of Argüello's bloody eye, Pryor came out and jabbed the wound. Refusing to fight a conventional style, Pryor followed his punches and ultimately landed out of position after each punch.

However, he bested Argüello when he landed a huge right hand—the best punch of the round—that pushed Argüello against the ropes. Pryor the performer also baited his opponent by feigning injury after taking a straight right from Argüello. He stepped back to buy some time and then kept punching. Whether Argüello was waiting for Pryor to punch himself out, he wasn't throwing enough punches. Pryor's head movement allowed him to avoid punishment.

At the start of the fifth round, Argüello looked confident and strong, but he couldn't match Pryor's pace. Few, if any, fighters could maintain such a pace, but both fighters were in superior condition. With one minute remaining in the round, Argüello landed two left hooks and a short right cross. He only managed to stymie the oncoming monster for a second as Pryor ended the round by jabbing and moving again.

By the sixth round, another cut had begun to form on the top left corner of Argüello's nose. Pryor had completely abandoned his ambush style and substituted it with effective lateral movement and less power punching, the exact style to frustrate a puncher like Argüello. Midway through the round, Pryor sneaked a quick shot that froze Argüello. The clean right hand exacerbated a cut over Argüello's left eye.

"After the sixth, Pryor was stronger and Alexis was no longer at his best," said Edgar Tijerino. "Each round was harder and harder for Alexis. But here in Nicaragua, we always had faith in Alexis."

Nearly at the midpoint of the fight in Round 7, Pryor's awkward style had completely befuddled the straight-on Argüello. With 1:30 left in the round, Pryor assumed control: He brawled or boxed when he pleased and danced or stepped back when he felt the urge. Everything Argüello did to stop him was futile. It was now a show with Pryor as the headliner. Nevertheless, Argüello had his moments. In that round, Argüello missed a left hook but followed with a straight right that nailed a stunned Pryor. A left hook also hurt Pryor to close out the round. To the boxing purist, Pryor adapted and changed as the fight progressed, while, at this point, Argüello could not.

Between rounds Lewis screamed at Pryor, "He's a blind man!" Going into the eighth round, unfortunately, Argüello couldn't follow up what he'd initiated in the previous round. Pryor defined the eighth with his retreating style and sneaky right hands. The performance prompted guest commentator Sugar Ray Leonard to say, "Very few men can stay in the ring with Pryor." Argüello landed some blustering shots to end the round, but his low blows had become a theme throughout and after the eighth round. Lewis urged Pryor to counter with his own low blows.

Argüello entered the ninth round with a sense of urgency and his floating right hands became sharper and on target. He would continue to be effectively aggressive over the first half of the round. The Nicaraguan landed his best punch of the fight to this point—a right hand that forced Pryor to duck and fall toward the canvas but his hand never touched it, so it wasn't recorded as a knockdown. Pryor landed seven out of nine shots on a defenseless Argüello, but the Hawk was off balance and clearly hurt, lunging at the end of the round.

Although the men traded punches in the tenth round, Pryor damaged Argüello's cut eye again. Argüello ducked down, fired, and landed a straight right to the head, which didn't hurt Pryor but managed to slow him down. Pryor countered with a beautiful uppercut, which had become his staple punch. As the round closed, Argüello sat back and crushed Pryor with a straight right. Nothing. Pryor didn't give him a sarcastic grin or even blink. The brash Pryor danced and goaded Argüello as he walked toward him after the bell. Cornerman Don Kahn continued to implore Argüello to "fight back . . . don't jab . . . you have to hurt him."

"I wasn't speaking directly to [Alexis], but as he kept coming back to the corner, he kept saying, 'Man, I am throwing everything I can at this guy, and he won't budge.' He was so frustrated, because he was hitting Pryor so much and he didn't blink," said cornerman Bagnariol.

Still fueled from the previous rounds, Pryor ran at Argüello to start the twelfth round. Pryor moved back to his boxing and movement. He landed five punches that clearly halted the rushing Argüello. Pryor had him against the ropes but ran into stinging counters. Both fighters landed significant punches throughout the round.

However, the lull in the fight gave way to warfare in the thirteenth round. Pryor's vicious left uppercut left Argüello reeling. Midway through the round, Argüello returned to snap back Pryor's head with a straight right hand. Few men would have still been standing after the punch. Pryor stepped back and took another less-damaging left hook, but he managed to stay out of danger as the round ended.

"When Pryor started to take those right hands and shrug them off, the crowd began to get a little worried," said promoter Walter Alvarez. "Then Alexis started to smack Pryor, and he's still there, the crowd looked around to ask, 'What's going on?'"

Between rounds, trainer Panama Lewis replenished his fighter with a concoction that would go down in history as the "mystery drink" that he himself specially mixed for Pryor. In the TV replay that was aired after the fight, Lewis continually motioned for his "special mix," which he later admitted included an antihistamine to increase Pryor's lung capacity. Rumors had surfaced years later that Lewis spiked the drink with a combination of cocaine, honey, and orange juice. Under Miami Commission guidelines, only water was allowed in the corner. At the bell, now fighting with new vigor and impervious to pain, Pryor leaped off the stool and beelined for Argüello.

Some may have challenged Lewis's belief that Pryor needed to win the final two rounds, but Pryor certainly didn't disappoint his boisterous trainer. Pryor jabbed to start the fourteenth, and a straight right sent Argüello across the ring. The end was near. He nailed the immobile and defenseless Argüello with ten clean punches against the ropes. Referee Christodoulou stepped in as three to four more punches landed on the helpless legend. As the punches rained down on Argüello, there was no mystery: the final chapter had ended mercilessly. Christodoulou stopped the bout at 1:06 of the round, thus averting a possible tragedy.

Argüello slumped down between the ropes before the referee could save him, leaving an indelible image for those who loved him. No one ever expected that such a powerful man would be reduced to falling in and out of consciousness. Before the stoppage, Pryor was ahead by three points on judge Ove Oveson's and referee Stanley Christodoulou's cards. Judge Ken Morita had Argüello ahead by two points.

"As soon as the fight was stopped, the ref looked at me and said, 'C'mon in, doc.' As a doctor you look to see if the fighter is still defending himself, but it happened so quickly, the punches like a rat-a-tat that the ref couldn't get to him quick enough," said ringside doctor Dr. Marshall Abel. "He was out for about two minutes. His eyes eventually opened, but they were glazed over. We gave him oxygen. The paramedics came in, and some reporters asked a few questions to confirm that Alexis was out."

Friends looked on in horror. "You can't put into words what I felt," said Bagnariol. "It's unexplainable as a fan and friend." Similarly, Don Kahn said, "He was like a son to me. When I saw him going down, my heart broke."

Associated Press writer Ed Schuyler Jr. observed Argüello's fall with trepidation. "I remember looking up and Alexis had fallen right above me. I thought he was badly hurt. They were cutting his shoelaces off. I thought it was serious. He's down and I am dictating. I am not looking around, but trying to concentrate on what happened in the fight. I thought Argüello went down mostly from exhaustion. But Pryor could hit and punch with power from all angles. To me, Argüello fought as well as he had done for every fight in his life."

On his way back to the dressing room, Argüello collapsed again on the Orange Bowl field. Later reports said that he had a severe concussion and received thirty stitches for his cuts. Stretchers were available, but Argüello did not need one.

In one dressing room, it was finally "Hawk Time." In Argüello's, there was silence.

"I visited Pryor's locker room first to do the post-fight check up, and everyone was yelling, 'What time is it?'" said Dr. Marshall Abel. "But Aaron had these huge welts all over his body, which you couldn't see unless you were up close. Then I went to see Alexis in his dressing room, and it was the saddest thing. He was sitting on the exam table, slumped backward and crying. He had this huge gash or hole under his left eye and you could see through to the eyeball. It wasn't on his forehead, but in a dangerous spot. There was an ophthalmologist there, a friend of his, who said he would take care of the cuts. Like Pryor, Alexis was also laying there covered in welts. We didn't say much, but I think he looked at me and said, 'Thank you.'

"When you are in your 20s, you can sustain a beating like that and come back. But when you get over 30, it takes so much of a toll, both mentally and physically."

As a member of the commission, chairman Jimmy Resnick met Argüello back at his dressing room to assess his state. Owing to the brutality of the knockout, most onlookers expected the worst.

"I ran to his dressing room and I remember it was this makeshift room. Bill Miller was in there. And he leaves and I am by myself with Alexis, and he turns to me and says, 'Resnick, I have been in a million fights, but this is the first time I got hit by two hands at once.' I felt so bad in that locker room, he was a beaten guy," said Resnick. "I never saw him like that because he was always full of life. There he was in that fetal position. His eyes were watering. I had been with Thomas 'Hit Man' Hearns after the fight with Marvin Hagler, but this was different. I felt pity for him."

Away from the locker rooms, HBO's Ross Greenburg and his staff were busy trying to take out the ambient sound of their videotape so they could hear what Panama Lewis had been saying to Pryor between rounds. The statement "Get me the other bottle, the one I mixed," would take on a whole new meaning after the fight.

Meanwhile, in the ensuing chaos, the Miami Boxing Commission blundered again by failing to administer the mandatory drug test to Pryor and Argüello following the fight.

Dr. Marshall Abel recalled that one of the two ringside doctors employed to work the bout, a Cuban doctor named Dr. Juan Rodriguez Acosta, had admitted to being a friend of Argüello's before the fight started. He was relieved of his duties because of a perceived conflict of interest. So, instead of staying and collecting the men's post-fight urine samples, the doctor left. Commissioner Resnick refuted that story and claimed that Acosta had no prior relationship with either fighter. The commission's oversight would be the focus of its meeting days later.

To Farhood and the rest of the journalists who were kept in the dark, the events that evening "would remain one of life's mysteries. Was it something Pryor was on? Was it the five pounds? We'll never know."

Despite the furor over Lewis's bottle and the local boxing commission's lack of accountability, Argüello couldn't escape the reality of what occurred in the fight. "That was his night," Argüello said. "Like it was my night against [Rubén] Olivares. What we do when we come in, they do to us when we go out. From the first ring of the bell, that was a freaking war. No remorse. I can tell you that I would do it again."

"The atmosphere at the Orange Bowl, everything. It remains thirty years later the best fight I ever saw. And that includes Leonard-Hearns and the others," said Farhood. "It was the best. The way I analyzed it only a couple of fights were determined when it didn't matter what the other guy did to his opponent. For Argüello, he had no chance.

"I got the same feeling with Ali and Frazier. No matter what, Frazier was going to win that fight. Argüello fought a winning fight. There was nothing he didn't do. With the punches he threw, to not knock him out was remarkable. But Pryor was fighting for everything. This was his ticket to stardom. I am not saying he wanted it more than Argüello, but he would have beaten the Incredible Hulk that night."

Until the last round of punches came down on their hero, the Nicaraguan people always felt that Argüello had a chance.

"To have done the fight he did, it had to be the best Alexis he could have been," said Tijerino. "[In the middle rounds] we always believed in Alexis. Here in Nicaragua, we always had faith in Alexis. In the tenth round, we didn't think Pryor would be able to stop Alexis's power."

Dr. Roman had watched the brutal bout near the exit with Argüello's wife Loretto, as they both took turns reciting the play-by-play. So when Roman, in tears afterward, tried to console the diminished champ, he focused on the rematch: "When I sat with Alexis and he was crying I told him that he was still the same Alexis Argüello and with the proper training he could beat Pryor anytime. I told him what happened to him could happen to most people, but you have to train hard and get back in the gym. Sometimes he cried after fights because of all the emotions."

Roman also was privy to Argüello's marital problems, which were addressed following the knockout.

"The day he lost to Pryor in the first fight, I remember he came back to the corner of the ring and said to me, 'Give me $1,000 and give Loretto $1,000,000,'" said Roman from his home in Nicaragua.

"I looked at him and said, 'You're crazy! Why?'

"Argüello replied, 'Loretto came up to me before the fight and said, 'My love, you're going to lose because you didn't behave.' If I had not behaved then I deserved to lose. Give her the money."

Ironically, those press members who had salivated over a Durán-Argüello showdown left the arena while Durán was fighting in his first swing bout against the light-hitting Jimmy Batten. Although the press conference after the Argüello-Pryor fight cut into most of the bout, reporters still had the opportunity to see the 157-pound Durán fight an unimpressive final four rounds against Batten. They would have seen that Durán's worst opponent was himself, but he did decision Batten.

For most observers, however, the boxing tragedy that occurred the following day superseded any reporting on the championship bouts. In a world title bout, Argüello's training camp partner, champ Ray "Boom Boom" Mancini, fought lightweight challenger Duk Koo Kim. In the fourteenth round, Kim collapsed in the ring and later slipped into coma. He died four days later. Meanwhile, the rumors about the Argüello-Pryor fight began to spread as soon as Panama Lewis's corner tactics were publicized. Even though the boxing community was still shuddering from the beating that Argüello received, "Bottlegate" had taken on a life of its own.

"If you can go that hard, take and give that hard, it was superhuman," said HBO commentator Barry Tompkins, who called the fight. "Knowing Panama, you knew he could do it [spike the water]. Where there's smoke, there's fire."

Tompkins's colleague Larry Merchant, who also worked the live broadcast, said, "I put a lot of credence in Panama Lewis's actions. I don't remember exactly, but we referenced it on air as it happened. It was there to hear and to question.

It wasn't until later on that we learned how notorious Lewis really was. So at the time there was no reason to be overly suspicious.

"That clip on HBO of Panama Lewis saying, 'Give me the special bottle,' to use a modern term, became 'viral' [widely disseminated] in the boxing world. I don't know what it was like outside the boxing world."

It is customary that after every big fight, the people involved in the fight congregate the next morning for breakfast at a designated hotel. Often, the celebration carries over from the previous evening.

At his breakfast, a victorious Aaron Pryor, still in his trunks from the night before, strutted into the room with a bottle of champagne. According to witnesses, the mood was joyous because Pryor finally got the credit he deserved.

"It was hard to tell during the fight about any controversy or if the guy was mixing anything in the corner," said Schuyler. "It would have been a greater controversy if Duk Koo Kim didn't just get killed in the ring. That death took all the play. So the conversation quickly turned to people wanting to ban boxing. Kim's death wiped it clean off the sports page."

Trainer Emanuel Steward knew of Lewis's capabilities when he said, "Whatever Panama had in that black bottle, I don't know if Aaron would have survived that fight judging by the punches that he was taking from Alexis. Then, that whole black bottle thing went all over the world. But Aaron certainly never acknowledged anything. You have a certain value system on the street with street kids. No snitching, that stuff."

Even with the "cheating" accusations directed at Pryor's camp, Argüello fell into a depression. The psychological debris left over from that fight would haunt Argüello forever. Later, locking himself in his bedroom and watching the haunting replay of the bout in his Kings Bay, Florida, home, Argüello refused all outside visitors. When Argüello walked into the ring against Pryor, close friends had seen that he clearly was distracted. Yet, some felt the controversy surrounding the mysterious bottle warranted a return match.

"When I went to his house a couple days later, I didn't see him depressed, but at the same time committed to next time to change whatever he did wrong during training the first time," said promoter Walter Alvarez. "He was ready to give up whatever he was doing wrong [inside and outside the ring]. But it was a dual mood. He also felt a little humiliated, but that eventually wore off and he focused on the rematch."

Bill Miller, Argüello's agent, recalled that after the loss, "Alexis was down because it never happened before. If you go through your career without getting beaten, and suddenly someone does it to you, it's hard to understand. But he never figured to be the victim."

Questions came from all angles, but the one that Argüello could never resolve was how his opponent managed to weather his venomous storm of punches. Rightfully so, the evidence was there for the world to see.

Despite Argüello's name being banned in Nicaragua, the sportswriters there did cover the historic bout. The *Barricada Internacional's* headline read, "A Great Champion Falls," while *El Nuevo Diario* used some political spin with the headline "KO to the Contras."

"In the Orange Bowl, I didn't know how that happened," said Argüello. "I asked Pryor a few times. I don't believe that with cocaine someone could perform like he did. Sugar or mint could give you extra energy. He told me it was mint in there. But sugar gives you that extra wind, that stamina."

The controversy surrounding the black bottle raged as Bill Miller filed a protest with the WBA and the Miami Boxing Commission on November 14, charging Pryor's camp with the use of stimulants and the fighter's refusal to take a post-fight urine test. Miller said, "We think there were enough irregularities to warrant an investigation and a rematch." He would later add that the Miami commission members were "inept" and took on "the role of spectators." Furthermore, he charged the commission with negligence (of which he was incorrect). Miller also asked the commission to confiscate the fighter's gloves, but it was never done. The bout was never declared a no-contest, which unnerved Miller, but his futility did help spur a rematch. At this point, Miller was busy running the day-to-day operations for Roman. When faced with the bottle controversy, Roman refused to face it head on. "In that moment I had no reaction," said Roman. "I had not been in boxing all my life. Nobody saw what the person behind [Panama Lewis] was doing. After I saw the fight again, I started to think in the alternative that something was put in there [to help Pryor]."

When pressed on the issue, lead trainer Panama Lewis claimed that the drink he administered was a mixture of tap water and Perrier to settle Pryor's stomach. Cornerman Artie Curley confirmed it was peppermint schnapps. At the time, both substances were illegal. The WBA officials and the Miami Boxing Commission prohibited the drinking of anything but water between rounds. Regarding the urine analysis gaffe, although the WBA does not require a urine analysis after every bout, the Miami commission agreed to take one for this specific title bout.

By July 1983, the protest was still pending, and Miller hadn't heard from the WBA or the commission. An exasperated Pryor responded, "I'm tired of hearing all the talk. I was around for two hours after the fight if anyone wanted to take a urine test. And there was nothing wrong with my gloves. I didn't do anything wrong or illegal." Some claimed that Miller was trying to capitalize on Panama Lewis's having had his boxer's license permanently revoked that July first after a glove-tampering incident.

Whatever Lewis mixed and called for between Rounds 11 and 12 and again between 13 and 14 stirred debate for decades. It represented another black eye for the sport.

After the vicious fight, Dr. Aaron Tuckler, a friend of Dr. Roman's since childhood, gave Argüello a clear bill of health to continue his career. "After the knockout in the first fight, we did a CAT [computerized axial tomography] scan on the brain. There was no such thing as an MRI [magnetic resonance imaging] at that time," said Dr. Tuckler years later. "We also took neurological tests. There was no concussion, and everything came out normal. The only thing we found were small holes around the eyebrow, but nothing special."

On February 15, 1983, Argüello officially relinquished the WBC lightweight crown, citing an inability to make the weight class. Argüello knew the rematch with Pryor was inevitable. Although promoter Don King tried to intervene and put Argüello against WBA 140-pound champ Leroy Haley, his ploy failed. Before Argüello could focus on a return bout with Pryor, he first had to deal with uncharacteristic criticism when a newspaper headline read, "Argüello Blames Futch for Defeat." Although it was a blip on the boxing radar, no one believed that the kind and generous Eddie Futch would undermine the great fighter. Many claimed Argüello was merely making excuses.

"I think I was cheated by [Futch]," Argüello had told a reporter when discussing his frustration with Futch's training methods. "He didn't care about my training. I didn't receive any advice from him as a professional. He didn't conduct himself as a professional." Argüello went on to add that "my brain was good, but my body was exhausted."

Spats between trainers and fighters were common in the sport, especially after a big loss. But Argüello prided himself on perpetuating lasting relationships with those in his inner circle. When he released Futch that February and replaced him with Sugar Ray Leonard's cornerman Janks Morton, the change raised a red flag.

Argüello once expressed his loyalty and the need for true friendship when he said, "I never had people telling me what to do. I had Don Kahn from Puerto Rico in 1978, and he became my buddy, my pal, my friend till the end of my career.

Those guys I considered my friends, not the leeches. When you have talent, you have a couple of guys who you attract, but they don't accept that they are leeches. They serve the guy, and that's the way they show that they are your friends."

Dr. Roman's theory about trainers was that in order to keep a fighter fresh and progressing, it is necessary to bring in a long line of trainers. Even though Roman never claimed to be a "boxing guy," he was deft at analyzing fighters' personalities, surrounding them with intelligent individuals, and, above all, always keeping order in the camp. In Argüello's case, Roman knew that there wasn't a trainer who could teach him anything new, but he was aware that even at Argüello's advanced level, certain fighters and trainers clashed regularly.

"I consulted with a lot of people to get recommendations for my fighter. I compared it to learning from five different professors, instead of learning everything from just one professor," said Roman. "The only real task I had was to make sure I had discipline on the team. If one of them got off task, then I had to cut them from the team. That was my job. That's the reason why I had so many trainers."

As for letting Futch go, Roman added, "Eddie Futch was a very good trainer and he was a very nice person, but he was not the Latin-type trainer. He was very square, not in a bad sense, but he had a methodology and you had to follow it. Eddie was more of a classic type, not a motivational type. But Alexis was intelligent enough to take something he needed from every trainer."

Meanwhile, new trainer Janks Morton and the Argüello camp readied for a rematch against the slippery Vilomar Fernández. A Dominican with no pop in his punches, Fernández (27-9-2) was tailor-made for a fighter who had recently sustained his first concussion in the ring. The bout would be only Argüello's third fight at the 140-pound limit. He had demolished Kevin Rooney and lost to Pryor, so the jury was still reluctant to give him passing grades at the higher weight class.

CBS Sports had agreed to use the Argüello-Fernández ten-rounder at the 1:30 p.m. slot during the *Sports Saturday* telecast. Argüello (72-6) and everyone associated with the sport knew that Fernández couldn't hurt him. They also knew that Fernández was a natural lightweight. Critics questioned the decision to fight the Dominican since Argüello had lost to Fernández five years earlier as a lightweight, and both fighters had slightly deteriorated since then. The junior welterweight clash was held at the Freeman Coliseum in San Antonio, Texas, on February 26, 1983. Argüello weighed in at 140, while Fernández was listed at 141.

In his first fight back, Argüello cut Fernández with that sledgehammer right hand early and often. Fernández was still the agitating, slithery fighter Argüello remembered, but this time Argüello skillfully cut off the ring instead of chasing his opponent.

"After Fernández ran like a thief in the first bout, Alexis wanted to set the record straight," said Bill Miller.

By the end of the bout, Argüello had opened cuts over both of Fernández's eyes, but the chase left both fighters frustrated and exhausted. The early rounds had been exact replicas of their previous lightweight bout, when Argüello ran after Fernández, missed punches, and occasionally walked into counters. The rat race stopped momentarily at 1:40 of the fourth round when Argüello raked Fernández with a left hook and right hand combination that sent Fernández down for a seven count. An anxious Argüello rushed at his opponent and landed punches with impunity, but by the end of the round Fernández had danced his way out of trouble.

A harmless cut formed under Argüello's left eye by the fifth. Many expected Argüello to use the knockdown round as a springboard to earning a quick knockout victory, but Fernández valiantly fought back in the fifth. Fernández relied on a jumping left hook to halt Argüello's forward progress and nothing more. The spray of punches accomplished nothing as Argüello plundered directly through them and battered Fernández along the ropes over the sixth and seventh rounds. In the seventh, Fernández ignited his countrymen as he passionately traded punches with Argüello for the second half of the round.

Then, Fernández ran for the remainder of the fight. In his best moments, Fernández ventured inside to land an overhand right and left hook, but during Argüello's best moments, he trapped Fernández against the ropes with wide hooks and a devastating uppercut. Then he made Fernández grimace from a slicing left hook to the ribs. As the final round started, it was clear that the rematch was no longer a carbon copy of the first fight.

When Fernández wasn't moving, he was pawing at the cuts he had sustained over both of his eyes. Blood splashed in his eye socket, impeding his vision and thus, blinding him to Arguello's combinations. Instead of trying to win the final round, Fernández ran, walked, feinted, ducked—trying anything to halt the incoming punches. Hoping for a continuation of the 1978 performance, Fernández's supporters were sorely disappointed. Argüello had learned from his mistakes and controlled Fernández this time around for a unanimous decision victory. The scores from judge Roy Ovalle (100–91) and referee Steve Crosson and the third judge (98–92 for both) reflected Argüello's dominance.

Argüello thought he had won an early evening after the knockdown, but Fernández showed his durability and spirit. After a decisive but not dominating performance, supporters could not determine if Argüello had completely recovered from the Pryor beating.

"I was trying to put my punches together, but he was hard to hit," said Argüello, now 73-5. "That's his style. Vilomar knew that trying to trade punches was wrong. He's a different kind of boxer. Chasing a good boxer is difficult."

For the first time in his professional career, Argüello relied on excuses to explain the one loss that haunted him. While preparing for an ill-advised celebrity pro-am auto race, Argüello spoke with a reporter regarding his loss to Pryor and the ramifications. The fighter complained about the exhaustion from the extensive promotions, the overtraining he endured under trainer Eddie Futch, and the lack of caution that the Miami Boxing Commission had observed.

"Going into such an important fight, I should have felt more loose with more speed and quickness, but I had nothing. I could not react with movements. I had no reflexes," said Argüello, taking a shot at Futch's training mentality.

Regarding the commission's inaction, Argüello said, "Every boxer has a right to be protected. The only way we have to be protected is by an honest commission."

Argüello later apologized to Futch, but he did not bring him back for the rematch. When training camp began, Mexican trainer Lupe Sanchez brought in a coterie of quick featherweights to acclimate Argüello to Pryor's speed. Between fights, Argüello dabbled in the celebrity race car circuit with actor Gene Hackman, while Pryor married his longtime girlfriend Theresa Adams, and stayed undefeated with a third-round technical knockout of a top but severely overmatched contender, Sang-Hyun Kim.

By April 7, 1983, numbers for the rematch were announced. Pryor stood to make $1.75 million and $500,000 would go to Aphrodite, his wife's company. Before Pryor could sign a contract, he had to settle his ongoing legal dispute with on-again and off-again manager Buddy LaRosa. Such highly publicized legal spats and ill-advised business decisions had plagued Pryor since the outset of his career, so no one paid much attention to his most recent conflict.

The Rematch

Time catches up with all of us.
—ALEXIS ARGÜELLO

On April 24, 1983, Argüello returned to face Trinidad and Tobago's Claude Noel in Atlantic City, New Jersey. Coming off a lackluster ten-round decision over Vilomar Fernández, Argüello wanted to impress his fans. At age thirty-three, Noel (29-5, seventeen knockouts) combined speed and lateral movement. The bout was televised on NBC's *SportsWorld* and competed with another card featuring the Eusebio Pedroza–Rocky Lockridge WBA featherweight title bout, which was televised at the same time on ABC's *Wide World of Sports*. Argüello, now 73-5 with sixty-two knockouts, held a four-inch reach advantage over the veteran lightweight. Having lost two of his last four bouts, including a knockout loss to Art Frias, Noel was clearly on the downside of his career.

The bout reflected Noel's flaws. Noel was down early in the first round after he succumbed to a blazing left hook. Before he threw the punch, Argüello baited Noel with a sleepy jab and then landed the hook. Noel quickly rose to his feet and stumbled ahead as referee Larry Hazzard administered the eight count. Noel took thirty seconds to regain his senses, and he avoided Argüello to survive the round, barely.

Noel returned in the next round to nail Argüello with a flash right hand. Seconds later, the fighters collided. Argüello clipped Noel with an imposing uppercut. Noel bounced off the ropes and used his experience to stave off the eager champ.

Few understood what occurred in the next two minutes once Noel landed in his corner between rounds. As his cornermen massaged his ribs, Noel could be heard complaining, "I can't stand up, man. I can't stand up." After some brief talks with the referee about his ribs, including incomprehensible chatter with his corner, Noel limped up and dramatically exclaimed he could continue fighting. However, after a three-punch combination, Noel's bravado had worn thin. He searched for

excuses. He grabbed his side and waved his hands as if to say, "Enough. I'm done."
A puzzled Argüello walked away as a disgusted crowd booed loudly. Hazzard called
the bout at thirty-seven seconds of the third round. Fight doctor Ferdie Pacheco
went to check on the beaten fighter. Noel showed him his right side and, squinting,
said, "[The pain is] in the ribs man, right here." He went on to add, "I want to
fight, man. But I can't." Referee Hazzard announced the stoppage at 12:37 because
of a hip injury, specifically a hip pointer. Fighters often looked for an escape against
Argüello, and this incident only reinforced that notion. In a bigger fight on a bigger
stage, Noel's decision would have been crucified as cowardly. At this point in his
career, his loss served as a steppingstone that put Argüello in position to face Pryor
in a rematch. Three weeks earlier, in his next defense, Pryor was forced to fight
a WBA-appointed mandatory bout against South Korea's Sang-Hyun Kim on
ABC's *Wide World of Sports* telecast. To accentuate the WBA's ineptitude, Kim had
been catapulted to the No. 1 ranking after beating a winless fighter, Canes Ibarra.
Pryor, however, needed only three rather pathetic rounds to dispatch Kim.

"It was a ridiculous fight," said New Jersey promoter Dan Duva. "Pryor didn't
want to fight it, and I didn't want to promote it." Duva, however, stayed with
the absurd proceedings for the prizefight in order to ensure Pryor's loyalty for
the Argüello rematch.

"Condoning the fight is a different matter," said Steve Marantz, who covered
the bout for the *Boston Globe*. "ABC paid about $300,000 for Pryor-Kim, gave it
a nice ride on *Wide World of Sports*, and hung out the WBA initials like they were
some sort of sacred inscription. ABC can play innocent, and rationalize its role
by saying it is not in the matchmaking business, but that doesn't wash any more.

"ABC made the fight go. Without ABC money, it doesn't come off. Duva lost
$100,000 despite ABC backing, and did it begrudgingly, so that Pryor will stay
with him for his potential rematch with Alexis Arguello in July."

The WBA's antics continued as the organization looked to disrupt the possibility of the rematch unless it was fought on their terms. Thus, they forced
Argüello's hand by making him earn his ranking by fighting WBA-sanctioned
bouts before he got back in with Pryor. Pryor reacted to the organization's
appalling actions when he said, "They made a terrible mistake in dropping
Alexis out of the rankings."

Decades later, Walter Alvarez concurred: "It was all political and money.
Alexis's loyalty was to Jose Sulaiman and the WBC, a bitter rival of the WBA.
Pryor, however, held the WBA crown. The WBA would not rank Alexis auto-
matically since Pryor stopped him."

Even after the first Pryor-Argüello bout was named 1982's Fight of the Year by those in the boxing world, the WBA sent a veiled threat by refusing to sanction the title bout because it did not rank Argüello as a top-ten junior welterweight. No one bought the transparent threat. Instead, many in the industry saw it as typical of WBA shenanigans. The corrupt organization tried to trap Argüello and force him to fight its guy Miguel Montilla under the promotional banner of WBA crony Pepe Cordero.

"I laughed," Argüello told a reporter. "If you saw Aaron's fight with the Korean guy . . . he was supposed to be the No. 1 contender. If he's the No. 1 contender, then I'm Superman."

Not one to be controlled by the WBA organization, Argüello scoffed at its underhanded dealings, beat its lightweight challenger Claude Noel, and then signed to fight WBC junior welterweight champion Billy Costello, a move that frightened the WBA powers. They knew if Argüello lost, he disappears, and the organization would miss out on the enormous sanctioning fees on the Pryor rematch. Conversely, if he won and added another belt to his collection, the WBA realized it might be upstaged, and have to share the Pryor rematch with the WBC. They frowned on either scenario. The organization quickly reneged on its previous threat and capitulated, giving Argüello the necessary ranking. The rematch was originally set for July.

If Argüello was going to succeed in the rematch, he had to restore order in his camp. By all accounts, in preparing for the first bout, Argüello called the shots and ran and worked out when he pleased.

"[Between those fights] we had a lot of conversations, but Alexis didn't need to be motivated," said Dr. Eduardo Roman. "I didn't need to tell Alexis the mistakes he made. Sometimes we sat down and talked to him, but he was very intelligent about the things that he needed to do in the ring."

Cornerman Don Kahn, whose personality energized Argüello and the other camp members, recognized the inconsistencies during the first fight. He lamented, "I was in camp with [Eddie] Futch, but [Alexis] was not the same. There were so many things wrong. Maybe he thought he could have beaten Pryor, I don't know. At that point, Miller called the shots, and Roman didn't come too close anymore. In fact, I never saw him again. I remember talking to him on the phone, but I didn't like a lot of things that were going on."

The fascination with the innate power and genius of Alexis Argüello led thousands to obsess over him. He elicited charm and inexorable warmth wherever he went. He expressed his warmth through a secure handshake, always conscious of looking the individual—a fan, friend, or family member—directly in the eye to show that he cared. All his life, he exhibited that grace. People knew where they stood with him.

But a change occurred between the knockout loss to Pryor and the eventual rematch. Some fans questioned if the tightly wound Argüello was unraveling. Those same people who had showered Argüello with praise and affection began to question whether their hero's place was still in the ring. He was getting hit with the same type of punches that he had once landed on a regular basis.

"It's the punch that you don't see that kills you," he said. "It's the position of the punch that does it. I got hit a couple of times and my ass was on the floor. I was like, 'Man, I didn't see the punch, where did it fucking come from?' Those that you don't see are the ones that screw you up.

"A strong punch, he might cut you, but a precise punch is the one that makes your brain . . . that's what causes the KO, because when you make the brain twist it's the position of the punch."

Whether he still could position that punch the way he did in the 1970s was not clear to fight fans. Argüello once said that he was fighting for his people. Still exiled from his country, the "people" now represented the Miami residents who had grown to adore him over the last decade. They would flood Las Vegas that September in what many considered Argüello's swan song. Moreover, the Nicaraguans hadn't lost faith in their national hero. One day he would return home, and those same fans would greet him like an old friend.

Living by a strict lifestyle had separated Argüello from his counterparts. To him, his entire life was one big training session with little time to enjoy the rewards. Even if many doubted his commitment to the sport, Argüello professed that he still lived by the credo that "it was my responsibility [to not let the fame take over]. I made a promise on my knees. A man who doesn't put his money where his mouth is, is not a man." Rumors surfaced, however, that Argüello lacked that same discipline that had defined him earlier in his career. As he headed into the second (and final) showdown with Pryor and after a long-running dispute with the WBA, Argüello settled into a No. 2 ranking.

That May before the rematch, Pryor's camp negotiated a settlement with Buddy LaRosa that guaranteed the ex-manager one-third of the $2.25 million that Pryor and his wife were set to make. It had been reported that Pryor also had signed a three-year promotional deal with Stallone's promotional company Tiger Eye Ltd. in conjunction with Atlantic City's Sands Hotel. According to promoter Duva, however, the new partnership had no bearing on the rematch and would come into effect after the bout. The rematch was tentatively set for August 13, but after several changes, the date was confirmed for September 9, only ten months after the first bout. The legendary rematch in Las Vegas would be promoted as a pay-per-view extravaganza and televised on ON-TV, SelecTV, and countless closed-circuit establishments around the country.

Both men were expected to actively promote the fight. However, during the week of August 12, Argüello was a no-show at a press conference at the Los Angeles Athletic Club.

No one gave a legitimate reason why Argüello skipped the press conference. Argüello, who had been ignoring reporters in Las Vegas, also threatened to skip another press conference in New York until promoter Dan Duva sent word that there would be dire consequences of a bout cancellation if Argüello continued his antics. Argüello's actions were so atypical that for the first time in his career, people questioned if Argüello was acting out his frustration at playing second fiddle to Pryor.

"I think it was a bruised ego that Argüello was suffering from," said boxing writer Michael Marley. "For all the nice things that I have said about Argüello, all fighters have tremendous egos. Argüello also had that superego, and he was looked at as the opponent for the first time. He was a very sensitive guy . . . he could be moody. It was out of character for him to act like that. But you have to remember he always thought he was the man."

Pryor, who had fired trainer Richie Giachetti and would eventually settle on Emanuel Steward as his trainer for the rematch, turned the press conference tour into "Aaron's Time." Immediately, Pryor began to snatch the momentum with precisely timed one-liners and highlighted what many considered Argüello's abnormal behavior.

"Even in the press conferences before the bout, Pryor was there before Argüello both times," said Steward. "He looked at Alexis and then looked at his watch when he walked in to say, 'Alexis, don't you know what time it is?' Everyone started to laugh. He really welcomed the change."

The lead-in to the September rematch proved tumultuous for both fighters. On August 21, Pryor was admitted to the South Lake Tahoe hospital for a severe headache and blurred vision but was reported to be in "very stable" condition the next day. He was released later that evening. Pryor's training regimen suffered because of the hospital stint. Dr. John Harris allowed the fighter to continue running but discouraged any sparring sessions for three days. Pryor's personal life and career were in constant turmoil. Pryor was running through trainers, was still connected to Stallone through an ill-advised contract, and was possibly facing a separation from his wife, Theresa. To add to the turbulence in his life, Miller continued to bring up the bottle controversy from the first bout, which many believed only worked to motivate the junior welterweight champ. That was the main difference between the two fighters: while Pryor thrived on chaos, Argüello self-destructed from it.

Ironically, on July 1, 1983, the New York State Boxing Commission had revoked trainer Panama Lewis's boxing license permanently for his role in a glove-tampering affair. He had been convicted of removing the horsehair padding from his fighter Luis Resto's gloves minutes before a fight against Billy Collins Jr. The Nevada State Boxing Commission honored the decision of the New York State Commission. Reports surfaced that Pryor was without a trainer twelve days before the bout, and a warning was sent out to Pryor's camp to keep Panama Lewis away from the proceedings. As noted earlier, Pryor eventually opted for Kronk mainstay and trainer Emanuel Steward.

Steward had a history with the flamboyant champ. "I've known him since 1972," said Steward. "A wild kid, a maniac. I remember in 1973, his first national amateur tournament. . . . I guess he was in a room afterwards celebrating and he got out of control. The other guys put him in the hall, and there he was, pounding on my door, buck naked."

Back then, Steward represented Detroit's Kronk Gym and helped fashion it as the breeding ground for the toughest and most skilled boxers in the world. World-class fighters such as champs Hilmer Kenty, Milton McCrory, and the incomparable Thomas "Hit Man" Hearns all hailed from the prestigious gym. Ironically, Steward had been in Las Vegas to work in Hearns's corner, and when the bout was canceled, Pryor saw an opportunity to reconnect with a man he had worked with on the amateur circuit. Pryor was in no position to be finicky at this stage, and his familiarity with Steward became a major selling point. Hearns showed some animosity toward the decision, but he did not cause any friction regarding the brief trainer switch. Personally, Hearns could not have been thrilled that his trainer was trading corners with a fighter who had beaten him in the amateurs and lived such a reckless public lifestyle that was so different from what Hearns enjoyed. Yet, according to Steward, Hearns told him, "You have a big decision to make." Pryor's people approached Steward two weeks prior to the Argüello fight, and after careful consideration, Steward accepted the offer.

Realistically, a trainer and his fighter want to spend at least a month working together before a fight, but with Steward joining the camp so late, they did not have that grace period. During their initial encounter, Steward immediately took the confused champ to task. "When I saw him," Steward said, "I asked him, 'Why have you been boxing 10-rounders in the sun with no headgear?' He responded, 'I got to get in shape.' I think he was psychologically dependent on Panama Lewis and his tricks. I said, 'Let me be clear. If you get hit, I am not going to have that black bottle waiting for you. If you have a heart attack or whatever, I am not going to be here. I won't do anything unfairly or damaging. I am not going to jail. I am here to train you. Do you understand?' He looked me straight in the eyes, and said, 'I understand.'"

Steward continued, "I told him, 'You are not going to get hit a lot. You are not going to have that energy for you because your last trainer is in prison.' He looked at me and said, 'You the boss.'"

Pryor did not look at Steward's threats with contempt. He knew that he was out of options and had no choice but to abide by Steward's plan. The respected trainer went on to dissect his new charge and rapidly began to like what he saw. More specifically, Steward publicly wondered at the fighter's organized rage during his intense training sessions and his turbulent yet charismatic personality.

Slowly but surely Steward acquiesced to Pryor's freewheeling ways and simply sought to add focus and shape to his fighter's uncontrolled fury. First, he cut down the damaging sparring sessions to ten rounds and brought in some of his talented sparring partners. He also conducted a fashion makeover, encouraging Pryor to cut his hair, dispense with the signature Santa hat, and dress in business suits. Steward wanted the public to perceive the wild fighter differently both inside and outside the ring. As he later put it, Pryor had to "get rid of that street mentality."

During the interim leading to the fight, Steward, who also had trained Argüello for a previous Vegas fight, effectively orchestrated mind games. First, he craftily questioned Argüello's chances when he asked a reporter, "How do you defend against madness?" Then he went on to say that Pryor was "a raving wild man" during training and appeared "immune to any punishment during those fierce training sessions."

Still, Pryor looked to mend psychological wounds. All Steward had to do was listen.

"Aaron was very welcoming to me," Steward recalled. "A lot of guys when you start with them are like, 'I don't give a damn what you say.' But Aaron was very accepting of me. When I have a guy like Aaron, I like to spend time with them. You don't just sit a fighter at the gym or tell your fighter to 'do this or do that.' You have to get to know him. We sat down and talked about life and family.

I spent quality time with him. I developed a relationship with him. It helped that he had a lot of respect for the Kronk fighters back then. My guys were always well dressed. I think deep down he always wanted to be like those guys."

By engaging Pryor the man before analyzing his ring progression, Steward was able to win over the Cincinnati native. In contrast to the Pryor who used to stay out all night before bouts in amateur tournaments, this Pryor stayed home and evaluated his sparring sessions while playing with his five-year-old son.

Meanwhile, Argüello worked out in the Tropical Park warehouse in Miami before the bout and moved to Johnny Tocco's Gym when he landed in Las Vegas six weeks prior to the bout. Having avoided distractions from his previous camp in California, Argüello worked with trainer Lupe Sanchez this time around.

Again he had to contend with the announcement that his countrymen would not be able to view his possible return to glory. Daniel Ortega and the Sandinistas were not only going to black out the fight in Nicaragua, but they also forced censors to remove any mention of Argüello's name on the airwaves or in the Nicaraguan newspapers. Pryor's name was also disallowed because of his association with Argüello. Their move was a far cry from the last-minute plea (and payment) they had made to broadcast Argüello's lightweight title fight with Jim Watt in June 1981. Loyal fans planned trips to Vegas and nearby Honduras and Costa Rica in an attempt to see the historic bout. Nicaraguan radio personality Mario Diaz summarized the people's love for Argüello when he said, "One way or the other, a lot of Nicaraguans are going to see or hear this fight."

Ten months after the first Pryor bout, the boxing world pondered the damage Argüello had suffered and posed the inevitable question: How much skill, endurance, and passion for the sport does Argüello have left? Judging solely by the manner in which Pryor had outclassed Argüello in Miami, it was a fair question. It was one that the great fighter continually also asked himself. Although he was battered by Pryor, Argüello never took an excessive amount of punishment to that point, and, unlike his colleagues, he always stayed in fighting shape.

"I wasn't sure that I could do it, because I failed the first time to win my fourth crown. I had the gut feeling that I wanted to do it, that I could beat this guy," recalled Argüello years later, ". . . but before the first and second fight, I believed that I could beat him because there's something inside of each of us that challenges [that] aspect of our lives."

Despite Argüello's inner strength and unequaled thirst for redemption, he was not without his contradictions. As Dr. Roman observed, "[Alexis] normally trained well with the exception of one or two times. And he trained well for the second Pryor fight. He didn't go out with the ladies or to the dances. [I remember] the night before one fight he was running from me because I had to give him a needle. It was a shot the doctor gave me so he could get energy. But as I got it out, he started running. I was like, 'You take those big punches, and you are scared of this little needle?' One time I had to put alcohol on his cut and he turned and said, 'Don't put it on me.' And I told him, 'I haven't done it yet.' That's the way life is."

The media flooded Vegas that weekend. Between the rumors of an undisciplined Argüello and an erratic Pryor, there was enough speculation to feed the boxing scribes' interest. However, the hype did not come close to the buildup of the first fight. The rematch stirred the boxing world, but many writers who chose Argüello the first time around had witnessed a swinging of the pendulum.

"I didn't think his heart was in it," said Michael Marley, who covered the return bout for the *New York Post*. "Sometimes you have to read a fighter's mind because they are not always upfront with how they feel. They don't always disclose their prefight thoughts. I think that first fight took a lot out of him mentally. I think he thought that he would beat Pryor easily. It was the first time that he had to look himself in the mirror and say, 'This guy is better than me.' It was like he gave it his all and he finally met his match. I am not sure if he believed that he could beat Pryor after that first fight. I know Alexis was a guy who read books, had a limited education, and he was a pretty sharp guy. If he were some big dummy, he would say, 'Pryor got lucky, the hell with him.'"

Marley continued: "I remember walking around in the lobby and hearing Pryor's guys yelling, 'What time is it? It's Hawk time!' And it was Hawk time. Mentally, Alexis was not the same. He took some real punishment in the first fight, which was aptly named 'Ring of Fire.'"

Meanwhile, Pryor was dividing his energies among reports of a separation with his wife, vicious sparring sessions with Fernando "Mad Dog" Martinez, and an ongoing business conflict with Sylvester Stallone. Yet, the chaos, unending anxieties, and effusive distrust were staples of a Pryor camp. He needed them, seeming to thrive on the disarray. One reporter appropriately labeled him the "prince of confusion." Only Pryor could deflect the distractions and use them as motivation. By making himself the victim, Pryor used his fists to fight back. Argüello would feel the brunt of the incensed champ's anger.

Meanwhile, Argüello also felt disrespected by the press, but he internalized the emotion. He was not willing to vocalize his discontent throughout his career. A day before the bout, the philosophical Argüello, with Loretto by his side, expressed his need to be accepted when he explained, "Boxing is a beautiful sport. This is my chance to be somebody in life."

Having worked the previous camp in Palm Springs, trainer and personal friend Kahn felt that Argüello was much more focused this time around but that he would need a near miracle to beat a twenty-seven-year old machine like Pryor.

"I was so mad after that [first] fight. I walked into the dressing room, took a shower, got dressed. Everyone was crying. I cursed everyone," Kahn recalled. "I told him the way it was. Alexis was laying down on the bench. That's why I told him not to take that fight. I went to Loretto, who was crying, and told her not to cry, but she should have cooled down with Alexis before the fight. Everyone told him he would beat Pryor in two or three rounds. And these were boxing people. I said, 'Don't listen to that shit.'"

Main Events and Dan Duva promoted the rematch, which was held at Caesars Palace in Las Vegas on September 9, 1983. Duva estimated the fight would be seen in 111 pay television systems, including 600,000 seats for 120 closed-circuit sites in 105 cities. Pryor would earn $1.75 million (divided among several law-suits) to Argüello's $1.4 million purse. Nearly 10,000 fans filled the arena. Argüello weighed 139 pounds, while Pryor topped the scales at the 140-pound limit. Bettors declared Pryor an 11–5 favorite, a significant turn from the first fight in which Argüello had been a 2–1 favorite. The crowd sided with the challenger as Pryor again took a backseat to the charming Latin king.

Steward's caustic words stirred the affair when he commented, "That beating [from the first bout] is still lying back in the closet. When something happens that closet door will open."

Nicaraguans, many of whom would find a way to view the bout, knew that Argüello still had the capacity to beat Pryor, even if the odds were stacked against him now. *Boxing Illustrated* journalist Randy Gordon encapsulated what the press thought when he said, "Most felt Pryor would win. Most wanted Argüello to win." Another publication, *International Boxing*, suggested that Pryor would "end the dream permanently," with a more brutal ending than the first bout.

"Still in the rematch, the journalists and the United States reporters thought Alexis still had a big chance to beat him," said journalist Edgar Tijerino. "All the reporters thought it would be a close fight; in the first he was a favorite, but now it was almost even. Nicaraguans thought he was going to win, but then toward the end of the fight, they lost faith."

Having experienced both camps, trainer Don Kahn felt that his Argüello had lost something along the way. "When we trained for the rematch, he didn't love boxing like he used to. At the time he was already thirty-one years old," said Kahn. "He did what he had to do in order to get in shape. For the second fight, we trained in Miami. We didn't go anywhere to train."

With the fight approaching, Steward wrapped Pryor's hands in an upstairs room in Caesars Palace, a move that departed from the usual wrapping procedures in the fighters' dressing rooms. Before the fighters met in the middle of the ring, Steward unleashed his final bag of tricks. As the energetic champ circled the ring, the soft-spoken trainer lashed out.

"I went over to Aaron while he was in the ring before the fight and told him, 'Do you hear that crowd? They are all here for Alexis,'" said Steward. "'He is still the darling after that first fight. He has all the popularity. The only thing you have right now is this towel. You are just a little poor ghetto kid with nothing. He's here to take away everything that you have. He wants to stop you from making a living, take away your family.' He was actually crying before the bell, tears were coming down his face."

Conversely, the moment he woke up the morning after the first fight, Argüello told Miller, "I owe Pryor something, and I want to pay him back." Whether he was physically capable would be evident after the first couple rounds of the fight dubbed "The Rematch."

After examining all the Miami Boxing Commission's errors during and after the first bout, there was room for caution this time around. Even after all the scrutiny, the fight card still got off to a rough start when singer Robert Guillaume forgot some of the words to the national anthem.

To start the rematch, Argüello nailed Pryor with a left hook. However, seconds later his bravado earned him a standing eight count. Argüello went down from a glancing straight right that revealed his carelessness rather than Pryor's power. Argüello pushed himself up quickly, and referee Richard Steele finished off his eight count. Yearning to end the fight in quick fashion, Pryor attacked Argüello with glancing head shots rather than moving to the body. The round ended with Pryor nailing his opponent with straight rights.

"[Pryor] was so wound up that he ran over to Alexis and dropped him," said Steward, replaying the round in his head. "That's what I wanted him to do. I wanted him to give Alexis flashbacks from the first fight, and not let him get into a rhythm. So I needed to get him wired up early. Psychologically, I didn't think he got over the beating from the first fight. He really got beaten up in that fight. Between the first and second fights, his confidence was not right. Alexis didn't have the same confidence that he'd had the last time around."

If fans wanted to see Argüello use head and lateral movement, he refused to comply. In fact, both fighters were content to go toe-to-toe in that second round, with Pryor shooting lead rights into Argüello's face over his careless guard. Too many wars and late-round stoppages had left Argüello a slower, more deliberate version of his old self. As Pryor ambushed him without repercussion, it was clear that the belt would only change hands if the young champ committed a colossal error. Pryor and Steward's plan was to force a faster fight, never allowing Argüello to set on his punches, and the strategy was working beautifully in those early rounds. Of course, there were minor setbacks.

As the round receded, Pryor committed an error and walked into a right cross that hurt him badly. It marked the first time in two fights that Pryor was backing up. He stumbled to the corner to prevent further damage, but Argüello wasn't finished. Argüello took the initiative and began to cut off the ring to maximize his strength. Two uppercuts to the body in a ten-punch combination gave Argüello an advantage. Struggling to create some space, Pryor absorbed an uppercut and a blinding straight right. Argüello finally landed an explosive right hand and followed it with a sharp left hook. A heady Pryor collapsed into the Nicaraguan's arms to halt the onslaught. It was the first clear-cut round that Argüello won in the two fights. Pryor, a glutton for punishment, only smiled and headed back to his corner.

"I told Pryor that he was fighting a beautiful fight. Alexis was having trouble and wasn't making good pivots," said Steward. "See, Aaron was hitting him from angles. At one point, I told Aaron he was 'relaxing a bit and he needed to get back to being alert.' But he was fighting a good fight."

Argüello was back on the defensive in the third round. Springing from his stance, Pryor cleanly nailed Argüello without resistance in the fourth round. Pryor ignited the second knockdown flurry first with a straight right mixed with a left hook. The telltale punch was a chaotic but brilliant left hook. Argüello went down, for the second time, from its force and was up by the count of three. Unfortunately for Argüello, Pryor had ample time to load up again.

He tore into Argüello, who'd obviously aged. A fighter shows his age through how hesitant he is in each move, each thought. This version of Argüello carefully considered each punch, and he no longer exhibited that natural feel of a true boxer. Yet, he quickly avoided a third knockdown by using his right foot for leverage. Any normal fighter would have been clinching desperately at this point. Argüello fought on, however, and absorbed more punishment.

Depression set in for the Argüello followers. There is always that one moment in a fighter's career where he falls for the last time. Even the casual fan understood the inevitable truth after the second knockdown: Argüello had nothing left.

In the same round, Argüello spread his legs to avoid yet another knockdown; Pryor sneaked a big left hook through his guard. Argüello somehow ended the round on his feet, punching away. The men began to crowd each other in the fifth round, and Pryor skillfully countered Argüello's reach. Pryor threw five-punch flurries and blocked any offerings with the outside of his left glove, while Argüello was reduced to desperately searching for one big punch. This pattern continued through the sixth round.

Aggressive and determined, Argüello quickened the pace at the outset of the seventh round. At the end of the round, Argüello landed a right hand just as Pryor was throwing his. Pryor quickly turned his body as a shield from another punch. Pryor ended the round in rapid retreat.

If Argüello pressed the action in round seven, a stirred Pryor charged at his opponent and unloaded ten to twelve punches at the bell to open the eighth round. Some punches landed cleanly, but Pryor also periodically left himself open for a short counter left hook. Pryor covered up and stepped back, giving the only hint that he was hurt.

They stood in front of each other and brawled again. It had to be demoralizing for Argüello to see Pryor so brazen and cocksure. This man doesn't feel pain like normal people, Argüello may have thought. Most men wouldn't have lasted a round with Argüello. Argüello landed a right to the head and followed with a left hook to the neck that put Pryor in a desperate state. Pryor searched for an escape route, but then he instead relished his crouch stance against the ropes. Pryor absorbed a low blow but didn't acknowledge it. Referee Richard Steele walked in, separated the fighters, and took a point away from Argüello for the illegal punch. The move drew criticism from those who suggested that Steele did not give the necessary warning. The move certainly represented Argüello's final shot at redemption, but it might have saved Pryor. The low blow provided Pryor a breather as he reverted to his dancing ways and faked a mini-bolo punch to close out the round.

The fighters spent the first forty-five seconds of the ninth round engaging on the inside, as Pryor took the initiative. For the first time, Pryor concentrated on the body and then moved to the head in a tactic that might have assisted him earlier. Blood seeped into Argüello's damaged left eye, as he completely ceded to Pryor's offensive output. Pryor forced his will on a beaten Argüello in what proved to be the tenth and final round. First, landing a jolting right cross and then a short but effective left hook, Pryor put Argüello in backpedal mode.

"No one that I remembered picked Argüello to win the rematch," said journalist Steve Farhood. "Argüello gave everything he had and got knocked out violently. Pryor was on an all-time high. Argüello had flashes of brilliance, but there was never a point where you thought he could win the fight. Pryor had that psychological edge. If the first fight was shocking, the second was predictable."

That predictability set in as the seconds ticked away in the final round. Pryor walked down Argüello, positioning him against the ropes. Pryor maneuvered his way inside with a hook and a jab. Argüello stopped punching; he couldn't lift his arms. A vicious uppercut pushed Argüello's mouthpiece to the other side of his cheek. Pryor landed one more uppercut as he watched a legend crumble to his knees. It marked the end of a man, an era, and a career as Argüello sat Indian style and looked ahead indifferently. As Steele counted, Argüello stared through the people who loved him. A blank-faced, hollow-eyed Argüello, hands on his knees as Steele reached the final count, came to the realization that his career was over.

At 1:48 of the tenth round, Argüello had mentally moved on. Argüello had once said that what Pryor did to him in the first fight would stay with him forever. And as Pryor's handlers could be heard asking, "What time is it?" the statement was confirmed. Argüello had no response as Pryor expedited his rival's rocky path into retirement. Instead of waking up from a near coma as he had after their first battle, Argüello balanced himself, walked back to the corner, and prepared to respond to a host of reporters wondering what his next step would be.

For a man to have given himself completely to a sport, many felt the later whispers of his being a coward and quitter were unfounded.

"Make no mistake about it, he quit. He could have gotten up," said Steve Farhood. "But I remember going back to the office and arguing with staff whether it was OK to quit. I said that you can't judge him by one fight. He earned a pass on that fight. He was beaten psychologically by Pryor, and nothing short of a baseball bat would have beaten him. So I said it was justifiable, and he was owed that one. That fight broke his heart and took the life out of him.

Farhood continued: "We viewed him as finished and wondered if there was a point of going on with his career. If he did come back it would just be another boxing comeback. It was very sad. I remember him crying at the post-fight press conference. He was crying out of frustration. It made me want to cry. It was an example of how brutally unsentimental boxing is. Here is a fighter who can't beat another man and he knows it. And there was nothing he could do about it."

Ringside reporter Michael Marley considered the stark reality that Argüello faced. "Now the party was over. For a lot of fighters it gets to the point where they ask themselves, 'What can I milk out of this?' Basically that was what it became for Argüello. I don't think the reality of the first fight arrived until the end of the second fight. This time there was no question about the fight, and now Argüello had a new reality . . . Pryor was stronger, faster, and younger. He hit just as hard as Argüello. I am not saying that Argüello was as Leonard used to say 'a punched ticket,' but I came away thinking that if they fought seven times, Pryor would win each time."

Journalist Ed Schuyler Jr., who also felt an affinity for the great fighter, added, "I saw a change in Argüello after the first couple rounds of the rematch. The change was 'I can't beat this guy.' He could have gotten up, but nobody held it against him. I think he was thinking, 'What was the point? Should I get myself killed in here?' He didn't quit, he just accepted the inevitable.

"Oh, and he was taking a beating again. And this time he didn't apply one to Pryor. I don't recall any boos at the end of the fight, just acceptance. It was clear that he couldn't win the fight."

Going into the final round, Pryor was ahead on all three scorecards. Argüello had to accept the fact that there was one man on earth he would never conquer. Although he voiced his admiration for Pryor, he would never be able to accept it.

"Alexis met my challenge today," said Pryor. "It was the best condition I ever had. I couldn't have done it without Emanuel Steward. He came into my camp and gave me a lot of confidence."

Argüello walked over and they embraced.

"It's over. God bless my good friend Pryor; he's a good man. I wish him the best," said Argüello as he greeted the champ.

"The left hook is silent now?" asked a reporter.

"The right hand too," Argüello responded. "I did my best. I want to say good-bye to the boxing business."

That night Argüello acknowledged, "The carnival is over," and he attempted to move on. Argüello's decision to retire was well received, especially after how the rematch ended. He had made nearly $5 million for the two bouts, so he was financially secure. Decades later when Argüello looked back on his career, he had no reservations about how the fight ended.

"Accept certain things?" he asked. "It's a fact, and it's something that I can't avoid. It's hard to accept, but it's good to accept. I did it with grace and just accepted that the guy beat me. Even though I lost the first fight, I didn't think he could beat me again. You could see that. Even though I did my best, in the tenth round, I accepted it, right there. I said, 'This is too much. I won't take it.

I'll just sit down and watch Richard Steele count to ten.' I didn't have the strength or the eyesight. When he hit me, he was so quick. He was throwing his punches, so that I didn't see them. When I was a boxer, I felt that I had all the skills to face him and win, but after that second fight I realized that I was too old for that. That was the difference."

While legions of fight fans still look back to those battles with Pryor with nostalgia, the bouts were the only two real blemishes of a Hall of Fame career. True fight fans understand that Argüello's legacy was cemented years before his legendary fights with Pryor.

"It happens to all of us, but you never notice because there are other people who get close to you. As long as you are an attraction to the media, the leeches are always going to be there," recalled Argüello. "After the Pryor fight, I fought a couple more fights and there were people there because there is always some-body who believes you can do it. The people were still there until I retired against Scott Walker, but it wasn't the same. It's normal because you don't make the same money, and money attracts a lot of people."

Throughout his life Argüello served his people and his family in a sport that couldn't pay him back. While the erratic Pryor entertained ideas of joining the ministry and arranging a bout with Ray "Boom Boom" Mancini, Argüello had to learn how to live again, this time without the constant cheers, the smell of the gym, and the paychecks rolling in after bouts. The moment a fighter decides to leave the ring, he's flooded with all the memories.

"[All great fighters] have to go through the toughest thing, that adversity within. Each is born with a natural instinct. We weren't born as fighters. For me it was meant to be. I was born as a star," said Argüello.

At times, the star dimmed. More devastating than the loss to Pryor was the damage Argüello had inflicted on his family. His wife Loretto did not ignore his earlier, and quite public, transgressions. Few knew the sacrifices that Loretto had made to establish a functional family environment. She raised A. J. and Roberto and ensured that they received a good education. She provided guidance and support during training sessions and developed strong relationships with people from Argüello's tight inner circle. From all accounts, she was Argüello's backbone.

Many wondered how Argüello would recover from what many considered his final bout.

"Alexis gave up," said Bill Miller. "Somehow he made up his mind. By that time, when you are mentally out of it, you're out of it. He said to himself, 'I am not going to get up.' And I agreed with him."

ROUND 12

Downfall

So I tried to replace one thing with another. I still feel empty.
—ALEXIS ARGÜELLO

With boxing on the back burner, Argüello looked for other pursuits to fill his time. War seemed a viable option.

In October 1983, five weeks after his retirement, Argüello sneaked into Nicaragua with the help of journalist Tomás Regalado and manager Eduardo Roman. Argüello described his reason for returning as a moral decision; others called his risky trip a desperate, impulsive plea for help. With no more daily routine or a fight in the near future, Argüello searched for an identity. Fighting, in any fashion, previously had fulfilled that purpose. He traveled across the border of Costa Rica and into the southern mountains of Nicaragua to join "Commander Zero," or Edén Pastora, and his four thousand troops who were strategizing against the communist regime.

Pastora, a handsome and charismatic revolutionary full of bombast, had an interesting backstory. An established Sandinista guerrilla, he had orchestrated the successful raid and capture of the National Palace with second-in-command Dora María Téllez in August 1978. That sensational raid represented the first violent insurrection that the Nicaraguan communist movement initiated. The guerrillas held more than fifteen hundred officials hostage and finally garnered the attention they had desired.

Edén Pastora, nicknamed "Indio" for his bohemian lifestyle, had shared command of the Southern Front, and the world recognized him after he boldly yanked off his ski mask during his escape. Because of his fame, the Ortega brothers, Daniel and Humberto, alienated the flamboyant leader. In *Unfinished Revolution: Daniel Ortega and Nicaragua's Struggle for Liberation*, Kenneth Morris writes, "The Ortega brothers simply did not trust Pastora with military victory, and therefore denied it to him. Their mistrust was warranted. On the eve of victory, Pastora contacted the United States and urged them to persuade Somoza to withdraw the National Guard from the south so that he, Pastora, would claim victory and deny it to the 'radicals.'"

Pastora's inexorable need for attention, combined with his renegade style, widened the chasm between him and the Terceristas. At one point, rumors spread of an FSLN-sponsored assassination attempt on his life. Ortega granted Pastora a position in the Ministry of the Interior so he could be carefully monitored. Nevertheless, Pastora switched allegiances by 1982.

At the eventual meeting with Argüello, his friend, Dr. Roman, and Regalado, Pastora was too astute to believe that Argüello physically would help his men defeat Ortega and the Sandinistas, even with U.S. support. The stubborn but politically naive Argüello wanted to join the soldiers on the front line of the Contra war that had raged since the 1970s, but Pastora rebuffed him, stating that his place "was in the trenches of international politics." Pastora and Roman knew each other from college, and they felt they had to protect Argüello, who would one day return to his beloved country, at all costs.

"For Pastora, Alexis was a good attraction for the people of Nicaragua—you know, the champ fighting beside him. It was a political move more than anything else," Roman confirmed. "The second time we were there, I left after five days, and Alexis stayed. He went back with some peasants. . . . But he never told me anything about that. We spent some days there, but there was no fighting. There were some airplanes in the clouds, but they didn't see us."

In 1984, the Sandinistas held their first election since they toppled the Somoza regime in 1979. It also marked the first time that the United States did not monitor the Nicaraguan elections since 1928. Daniel Ortega won easily, earning 67 percent of the votes. The result drew the ire of newly elected U.S. president Ronald Reagan, who was clearly concerned about the illicit ties among the Sandinistas, the Cubans, and the Soviets.

By October 18, 1984, a headline in the *Los Angeles Times* read, "Alexis Argüello Is Now a Rebel with a Cause." The Associated Press account reported that Edén Pastora fiercely opposed the unrealistic move to have Argüello fight. Instead, Pastora told him to "go to Miami, to Latin America to talk about our way of thinking, our needs, to people who don't know us."

Pastora continued to relish the national attention that the handsome champ's pro-war rhetoric attracted. The commander dramatically called Argüello's influence a "mortal blow, a jab to the liver," of the Sandinista government. Despite Pastora's infectious optimism, however, he was not without his flaws.

"My personal opinion of Pastora was that he had the balls of a lion, but his brain didn't match his bravery," said acclaimed Cuban author Enrique Encinosa. "He was a decent field guerrilla officer, who would do suicidal things. And he even helped bring down the government when he was with the Sandinistas. But as a political strategist and analytical thinker, he was a country bumpkin. As a military commander, he also was limited in supply and organization.

"Alexis and I talked about his time with the Contras. There was no way they were going to risk an icon. If you were a military commander, and they sent you Alexis Argüello, you would put him in a place with no danger, where the Sandinistas were like two days away. You don't put him on the next patrol; he was worth much more as a symbol."

Argüello returned to Miami, but he would visit the camps three more times before making his final decision. The press reported that by mid-December Argüello had ignored the precautions and planned to join Edén Pastora and the Contras that Christmas. Argüello's developing reputation for instability, detachment from reality, and political naïveté were enhanced in his melodramatic pronouncement that he was "looking forward even to being killed one day." Few Nicaraguans, however, were concerned that their hero would truly risk his life in the war. Perhaps, even after years of detachment, Argüello's people knew him better than he knew himself.

"He never fought for the Contras. Alexis didn't have a strong relationship with the Contras. The Contras had established a base in Miami to raise funds and support; like a lot of people they used Alexis to recruit people to their cause. But he had a very short-lived career with the Contras during this time period," said former judge Sergio Quintero. "Pastora was a subject who would go with the wind and was weak psychologically. He left the Sandinistas because he wasn't appointed one of the nine members of the leadership, and then they appointed him vice-minister instead of minister. Thus, he was disillusioned and felt as though he wasn't being included. He didn't leave because he was ideologically opposed, but rather because he felt slighted by them."

Argüello, at the time, was no longer the heroic exiled figure releasing those crackling right hands to thrill opponents or the charming gentleman of the ring who could do no wrong. Now, he was acting as a selfish, easily led caricature who was still searching for glory, but he ultimately would not find it in war. He attributed his decision to support the Contras to his need to stop the communist regime from destroying his country, but his wife and children suffered because of his actions.

"I am losing my wife Loretto because she doesn't want me to do this," said Argüello told a reporter. "But I don't care. Now I'm trying to do something for my country. They want me to be their representative."

Argüello was attempting to balance the gaping hole left by his boxing career with his love for his people. Roman helped get Argüello stationed in an area controlled by the Democratic Revolutionary Alliance (ARDE). Using the publicity surrounding his client, manager Eduardo Roman rerouted Argüello from Costa Rica to the ARDE territory. Two months after Argüello joined the ARDE guerrillas, reportedly Pastora pleaded for assistance because of the influx of volunteers and the lack of food, resources, and weapons.

Regarding Argüello's time with Pastora, journalist Edgar Tijerino said, "It was a way that he could protest and set his mind. The Contras used him as a public figure. It was important to them that they were able to use a figure like Alexis."

Not long after he arrived in the mountains, Argüello became disenchanted with the war's contradictions. He had gone to Nicaragua for his people, but, according to Argüello, Pastora and members of his directorate lived an elaborate lifestyle while showing a lack of genuine concern for the people's welfare.

Roman addressed Argüello's critique of Pastora: "When Alexis talked about Pastora going around holding a lot of money, I think he didn't understand. He had a very naive way of looking at that situation," said Roman. "What I mean [is], Pastora didn't have a bank. It was a very naive type of criticism."

Argüello acknowledged that he once was involved in an ambush in San Juan del Norte, and a friend of his died, but most of his time with the Contras was spent anxiously anticipating battle and finding ways to pass the time. Ironically, with the exception of the brief gun battle, which Roman did not recall, the war was not unlike Argüello's existence in Miami, where he had searched desperately for something to stir him. Argüello spent more time waiting than fighting. Instead of dedicating himself to the struggle as his compatriots did, Argüello found an escape route in war. He hoped that surviving in the trenches with Nicaraguan comrades would bring him a similar high to that of the boxing ring. Yet, the entire war episode represented another venture that Argüello blindly entered without considering the alternatives. Argüello clearly felt uncomfortable in his own skin no matter where he was.

"Alexis wanted to fight, and he even went to the training camp," said Roman. "He thought that he was going to take a weapon and going to fight. That is not how things worked. Besides that, there was not a real, organized movement."

By March 1985, Argüello had returned home to Miami, primed for a boxing comeback and to reconcile with Loretto. Most of his money from his boxing purses and sponsors was tied up in Alexicore Inc., his corporation located on LeJeune Road in Miami, which was run by Roman. Although the fighter earned nearly $5 million for the Pryor bouts, he had not handled it wisely. His agent, Bill Miller, suggested that his fighter was "floating" through life, referring to Argüello's inability to handle his finances, his unsuccessful stint in Nicaragua, and his fragmented family life. Although Argüello stressed how much he missed the sport, his sentiment lacked conviction. It appeared to be more of a knee-jerk reaction to the tedium of daily life. It was also during this time that reports of his drug use had become public knowledge in boxing circles.

Argüello vividly recalled that devastating time when he lost his way and slipped deep into a personal abyss. "I remember because I was missing what I did so good," he said. "So I tried to replace one thing with another. I still feel empty. That part of my life is still attached to me. Even family can't replace it. It's just different. It's something outside of you."

If the reckless Contra affair crystallized Argüello's delusional state, the revelation of a suicide attempt in front of his son confirmed what many thought: Argüello was completely devoid of hope or rational thoughts. One afternoon a year earlier in 1984, during his hiatus from the ring, Argüello and his son A. J. went out on his boat off the Miami coast. While at sea, Argüello contemplated ending his life with a loaded gun. His sobs collided with A. J. crying, "Don't do it, Dad! Don't do it." Conceding to his son's pleas, Argüello put down his gun. Years later, A. J. claimed there was no truth to the story and it was merely an embellishment by his father. Whether the story was valid or embellished, Argüello was desperate.

Argüello's comeback originated in February 1985, when Argüello contacted Bill Miller and asked him to help organize his finances after Roman had left Miami and returned to Nicaragua. Miller would not sign on until Argüello proved that his desire to fight was more than a whim to get back in the ring. Miller put Argüello through an intensive workout, which he passed easily, and then he brought in a physician to conduct blood tests, a CAT scan, and an electroencephalogram (EEG) on his brain.

"[Alexis] called me desperate. He just said, 'I am ready to come back.' I asked him if he was sure he was ready. He said, 'I am in,'" Miller recalled years later from his home in New Hampshire. "He first called and said he wanted to be a promoter, but I told him, 'You can't spell promoter.' Then he told me to come back to Miami to help him out. That's when he told me he wanted to return. It was a cry for help.

"My wife and I went to Miami for a visit and the first thing I did was to kick out all the Contras in his office who were just taking advantage of him. It wasn't a problem with Alexis, but the people around him. My wife went through his closet and took all the mail. There were liens, everything; Roman didn't even pay his taxes. So we spread the papers on the floor, organized everything, and made a schedule to pay the IRS and his creditors."

"When I asked him about going after Roman, Alexis said, 'No, I love him too much.' I told him he should strangle him. But Roman was long gone, and there was no way to find him. That was the last time I saw him."

"It's true," added Don Kahn. "The IRS put a lien on Alexis' properties. He dealt with the money and then he was gone. I even asked Alexis, 'Why don't you get a CPA?' He said, 'No I trust Roman too much.' He would not check the books. He just wouldn't do it, so he had to go back to boxing. At the time, he had a couple of buildings and a travel agency."

Roman responded to the charges by stating that Alexis spent and lost all of that money on his own. "I tried to put money in places where he wouldn't touch it," he told a reporter. "Alexis didn't lose all that money—he spent it."

The chasm between Argüello and Roman became a difficult one to tackle. First, when Loretto came on the scene in the late-1970s, she began to oversee her husband's finances. Thus, Roman no longer had complete control of Argüello's finances. Second, Argüello's life had started to spin out of control, he showed no ability to manage his depleted finances, and Roman didn't stick around to reconcile the problem like he always had for a person he considered a "son." Third, Roman may be at fault for not following through with Argüello's taxes, but it is difficult to believe that he stole from Argüello. Those close to Argüello refute such accusations. Ironically, the financial issue revealed more about their unbreakable bond than any differences they had. So when the conflict faded, friendship prevailed. Roman was the man who gave Argüello a chance, extolled the virtues of education, taught him how to act, and now his disappearance had created a rift. Yet, it was through this type of adversity that people learned about Argüello's true character. He viewed Roman as the father he never had, and even a financial issue of this magnitude could not disrupt that friendship. As sensitive as Argüello was, he was just as loyal when it came to Roman. "When I left Miami, I let him know I was leaving. I was in touch with him all the time. We never lost touch," said Roman in 2012. "I went back to my position at ENALUF as the vice president of finance because they still considered me even after I worked in boxing in the United States." Even if he believed that Roman mismanaged the money, he always believed he had the capacity to make another fortune. Yet, there was only one Roman. He would have never risked it.

"Alexis was a bit strange. He didn't give his friendship up to everybody. He kept people at a distance. He ended up trusting the one man he shouldn't trust—Roman. In fact, after me and Roman, he never trusted anyone like that again," said Kahn. "Later Alexis saw him again in Nicaragua, and he forgot all about it. That's just the way he was."

Nothing was ever proven, and the Nicaraguan public never fully condemned Roman. Although Tijerino admitted that there was suspicion about the swiftness with which Roman disappeared back to Nicaragua, the truth never surfaced. More importantly, the relationship never suffered.

With $600,000 of debt looming over his head and one last itch to scratch, Argüello announced his return to boxing and hired financial advisers Landon Thorne and John Spittler to organize his finances. He agreed to fight fringe lightweight contender Howard Davis Jr. on August 21, 1985. Now that Roman was no longer on Argüello's radar, the fighter relied on Miller to do all his negotiating inside the ring, as well as life counseling outside of it. Argüello had to liquidate all of his belongings—his four houses and an apartment in the Miami area, his yacht, his BMW, his Mercedes, and the houses he purchased for his mother and brother—and would apply the fight purse to finish paying off his debt. He was able to keep his beloved Rolex watch, but he had to discontinue his role in the popular Miller Lite beer commercials, which that had netted him $25,000, after announcing his return to the ring.

Despite his financial losses, Argüello exhibited a renewed vigor as he envisioned his return to his boxing roots. Argüello was not alone in his dire economic state, as his Latin colleagues and fellow 1970s icons Wilfred Benítez and Roberto Durán both had fallen prey to a host of leeches, bad investments, and their own reluctance to save any of their earnings from the ring.

As Argüello strategized his historic return, which was temporarily slated for Madison Square Garden, the press reported Pryor's downfall, complete with accounts of his party binges and his refusal to train consistently. He had divorced his wife, Theresa, and had a falling out with his bodyguard, but never had he been so close to self-destructing. In the fall of 1985, Pryor, who felt victimized by friends, family, and business associates throughout his short career, was living a vagabond lifestyle in Liberty City, Miami. Sources described seeing Pryor entering and leaving free-base crack houses and handing out hundred-dollar bills to random people in the streets. The man who was once characterized as having an infectious spirit and spontaneous aggression had disappeared. Pryor was a gaunt, disheveled caricature of his former self. The ring, the one place where no one could touch him, was miles away. "Hawk Time!" was over. What so many people suspected had finally surfaced that September. Pryor no longer denied his drug problem, and boxing people began to voice their disapproval.

"Whether he's broke now or broke in six months, it's just a matter of time," said Top Rank's Bob Arum. "Until he undergoes a radical transformation, he's through boxing."

When interviewed by Miami Herald reporters, Pryor sat under a tree and admitted his flaws: "I don't know if I will be around to watch the script. My hardest fight is [with] myself. . . . It's no fun when you're on top, enjoying your own success. I always feel like someone is watching me. In Liberty City, they accept me with no money and no jewelry."

Pryor, trailing off, added: "God bless me if I can find a friend. I haven't found one yet."

Ironically, the one fight that was supposed to have brought both men financial stability and personal fulfillment had left them both decimated. Pryor couldn't handle the limelight; Argüello couldn't stay away from it. The megafight that brought so much joy to so many people indirectly left both fighters lonely and confused about the paths of their lives. It had only been a couple years since Pryor had rebelled against public sentiment and sent Argüello into retirement, only a couple years since Pryor was a superstar, mentioned in the same catalog as the all-time greats. But addiction sucked the fighting spirit from his body. Now he was exhausted and needed a miracle.

"I didn't see him for a while after the fight. I ran into him in Detroit, and it was right after he was in a clinic or jail. He had turned around and completely changed. . . ," former trainer Emanuel Steward said years later. "I was proud about what I was able to do with him during such a short period of time. I had him fine-tuned, boxing well, and he even made such a character change. If I had stayed with him, he might have never gotten back involved with drugs."

Although Arum and other promoters in the press denigrated Pryor, Steward looked at the boxer's tragedy from a different angle: "It has to do with environments. . . . It was a hotbed; you became what you were associated with. It was a Panama Lewis–type camp. When you have that poverty type of situation, you become what you are associated with. Aaron totally changed with me. But you often go back to doing the same habits, to the person who you were when you come from that type of environment."

Boxing was experiencing a post-Argüello hangover. Ali, Leonard, and Durán were either retired or taking sabbaticals, and critics began criticizing the lack of safety measures for boxers. The cable and pay-per-view television movement had replaced the ubiquitous Saturday afternoon matches. The sport needed Argüello, but in what condition would it receive him?

After passing all the necessary medical tests to start fighting again, Argüello, then age thirty-three, agreed to a three-year contract with Miller on July 4. Argüello regained his discipline in New Hampshire, near Bill Miller's home. He did the majority of his training at the headquarters of the Aavid Engineering Factory in Concord, New Hampshire, against little-known sparring partners such as David Savage and Emilio Rabago. In the morning, Argüello did his runs on the Laconia Country Club's golf course. In an interview, Argüello, who loved the secluded training camp, revealed that he looked to the ring to save him from himself: "I don't trust myself. I have accepted I am a weak person. When I am boxing, I have no right to screw off."

For the comeback journey, Argüello returned without the man who brought him to prominence, Eduardo Roman, and re-enlisted the man whom he blamed [and then apologized to] for his downfall, trainer Eddie Futch. He was back for money, not the fame. To test his wares, Argüello participated in a six-round exhibition bout against Manny Madeira in the Lowell Memorial Auditorium in Lowell, Massachusetts on August 28.

"Futch was terrific, a very good boxing man," said Miller. "He would do anything for Alexis. [As for the money problems] Alexis never complained about the money. The only thing that bothered him was dealing with the IRS."

For a professional athlete, idle time is worse than any opponent. Argüello was not returning to the ring because he missed the camaraderie or a feeling of accomplishment; instead, he returned to a familiar routine to save himself from a life of monotony where he was forced to deal with his inner demons. The ring represented a protective enclave; unfortunately, it was the only space where he could trust himself. The low-key Miller encapsulated Argüello's struggle when he said, "You can only go fishing so much."

Meanwhile, the bout with Howard Davis Jr. fell through, and Argüello's comeback bid was put on hold because of TV scheduling conflicts. Argüello had linked with Sam Glass and Tiffany Promotions for the bout, who copromoted the fight with S Productions of Eugene, Oregon. Andy Nance was originally named as his opponent, but Argüello's camp would settle on a bout with lightly regarded Oregonian Pat "Lightfoot" Jefferson (24-5, eight knockouts) in

Anchorage on October 25, 1985. Jefferson replaced Nance after the fighter was cut during a sparring session. Argüello arrived there weeks ahead of time to adapt to the climate and the surroundings. The three-time champ had begun to steel his body for the pounding and arrived in Anchorage mentally and physically prepared for the junior welterweight battle.

Argüello (74-7) stood to earn $100,000 for the bout. He weighed in at 141½ pounds, while Pat Jefferson entered at 143¾. Jefferson was ranked seventh by the lightly regarded USBA. The bout marked the first time Argüello stepped into a ring for a professional bout since the fateful Pryor rematch on September 9, 1983.

After a two-year layoff, few people expected to see the vintage Argüello. Early on, spectators settled for the unbalanced Argüello trying to rid himself of the rust that had accumulated during his self-imposed exile. Argüello ended the bout by sending Jefferson to the canvas three times in the fifth round. The referee stopped the fight officially at 2:47 of the round in accordance with the three-knockdown rule, which stipulated that three knockdowns in a given round results in a technical knockout. All indications led to a next showdown with a bigger threat, former junior lightweight champ Billy Costello. More importantly, this was a new Argüello. He was content with his performance, had resolved his differences with Loretto, controlled his drug problem, and began to live a healthy lifestyle again.

Another tragedy beset Argüello when, in 1986, his mother, Zoila Bohórquez, who had resided in Miami in the early 1980s for a year, passed away in Nicaragua. Since the controversy with the Sandinistas was never resolved, Argüello was forced to bid his mother farewell from Miami, while his brother took care of the burial and funeral proceedings. Of all the offenses that the Sandinistas committed, Argüello would never forget this one.

"I stayed in the United States until 1986. That was the year my mother died. She was living in Miami [in a house Argüello bought her], but I brought her back to Nicaragua because she wanted to [go home]," said Argüello. "She got sick, and I went to the consul in Miami to ask permission to leave to bury her, but I couldn't come because I was considered persona non grata. The consul told me I couldn't come. My name was banned here in Nicaragua. I couldn't come because I would go to jail; that's what they told me. They confiscated my belongings and thought that I was a Somozista. I couldn't come because they thought I was an enemy of the land. Can you believe that?"

At the time, the pressures from the Internal Revenue Service as well as the steep deductions taken from the Jefferson purse for Miller, Kahn, and Futch began to weigh on Argüello, who quickly became disillusioned with his come-back. Still, Argüello, now thirty-four, turned his attention back to the ring. He set his sights on Billy Costello, a talented and brash twenty-nine-year-old, 140-pound welterweight from New York.

Questions were still swirling regarding Argüello's return to boxing. If Argüello could access that fantastic reservoir of skills on his way to one last hurrah, Costello represented the ideal litmus test. The fight was appropriately billed "Four the Hard Way," alluding to Argüello's try for four titles.

People in the sport noticed the rapid progress of the conventional 135-pound amateur. By 1978, Costello had already captured the New York Golden Gloves 135-pound open division title and sought help from a local manager, Mike Jones. A year later, under Jones's watchful eye, Costello decisioned Angel Ortiz in his professional debut at the Felt Forum.

With Jones fostering his boxer's growth by choosing a queue of immobile opponents, Costello became a New York favorite and won his first twenty-six bouts under the tutelage of trainer Victor Valle Sr. Back then, Valle stressed Costello's lack of polish but marveled at his power. Costello cultivated a local following by winning the majority of his fights in Kingston and Westchester County.

After beating Bruce Curry for the WBC 140-pound title in January 1984, Costello defended the world 140-pound title three times in Kingston, New York, and won unanimous decision victories in each bout. Unable to savor the ben-efits afforded a world champion, Costello, now 30-0, sauntered into Madison Square Garden on August 21, 1985, as a heavy favorite against undefeated Lonnie Smith. "Lightning" Lonnie had not beaten a notable opponent in twenty-one fights and was viewed as mere fodder for the champ. Eight rounds and five knockdowns later—Costello went down twice in the second round, once in the fifth, and twice in the eighth—Costello was no longer a world champion. The Kingston native hastily retired without considering his alternatives. The brief escape from the ring categorized Costello with thousands of fighters willing to give up the sport after one loss. To no one's surprise, Costello was back nearly four months later and knocked out unknown Rick Kaiser in two rounds on December 13. Costello weighed 151 pounds for the bout, a sign that he hadn't thought much about boxing during his hiatus.

Even if the Argüello-Costello fight matched one fighter way past his prime against another trying to resuscitate his not-so-far-off glory days, the showdown held serious implications. For boxing experts, the fight would be used as a barometer to measure Argüello's progress, if any, after coming out of retirement; and the "Costello Crazies" could finally confirm if the loss to Lonnie Smith was a fluke or a harbinger of what was to come.

No one had to convince Costello to fight. "I was positive I could beat him," recalled Costello from his home in New York. "I didn't have to fight Argüello. But he had a good name. I knew that he couldn't beat me. He was a great fighter. I watched him on TV, and he couldn't change. I knew if I moved around, I could beat him."

Argüello moved his camp back to Miami for his second comeback bout. By mid-January 1986 Argüello was with his family and in his comfort zone. He trained at the Tropical Park (formerly the Tropical Park Race Track), the boxing gym on the grounds of a neighborhood park. Two weeks prior to the bout, Argüello moved to the Eldorado Hotel in Reno, Nevada. His old charm reverberated as he donned a tuxedo for the press conference tour.

Futch expressed his satisfaction with the fighter: "I thought it was an exercise in futility. After a two-year layoff, and after seeing him in that second fight with Pryor, I thought he'd had it—he was all done. When I went to see him, I didn't expect to find anything. But it was like he'd never left."

On February 9, 1986, CBS broadcast the ten-round welterweight affair in a 1:30 p.m. time slot, jumpstarting a boxing Sunday that included ABC's light-heavyweight title fight between Leslie Stewart and Marvin Johnson. The Argüello-Costello bout was held at the Lawlor Events Center in Reno and promoted by Sam Glass and Tiffany Promotions. In Vegas, Argüello was the 2–1 favorite. In ruins financially, Argüello would earn between $150,000 and $200,000 for the bout. Argüello (75-7 with sixty-four knockouts) came in at 143 pounds, while Costello weighed 144 pounds.

Prior to the fight, controversy ensued. Costello's trainer, Valle, walked over to Argüello's dressing room and demanded that the fighter rewrap his hands. Valle claimed that Argüello used extra padding, which gave him a decided advantage over his fighter. Duane Ford, vice chairman of the Nevada State Athletic Commission, backed the Costello camp's assertion. Furthermore, Ford noted that Argüello had used eighteen yards of gauze rather than the allotted ten yards. An enraged Argüello felt slighted by the accusations. He threatened to storm off the premises and out of the bout.

"When I told him he had to rewrap," said Ford, "he said he wasn't coming out for the fight. I said, 'OK, go tell the media.' He sure started rewrapping fast enough."

Argüello, known for his composure, entered the ring for the first time in eighty-eight fights in a feisty lather. He did not want Costello to pay; he wanted to destroy him for the humiliation.

"What happened in that fight with Costello was an issue over handwraps. It had nothing to do with Costello," said Thomas Hauser, author of *Black Lights: Inside the World of Professional Boxing*. "They made Argüello rewrap and he was steamed. He threatened to not fight the bout. But his anger wasn't directed toward Costello."

Costello recalled the prefight hysteria. "Argüello got pissed off and said he wasn't going to fight. But I knew he had to fight. He needed the money. I wasn't threatened. People wanted to fight me."

After Argüello agreed to rewrap, the men went back to their dressing rooms. The damage was done; Argüello, caught off-guard, was flustered and cold. Unable to warm up with Futch properly, Argüello walked into the ring dry and still simmering over the prefight glove issue. A calm Costello was aware of the glove repercussions and how irritable Argüello had become.

"I was in the dressing room with Costello and Mike Jones," said journalist Michael Marley. "We told Costello, 'What you can't do is to lay on the ropes.' He told us that he was going to knock out Alexis. At that time, Alexis was finished as a great fighter. . . . To me you're a great fighter if you can still show something special after your prime."

After the early distractions, the combatants entered to the cheers of 4,123 fans at the Lawlor Events Center. Early on, Costello, who was built like a Greek god, used his strength on the inside to offset Argüello's stinging jab. By getting inside his long reach, Costello not only neutralized the jab but also imposed his will on a rusty fighter who was still visibly stirred from the glove incident. Whatever fallout there had been from the Lonnie Smith upset, apparently Costello had recovered. The Costello faithful watched as their idol intuitively evaded the right hand and stung Argüello with solid counterpunching. Costello's quickness befuddled the comeback kid, and his strength allowed him to bully Argüello. Most of all, he realized that Argüello was fueled by a negative energy, and he turned it against him. He heeded the advice of his confidants and stayed in the middle of the ring, aware that the ropes represented a death sentence.

More of the same one-sided domination occurred over the next three minutes. Costello beat Argüello to the punch, hooked off his jab, and confounded the veteran with speed and movement. As the seconds ticked off the clock, the great champ's deterioration was evident.

Costello recalled those early rounds: "Nobody showed me respect before the bout. It hurt me more than anything. But that's just the business. Of course, he had a great name, and everybody idolized him. But the time comes for any athlete: They get a split second slower. Nobody stays on top forever. I was pissed off mostly because it was mostly Argüello fans. But when I watch that fight again, I noticed that their mouths were closed. I was whipping his ass."

Creeping closer with that right hand, Argüello stayed patient, but he became aggressive in the third round. Yet, his methodical style was tailor-made for the fleet-footed Costello. Argüello's glancing shots gave his people hope; however, they did nothing to extinguish Costello's fire. As Costello heard the sound of the bell ending the third round, he went back to the corner, basking in the Reno spotlight. He was methodically stripping the confidence from one of the greatest fighters of all time. His fluke loss to Lonnie Smith becoming a distant memory, Costello was on his way to sending a legend back into retirement.

Then Argüello woke from his slumber.

A minute into that fourth round, Argüello shed his anxieties, tamped down his anger, and trapped his opponent against the ropes. As Costello threw a right hand, Argüello subsequently connected on a vicious right hand that was supplemented by a textbook left hook that sent Costello to the canvas. Costello crumpled, lost his balance completely, and landed on the side of his face. He struggled to his feet by the count of eight. Costello hadn't inherited his father's steely disposition as a confessed pool hustler; thus, the Kingston native panicked. Less than a minute later referee Mills Lane stepped between the combatants to end the bout at 1:42 of the round. At the time of the stoppage, judges Dave Moretti, Doug Tucker, and Keith Macdonald all had Costello ahead, 30–27. The victory positioned Argüello back in contention in the junior welterweight division.

Argüello sat down years later and winced at remembering the person he had become that night: "That was the one time where I got angry in the ring. That was the time when I thought I should leave this sport. There was too much anger inside of me. It was a beast inside of me. It wasn't me."

Watching from the crowd that afternoon, Hauser vividly remembered the turn of events. "I wondered if Alexis didn't take something off his punches early in order to lull an opponent into a sense of complacency," he said. "Billy didn't have the greatest chin. He was a good offensive fighter. His manager kept him away from punchers. He was doing well in that fight. Then, Argüello turned it all around with that punch."

Years later Costello still felt victimized and expressed his frustrations: "When he hit me, I fell down, got up and the problem was I couldn't move my legs. I was still catching punches. But after that fight Mills Lane came up to me and said, 'Billy, I am sorry. I shouldn't have stopped that fight.' But he was doing what he thought was right. I beat his ass for four rounds. That's how the business goes."

Unbeknownst to fight fans, the Costello bout marked the last time Argüello would display his God-given ability. Before he left the arena, Argüello walked into the post-fight press conference and apologized to everyone for his behavior before the bout. In typical Argüello style, he was gracious, kind, and genuinely embarrassed by his actions. Argüello had beaten a legitimate opponent who had only recently lost his title, and he now subscribed to the motto "An old man can do it." Argüello's ultimate goal to win four titles was still alive. Early reports named former junior welterweight champ Gene Hatcher or Patricio Oliva as the next opponent on Argüello's comeback trail, but the fight eventually fell through.

There were hints that the Costello fight only provided a brief respite from the emotional strain that plagued Argüello. That March, the old Argüello resurfaced. He broke down during an interview with a *Washington Post* reporter.

ROUND 13

The Struggle

What you do to them on the way in, they do to you on the way out.
—ALEXIS ARGÜELLO

Details from the months after the Costello win are muddled. In April 1986, two months after Argüello's bittersweet victory over Billy Costello, the champ learned from his personal physician Dr. Aaron Tuckler that he had coronary artery disease and would have to forgo his attempt to win a fourth world title.

"The results of the tests we did were abnormal, so I got a second opinion," said Dr. Tuckler. "All of the doctors agreed with me. Then I gave [Alexis] the diagnosis. He had angina or coronary heart disease. He was very sad to know about that. He was not angry, but he questioned me about his problems about the disease. He retired."

Argüello responded, "I don't want to take any chances at my age." To many of Argüello's supporters, the diagnosis was a blessing in disguise. Now their friend could focus on getting his life on track.

Months later, outside the ring, Argüello welcomed another addition to his family as Loretto gave birth to a son, Diego, on November 11. Now he had two sons, Diego and Roberto, with Loretto; A. J., Andrés, and Dora were his children from past marriages.

As he moved into his second retirement, it was unclear why he had left boxing again, especially since several doctors had given him a clean bill of health before the Costello bout. Many believed the new diagnosis was a mere pretext and that Argüello needed an escape route.

"He never said anything to me about his heart condition," said Bill Miller. "We paid him, and then we went separate ways. I don't think it was a heart problem. He'd just had it."

Prior to Argüello's second retirement, talks about a three-fight package with Walter Alvarez and Sam Glass had made the newspapers. A June 29 date in Reno, Nevada was open for Argüello to face Gene Hatcher.

"We had talked about it," said Alvarez. "Hypothetically, it was a done deal. But Alexis didn't give priority to it. So it never really heated up."

Despite the pain of leaving the ring for a second time, Argüello hung up his gloves and prepared both for an anticipated glorious entry into the International Boxing Hall of Fame and a smooth transition to a role as a boxing commentator or trainer. He still had movie star looks, a slew of contacts from his fighting days, and an engaging personality. At 81-7, with sixty-five knockouts, Argüello had earned a place in boxing lore and the guarded fraternity of fighters who deserved the highest accolades possible. No longer was he analyzed solely as a "Latin" icon; instead, he was considered one of the greatest fighters of all time. He accomplished everything he set out to do in his career except win that elusive fourth crown. Not only did he win three titles, but he also never lost any of them in the ring.

"All Latin fighters are tough fighters with big hearts and courage, especially Roberto Durán, who was a big hitter," said Argüello during a visit at the Hall of Fame in 2002. "But on the other side, you have good boxers with a heavy punch like Argentina's Carlos Monzon. In Latin America, there has been a variety of styles: Miguel Canto of Mexico, who was a great boxer, or Monzon, a heavy hitter with good height, and Durán was short, but a heavy puncher with good movement who threw good combinations. Every generation brings a different fighter."

People debate Argüello's place in the pantheon of great fighters, but it is hard to argue with his results. First, he destroyed Mexican legend Rubén Olivares in the thirteenth round of their famous matchup in Los Angeles, and the headline in *La Prensa* read the next day, "The Mariachis Silenced." Of course, he never faced another fighter of Olivares's quality over his two-year reign at 126 pounds, but Argüello dominated the division of underrated fighters such as Leonel Hernandez and Royal Kobayashi. The three-time champ went through such torment to stabilize himself at 126 pounds that he was relieved to move to the super featherweight division.

Many consider Argüello to be the best 130-pound boxer of all time. Despite experiencing a turbulent life outside the ring, Argüello refocused and engaged in two battles with Puerto Rican stalwart Alfredo Escalera that rivaled the final trilogy fought between Roberto Durán and Esteban De Jesús. Fans learned more about Argüello's courage, character, and resilience in those two fights than they did in his epic battles with Aaron Pryor. For two years (1978–1980), Argüello left his imprint on a division comprised of such men as the excellent and undefeated Ruben Castillo (46-0), the fading Bobby Chacón, the combative Alfredo Escalera (twice), and the dirty but skilled Bazooka Limón, who went on to regain his world title. With the exception of a forgettable loss to the quick-footed Vilomar Fernández, Argüello had moved up and victimized the 130-pound class of tough fighters with veritable ease. Some fighters do win three, four, or five titles at different weight classes, but rarely does a fighter move up and sustain the same level of destruction. When assessing the greatest 130-pounders of all time, the conversation starts with Argüello and includes the greats Julio César Chávez, Floyd Mayweather Jr., and Azumah Nelson. *The Ring* magazine named Argüello the top junior lightweight of all time, and in 2002 the magazine also recognized him as one of the twenty best fighters of the last eighty years. One can argue about each of these fighters' prowess in their prime, but the standard that Argüello set in that weight class can never be debated. The dominance, dedication, and class that he exhibited during his two years as a super featherweight opened the doors for the next batch of great fighters. Even when Argüello strung the challenger and his audience along for ten rounds, everyone in the arena knew that he was setting a trap for that one perfectly placed punch.

When Argüello finished his eight defenses at 130 pounds, he sought greener pastures in a 135-pound weight class that Roberto Durán previously owned. Before Argüello fought for the title, he beat a dangerous Cornelius Boza-Edwards and survived a controversial victory over José Luis Ramirez. At this weight, Argüello finally appeared to hit his peak physically. Although he was exciting but at times weakened at 130 pounds, he was as violent and destructive—perhaps more so—when he was five pounds heavier. Of his three titles—featherweight, super featherweight, and lightweight—the title bout against Jim Watt was the only one that didn't fulfill expectations; however, Argüello's successive lightweight bouts over the next two years did. Argüello went 6-0 in his lightweight bouts, and four of them were title defenses. But it was the way he finished off opponents that had lifted the boy from the Barrio Monseñor Lezcano neighborhood to superstar status. After nearly decapitating Ray "Boom Boom" Mancini, breaking Roberto Elizondo's jaw, catapulting James Busceme across the ring with a straight right, and leaving Andrew Ganigan slumping along the ropes, Argüello had developed into the puncher that other fighters aspired to be. When he hit fighters, the impact reverberated throughout the arena. More importantly, Argüello had the power to knock out an opponent with three punches: his straight right, the vaunted left hook, and the equally destructive uppercut. Most of his opponents knew the punch was coming, but had no recourse to avoid it. This was one of the qualities that made the mild-mannered Argüello so intimidating.

"To me, 135 pounds was my best weight class," Argüello told me. "That was where I made [eight] defenses." As for the classic style that he perfected, Argüello added, "I was certain that my movement helped put me into a good position. If I used more movement, I would've lost my power."

When other fighters were struggling to extend themselves to twelve-round bouts, Argüello had perfectly conditioned his body to be as fresh in the fifteenth round as he had been in the first one. As noted earlier, Mancini, who fought Argüello in 1981, observed that the champ "never got rattled, never. He always believed that he could weather the storm."

How long could Argüello have lasted as the king of the 135-pounders? Argüello could have stayed and dominated the lightweight division, but he wanted to face Aaron Pryor, the big money fight he deserved. In fact, Argüello could have easily captured that fourth crown against a lesser opponent, but he opted for the best the sport had to offer. Once he encountered a bigger, stronger, and faster fighter in Pryor, however, the thirty-year-old Argüello struggled to find his rhythm. With or without the corner stimulant, Pryor was an uncontrollable force. He was the one man Argüello could not program.

"That's the nemesis of every story," Argüello told me at the International Boxing Hall of Fame. "You have your story and I have mine. It's part of the cycle that sports has shown us that you guys don't talk about. It happens to Sugar Ray Robinson; it happens to Muhammad Ali; it happens to George Foreman, and it happens to me. I did to Olivares what Pryor did to me fifteen years later. That is a life cycle that none of us can avoid. It's something that whatever has been done to someone, it comes back and happens to him. That's the cycle."

Toward the end of his career, Argüello exhibited a remarkable ability to adapt to any situation against much younger fighters. For example, against Ray Mancini, Argüello bided his time until he was ready to pounce on him; he applied the hammer-like jab against Elizondo, who was 23-1 at the time; he went to the body against Cornelius Boza-Edwards; he wore down courageous Alfredo Escalera; and he matched Bazooka Limón's dirty tactics. The bodies he left behind, however, didn't define his legacy.

Of all Argüello's magnificent traits, his consistency should be celebrated. Some fighters have logged more than a hundred wins, but how many are legitimate victories, and how many are merely a mass of easy victories compiled during the third leg of the good-bye tour? Were there better fighters than Argüello? Of course. Were there 130-pounders who would have given him fits in his prime? Yes. But when assessing his career up to the second Pryor fight, one thing Argüello never did was let down his audience. All great fighters are guilty of "punching the ticket" against inferior opponents, but Argüello refused to succumb to that way of thinking. Sure, he could have beaten Vilomar Fernández, whom he later beat at 135 pounds, or looked better against José Luis Ramirez, but he never disappointed his fans. He always fought to his potential and never slacked. His losses didn't diminish his legacy and the way his fans perceived him. Furthermore, he never took a night off simply because he could.

Away from the ring, Argüello was always a consummate professional. He never ballooned uncontrollably between bouts or mocked his opponents to get attention and to sell tickets. Another quality that separated him from other great fighters was that, with the exception of his loss to José Luis Ramirez, he never relied on the judges to give him a "gift" of an easy victory. All of his victories were decisive, one-sided wins without the taint of controversy. When defending his titles, Argüello went 16-0 with 15 knockouts: 4-0 as a featherweight, 8-0 at super featherweight, and 4-0 in lightweight defenses. Overall, he faced fourteen world champions, beating all of them except for Ramirez and Pryor. Few fighters could accomplish the feat, and Argüello did it without significant hand speed or foot movement. He beat guys with precision, control, and timing or, more specifically, an innate understanding of when to punch.

"He won titles and never lost any of them," said former world champ Jim Watt. "I don't think that has happened since. He had great battles with Pryor and conducted himself well in every division. His greatest fights may have been with [Alfredo] Escalera. He conducted himself like a champion should. But I think he was a better lightweight because he didn't have to struggle to make weight."

People have it wrong when they put Argüello in a list of top-100 fighters and place fighters with better records ahead of him. They misunderstand what Argüello meant to the sport. Even attempting to measure Argüello in such a way demeans his legacy. He represented and upheld a model that can never be repeated. And his legacy has nothing to do with the inevitable three-punch combination that became his staple and ruined so many careers.

When Argüello learned English, he quickly became more marketable and separated himself from other Latin fighters. He treated everyone the same, from the hotel bellboy to the guy at the gym handing out towels, because he was courteous. It would be unfair to say Argüello wasn't fueled by a huge ego, but he wanted the people around him to feel just as special as he did. Whether it was asking a reporter about his family, remembering the name of an opponent's child, or bringing a birthday cake to an opponent, Argüello received as much happiness from seeing other people were happy as he did from winning the belts. "He was my idol. I got friendly with him at the Main Street Gym," said photographer Carlos Baeza. "He was very unique about our friendship. I felt like I had known him forever. And he gave me that same feeling too." And, until his later bouts with addiction, he tried to follow that premise in every aspect of his life. Thus, later on, he reveled in his role as mayor of Managua, even when others believed he didn't have the intellectual capacity to excel in the political spectrum.

"I think that boxing fans regarded him as one of the best fighters of modern times," said boxing journalist and TV commentator Larry Merchant. "He and Roberto Durán were immediate forerunners of the Latino dominance of the sport in the United States. Argüello wanted to be respected and likable outside the ring, and Durán didn't give a crap. . . .

"They were marketable stars. There are a lot of champions, outstanding fighters who don't necessarily become stars. They transcended sports. . . . Argüello was one of those guys."

President of the International Boxing Hall of Fame in Canastota, New York, Ed Brophy spent several Hall of Fame weekends with Argüello. He recalled, "Alexis was the type of person who enjoyed people and was interested in what they were working on at the moment. And it stuck with him the next time he saw them. He would listen to people and cared about them. He would ask people about their interests and their family. That made him who he was."

But for Argüello, in the end, there was no sunset in the distance, no goodbye parties replete with well-wishers. Even before his Hall of Fame induction in 1992, Argüello had spiraled into a state of delusion and pain. The contradictions bedeviled everyone who loved him. How could a man so intelligent, sensitive, and caring get embroiled in an addiction so violent and destructive?

Argüello had never prepared for a life after boxing, and when he left the sport in 1986, all of the flaws and problems that plagued him throughout his career bubbled to the surface. Ironically, what fighters detest the most—the workout—is also what keeps them sane. Argüello needed the routine, the training, and the early runs to keep his wandering mind away from the chaos and inevitable loneliness that all fighters must handle. For many fighters it's impossible to imagine that one day, without warning, something or someone is going to let them know that they can no longer do what they love anymore. Without an education, they struggle to answer the inevitable question: "What's next?" Some claim that Argüello's downfall started in Miami after his first loss to Pryor, while other suggest that the boozing and drug addiction took its hold more than three years later, after the 1986 Costello bout. Argüello's frenzied private life, specifically his divorce from his devoted third wife, Loretto; his juggling of girlfriends; the fractured relationship with Roman; and caring for numerous children had begun to impact the fighter negatively years before his decision to retire. No matter how or when he reached his personal abyss, Argüello floated through the next ten to twelve years without any structure. He was looking for an escape but refused any real assistance.

"Alexis was approached by some bad people," said longtime friend Renzo Bagnariol. "He wasn't busy like when he was training. He started to go down the wrong way and got caught on this thing. So many years restraining himself . . . these people were able to take advantage of his spirit at the moment."

From 1988 to 1990, Argüello moved back and forth between homes in Las Vegas and Nicaragua. After spurning a $775,000 offer to fight Pryor for a third time, Argüello settled into life away from the sport. His good looks and warrior mentality warranted film offers. In the late eighties, directors cashed in on the boxer's appeal as Argüello was cast as a hit man in *Moving Target* (1988), a hoodlum in *Cat Chaser* (1989), and "the good guy" in *Fists of Steel* (1991). He also had previously enjoyed cameo roles in several *Miami Vice* episodes as Pepe Moya.

He agreed to a two-year contract to broadcast fights for the Spanish-language network Telemundo and signed up for grammar classes to polish his English at Clark County Community College. Argüello also used his celebrity to negotiate a contract with Trump Castle in Atlantic City to work as a "goodwill ambassador," or greeter, at the casino. All indications were that Argüello's lack of stability and fluctuating moods had become public knowledge.

"I was hired by [Donald] Trump to be a celebrity sponsor," said Argüello, "before they made the Taj Majal. I signed a five-year contract to work for Trump in public relations for the high rollers. This was from 1985–89. I drank more booze in all of my life. I was crazy."

Meanwhile, Argüello began to plot his return to a country that had exiled him for more than a decade. Nicaragua's new president, Violeta Chamorro, presented a welcome image of democracy for the country, and Argüello was eager to revisit his home and collect the estimated $1 million that he was owed from the 1979 seizure. Having already envisioned his glorious return, Argüello finally could confirm his flight on February 25, 1990, when the Sandinistas and Daniel Ortega, who had run his reelection campaign with the slogan "Todo sera mejor" (Everything will be better), gracefully welcomed Chamorro and her new government. Ortega urged his followers to accept a peace and eschew rioting, and his message allowed for a smooth transition. When the Supreme Electoral Congress announced the results to the rest of the world, Argüello rejoiced. To Sandinistas, the new government marked the end of their war with the Contras; to Argüello, it meant a new beginning.

On May 8, 1990, Argüello, age thirty-eight, finally kissed the ground of his homeland. He received a hero's welcome at the airport. Sports Minister and journalist Sucre Frech welcomed Argüello after his being persona non grata for eleven years.

"I am glad to be back in my country again," said an elated Argüello.

For a short time, Argüello was handed the reins to bring Nicaraguan boxing to a world stage. The Sandinistas had banned the sport in 1981, so Argüello had the responsibility of resurrecting it. He reopened his gym, which the Sandinistas had seized, and retained one of the homes they had confiscated in 1979. Chamorro appointed Argüello as the commissioner of boxing. Then, Argüello began to organize boxing cards and provided guidance in and out of the ring for young fighters.

"The gain is, I'm in my land again," said Argüello, "and we have to make this work."

Longtime friend Don Kahn remembered that Argüello "was happy. He was the director of boxing for the government, ran a gym, and even helped to train and manage a couple fighters. He bought some equipment and worked with some fighters."

Unfortunately, after the celebrations died down, Argüello struggled to retain his fortune. He continued in a downward spiral as later he relied on old friends for loans and a place to live.

To Argüello, the only answer to his problems was to return to the ring. Buoyed by his work with young fighters in Nicaragua, Argüello felt that he could still achieve something in the sport. Disregarding his previous diagnosis of coronary artery disease, Argüello decided to return to boxing for a third time. Not having completely exorcised his demons, however, the ring was the last place that Argüello should have been.

"It was a risk for him to come back, but he kept a strict diet, he improved, and he felt good," said his friend and former personal doctor, Dr. Aaron Tuckler.

Those who facilitated this fight were to blame for Argüello's final round of self-destruction. He announced in 1994 that he would fight again that summer and face light-hitting Mexican Jorge Palomares. Now age forty-two, Argüello needed money, and he chose a fringe fighter for his return.

Nearly three decades since fighting Cachorro Amaya in his pro debut, Argüello teamed with promoter Jim Browning to make one last bid for a fourth title. No one had stuck around from previous camps, so Argüello relied on veteran trainer Jimmy Montoya to advise him in his return bout. Although boxing had once saved Argüello, it would destroy him now. While training in Louisiana for the bout, Argüello went to Saint Patrick's Hospital in Monroe, Louisiana, after suffering broken ribs during a sparring session with prospect Gregory Balcazar. The bout, originally scheduled for May, was moved to August.

"Before that fight, Jimmy Montoya brought Alexis to Louisiana. He called me to come to Louisiana. I said, 'Listen. Don't put Alexis in this fight. Let him commentate on the fight.' So I had Alexis put on the gloves and get into the ring to spar," said assistant trainer Don Kahn. "He broke his ribs, and I said, 'Go home. You're not ready to box.'"

Despite the setback, Argüello forged ahead. From a financial standpoint, the fight would give him breathing room. Although Palomares was billed [built up to market him] as a fighter with a record of twenty-two wins and eight losses, in retrospect, promoters had embellished his record outlandishly. It was more likely that he had lost ten of his previous eleven bouts and walked into the Argüello fight with only two victories. Thus, he presented absolutely no threat to Argüello.

The event reached full capacity as twenty-five hundred people packed the Miami Convention Center on August 27, 1994. After an eight-year layoff, Argüello entered the ring at 142¼ pounds, slightly lighter than when he fought Billy Costello. Palomares, a thirty-one-year-old southpaw, entered at 141¼ pounds. Although Argüello had not fought professionally in nearly nine years, he was not alone in making a comeback. In the same year, heavyweights George Foreman and Larry Holmes and middleweight Roberto Durán—all in their forties—had returned to the ring as well. Broadcasters and fans alike, however, questioned if Argüello had any power left.

As the fight began, Argüello relied solely on his right hand, and the powerless Palomares would slip his punches to land a left-right combination. Unlike in his golden years, Argüello now used no head movement and suffered frequent lapses in defense. The champ had been severely limited since the second round when he broke his left hand, the same hand that he had broken in 1972 during his bout with Jorge Reyes. Benefiting from his vast experience and potent right hand, Argüello courageously fought the last eight rounds on heart alone. Still, the hundreds of Nicaraguans who had traveled to Miami to see their hero one last time enjoyed a brief glimpse of Argüello's power when he used a body punch and set up a right cross that sent Palomares down in the sixth round. Some fans reveled nostalgically when Argüello knocked Palomares down again in that same round.

Argüello pounded out a majority decision. Judge Billy Ray scored it even, 94–94, while Rocky Young and Frank Skilbred had it 95–93. Argüello opened three cuts, one inside Palomares's nose and one over each eye.

"When I threw a jab and a left cross, I felt pain and I knew I hurt my hand," said Argüello after the fight. "I am an old-time fighter. I am old school. We don't run that easy. My trainer Jimmy Montoya told me not to show my pain."

When asked about his future, Argüello wanted to get his hand looked at first. On the surface, the casual fight fan had the opportunity to see a legend one last time; in reality, for the learned boxing observer, Argüello earned accolades for his bravery, but he had shown little against a below-average fighter. That August, Argüello went back to Nicaragua and had his trusted physician Dr. Jaime Granera examine his fractured hand. He was cleared to fight again.

Argüello's hand healed in time for a January 21, 1995, Top Rank–ESPN showdown with Scott "Pink Cat" Walker. A unique character, the challenger wore pink suits to weigh-ins and entered the ring to the "Pink Panther Theme." Adding to the attraction, Walker paid homage to his idol, James Dean, by slicking back his hair. Twenty-five-year-old Walker had won seventeen victories and dropped only three bouts. By comparison, the Hall of Famer, who was seventeen years older, was searching for his seventy-seventh victory in ninety fights. Although many criticized Argüello's decision to keep fighting, no one could argue with his credentials.

The bout was held at Arizona Charlie's, a neighborhood casino in Las Vegas, Nevada. Nearly eight hundred fans crammed the small arena for a glimpse of the great Argüello, and a thousand others were turned away at the door. Argüello earned $20,000 for his second comeback bout.

As the only active Hall of Famer still boxing professionally at the time, Argüello deserved the utmost respect. In the ring, Walker didn't give it to him. He did not look at Argüello as a legend but as simply another opponent. The stylish boxer battered Argüello in the first round, danced and scored at will in the second round, and managed to dispel any possible rumors that had surfaced in the Palomares fight that Argüello was back in form. Walker confirmed the inevitable: Argüello was finished. Argüello's futile attempt in the tenth round was admirable, but it was not enough to convince the judges to give him the fight. Walker walked away with a unanimous decision as Chuck Giampa and Jerry Roth scored the match 95–94, and Paul Smith had him ahead, 98–91.

Once a headlining attraction, the bout received nothing more than a mere blip. In the loss, Argüello reinjured his left hand in the fourth round. He claimed to be proud of his performance. Walker, however, summarized the ebb and flow of the evening: "He was a great fighter and I remember watching him as a kid. He's still a good fighter, but he's not what he used to be." Ever the self-deprecating elder statesman, Argüello told reporters, "I guess I am a self-masochist."

A year later Argüello's twenty-four-year old son, Alexis (A. J.) Argüello Jr., made a late start in the sport in upstate New York and won his first five amateur bouts. He relied on the same three-punch combination that his father had perfected decades earlier.

Meanwhile, any plans that Top Rank had to put Alexis on a future ESPN card quickly diminished. For the first time in his career, Argüello had been completely outclassed. His limitations were evident and alarming. Argüello had been reduced to a plodding, old, and hesitant fighter as Walker agitated him with quick combinations and movement. Those observers who had sugarcoated the victory against Palomares were silenced as Argüello went directly to his dressing room to seek help for his hand.

Without boxing, Argüello thought he could control his addiction as easily as he had picked off punches in the ring, but the drug abuse only ravaged him more in the late nineties. More important, even when Argüello knew that the addiction had a fierce stranglehold on his life, he refused any assistance.

By August 1999, forty-seven-year-old Argüello was living in the Las Colinas neighborhood in Nicaragua. At the time he was married to his fourth wife, twenty-seven-year-old Alicia Esquivel, with whom he had two children, Benjamin and Sixela, or Alexis spelled backward, a daughter they had adopted. Only four years after he ended his career once and for all, Argüello was living in a veritable hell. His body was emaciated and his mind controlled by cocaine. Further, Argüello found no solace in the comforting words of his friends. Before he could accept their help, Argüello had to accept his sordid state, or hit rock bottom. His self-destructive ways had reached the newspapers, and one headline read, "It Is the Final Round in the Life of an Idol." In an eight-day span, Argüello had suffered two car crashes while driving drunk and fractured his ribs in one of them. In one incident, he crashed into the wall of the Embassy of the Dominican Republic. When approached by reporters, Argüello shrugged off the accident.

"You can not cover the sun with a finger," said Esquivel, regarding her husband's addiction. "His condition is grave and he needs help. I personally think the people should find a way to help him because his condition is grave."

Yet Argüello failed to heed the advice of friends and family members. In September, Argüello was incoherent during a radio interview, and at one point he stated, "Yes, I want to die." It wasn't until Argüello became involved in a physical altercation with his wife at a party at the upscale InterContinental Hotel, however, that Argüello recognized the personal abyss into which he had fallen. Two weeks later, Argüello looked for help.

Then, when he needed them most, his friends entered the picture. Childhood friend Donald Rodriguez and WBA member Renzo Bagnariol saw firsthand the steep mental and physical decline of their dear friend. Bagnariol, the international coordinator for the WBA, had begun his relationship with Argüello as an avid fan and often accompanied Argüello camp members to title fights. However, the relationship took shape after Argüello returned. When Argüello returned to Nicaragua in the late nineties, they treated each other as brothers. It was rare that a day went by that they did not meet for lunch or a cup of coffee. At first Bagnariol was hesitant to intervene in the problem, feeling that it was not his place; instead, he waited for Argüello to take the initial step.

"[Alexis] didn't want to go to rehab," said Bagnariol. "Then he realized for himself that he was at the bottom of the world. He asked us to help him. He made a phone call to Donald [Rodriguez] and said, 'I want to get help.' We took him, but he first asked us for help."

By this time, Esquivel, who was fearful of the impact the drug addiction would have on their children, had left Argüello. Of all the people Argüello counted as friends, he felt he could only trust a handful. It is safe to say he trusted Bagnariol and Rodriguez with his life. During their entire relationship, Rodriguez had never asked Alexis for anything. Now, in early 2000, Argüello summoned his friends for assistance to help save his life, and they did not hesitate.

"When he said he was coming back to Nicaragua, I picked him up at the airport and [told him] here was a room for him. My wife realized he didn't sleep. Later I found out he had some drug problems. I didn't know he had drug problems, and when I found out we sat down and talked about it. I told him that I knew he couldn't sleep and he had some problems. He denied everything," Rodriguez recalled. "After a while he told me the truth. But at the time he was more comfortable in Nicaragua and started going out, and out there, there were always people that are willing to do something bad. So he had some friends who were drug addicts.

"So a group of friends that were always near him helped him any way we could. Later on he asked me to take him to rehab. I took him to one in San Marcos for two months in a place called Hodera and then he went out and had to go to some supporting groups."

Located in the town of San Marcos, Hodera is a treatment center for addiction. Situated on a modest-size farm, it is tucked away from the chaos of Managua. The center was run by former addict and current FSLN treasury secretary Francisco "Chico" López. During his stay, Argüello worked the land with dozens of other recovering addicts—a sign was erected in his honor that read "Alexis Argüello dug this ditch"—and sorted out the issues that had left him emotionally bankrupt. Often, he received visits from concerned friends.

"Alexis was brought to the rehab facility very close to my house, and he was working the land all day long," said Dr. Eduardo Roman. "He was very dark. He said, 'I am doing well and I am working hard. I am very happy.'"

Argüello spent two and a half months at Hodera and became close friends with its president. López facilitated Argüello's smooth transition back to the Sandinista Party and later orchestrated a meeting with Ortega. Spiritually, Argüello had strengthened himself, not unlike his strict training camps did; financially, he had no choice: whatever transgressions the Sandinistas made in the past he had to forgive.

"Francisco López owned the place," said Bagnariol. "He was a former addict himself. That is when they met for the first time. López was very emotional about helping people. There were about forty to fifty guys there. Once [Alexis] got out, his heart changed, and he forgave everything that happened with the Sandinistas."

Friends and family close to Argüello saw an immediate transformation once Argüello left Hodera. No longer was Argüello the gaunt, desperate soul searching for a replacement for the inexorable high of the ring. Instead, he talked about hope and forgiveness. Argüello believed that with persistence and dedication, he could become the person and role model that he once was. Still, there was time for celebration.

"The day he got out we made a big party at this place with Coca-Cola. He said, 'I want a party with Coca-Cola.' And every year on his birthday, we celebrated the same way," Bagnariol recalled. "We did it that way for five years, and on the fifth year, we even got a mariachi band."

After Argüello left Hodera, he reunited with Daniel Ortega and was appointed sports and youth minister in 2002. Argüello ran the Roger Dershon Gymnasium in San Judas. He was personally responsible for alleviating the issues that plagued boxing in Nicaragua. Argüello appointed Gustavo Herrera, Marlon Amador, and Ratón Mojica as trainers and Maritza Norori as his secretary. Then Ortega put Argüello on the FSLN victory ticket in 2004 as the vice mayoral candidate in hopes of facilitating the rise of then-mayoral candidate Dionisio Marenco. Argüello had not only reunited with Ortega, but he backtracked on a statement he once said, to "spit in my face if I ever get into politics," which resurfaced once the news spread of his political ambitions.

Dr. Roman, who remained close to Argüello until the day he died, rejected what he considered as the Sandinistas' ulterior motives. Roman was concerned about the Sandinista Party's manipulative ways and Argüello's fragile mind-set. "[Alexis] didn't want to go into sport. The FSLN offered him the position of the Minister of Sport," said Roman. "I explained to Alexis that there was no such title."

"When he retired, he moved back to Nicaragua and became the Sports Ambassador. Then he ran for office and was used by the Sandinistas. They used him to gain popularity and win the election," said former camp member and friend Don Kahn.

Many publicly challenged Argüello's risky decision to mend a relationship that had been hostile for more than two decades. By forgiving the party's past offenses, Argüello sought a second chance to help the poor people who had supported him unconditionally since he first stepped in the ring.

"I was born with the forgiveness. Right now in my country all the people can say, 'Alexis is an asshole,' because they took a ninety-acre farm, my boat, my houses, money in the bank, everything. But when the war came it was a country with no law; when the revolution took over it was a country with no law," Argüello recalled in 2008. "The guy that was carrying the fucking gun or rifle, he was the king of the neighborhood and that was the truth. Those days every kid with a fucking gun was a hero. Look, a kid that was born in a poor neighborhood. They destroy it. There was no law."

He continued: "The Nicaraguan people are respectful. Can you imagine how rageful they were at that moment? Maybe the excitement of overthrowing a dictator of thirty-five to forty years. The law wasn't there. I understand that. You can't avoid something like that: Anarchy. How can you avoid that? The people! I wasn't here. The poor people were the kids of the block in 1979."

While sitting in the lobby of the InterContinental Hotel in 2008, Argüello explained why he decided to make amends with Ortega and the party: "When I talked to Daniel Ortega he said, 'We apologize. I personally apologize. We took everything . . . your career.' I said, 'Look the past is past. Let's work forward to enhance our people, the country. Let's enhance the revolution to give the poor people what they deserve: health, education, housing. And you know that the nation won't be developed in five years. We're going to take twenty to twenty-five years. We have to show that we are going to do the right thing for the poor people, creating better health and housing programs . . . the little things that people need to get ahead.'"

Some notable moments over the next couple years included a rousing exhibition bout in the Bronx with former opponent Alfredo Escalera on August 6, 2001. By 2004, Argüello was brimming with hope at the International Boxing Hall of Fame when he told reporters: "I haven't had a drink in five years. I ask God every day to give me strength. I am happy I found myself."

Naturally, Nicaraguans wondered why Argüello, who had spent decades railing against the seizure of his funds and the socialists' ways, would consider reconnecting with the Sandinista Party. Although Argüello claimed forgiveness, others pointed to their promise to repay all the money they had taken from Argüello in 1979. Some felt that Argüello had no choice in the issue. Having reunited with the Sandinista Party, though, Argüello had regained his focus in his life. After winning the position of vice mayor of Managua in 2004, Argüello would hold that position for three years.

Still, Argüello gave in to his addiction one more time and disappeared in early January 2005. The news hit the press, and his close friends struggled to find answers, yet again.

"He fell off after that fifth year, and suddenly he was able to recuperate on his own," said Bagnariol. "He didn't need our help."

No one assisted Argüello during this recovery period. He showed the strength and fortitude to overcome the disease one more time. According to his close friends, that episode marked the last time Argüello suffered a setback.

In November 2007, Argüello vacated his position as vice mayor in order to run as the party's nominee for the mayor of Managua. While working for his people became the focus of his energies, in August 2008, Argüello relived some of his boxing glory when he bore the Nicaraguan flag during the Olympic Games' opening ceremony in Beijing. Behind him was Manny Pacquiao, carrying the Philippines' flag.

ROUND 14

Good-bye, Champ

Everybody has to go through their own hell in order to see if you are willing to come out of it.
—ALEXIS ARGÜELLO

Despite the fierce opposition that Daniel Ortega faced after he engineered the Sandinista victory in 1979, he always seemed to survive. First, Ortega was an integral part of a movement that overthrew Somoza's corrupt dictatorship in 1979. Second, he and the Sandinista Party overcame the U.S.-backed Contras. Decades later, Ortega reinvented himself and returned to power in 2006 against a divided opposition. During that election, Ortega turned away Eduardo Montealegre, candidate of the center-right Constitutionalist Liberal Party (PLC). With the coming municipal elections in November 2008, the opportunistic Ortega felt he had chosen the ideal candidate to oppose the popular Montealegre. The Sandinista Party had exercised control over Managua for the past eight years, and Ortega knew that Alexis Argüello was the only man who could keep the streak intact. Also, gaining approval locally in Managua would make Ortega's life easier. Critics, meanwhile, questioned Argüello's qualifications and capabilities against Montealegre, a proven leader.

The mayoral campaign presented the ultimate test for Argüello. Socially, he had found his comfort zone again, and had gotten remarried to Karla Rizo, a woman he had met while working out of the Roger Dershon Gym in San Judas. Politically, Argüello had a lot to learn. Many wondered how as a politician he would respond to the vitriol and contempt from the same people who had revered him as a champion. Would he be able to contend with deft political minds and endless intellectual debates? More important, how would he defend himself against the rampant corruption that besieged Nicaraguan politics? As always, Argüello threw a straight, conventional jab when he told his people: "I gave you three titles, I represented you honestly, and now I need you."

During his mayoral campaign, Argüello stressed issues such as better housing, the health system, and overall development. He looked back on the years
he'd spent in exile and considered the decisions he had to make when he said,
"Someone who leaves his country and gives up his nationality is an asshole.
That would've been like putting a knife to my throat. I couldn't look my people
in the eyes again. Like my umbilical cord is burned."

Astute and ambitious, Argüello knew what he was getting into when he gave
up his vice mayor position to campaign for mayor of Managua. And he had a
broad vision for his people.

"The end is not here yet," said Argüello. "This is the beginning of a beautiful
relationship. We as humans can start to develop a good nation, a nation in a little
shitty country. Without humanity, do we have the courage to fight for the rights
of the poor people? That's the remaining question mark. Only time will tell."

Longtime friend and consultant Dr. Henry Castillo spent endless hours campaigning with Argüello and marveled at the sacrifices he made and the class he
exhibited. Castillo had grown close to Argüello during the eighties and early
nineties when both men lived in Miami. They reunited when Argüello became
deputy mayor in 2004. Castillo worked as an adviser at a clinic for the local
government and was responsible for assessing medical needs, so Argüello sent
him patients. Often, they worked together to raise money for donations or medical supplies.

"Alexis loved to help people," said Dr. Castillo. "He would do anything to
help the poor people. He never wanted to show what he did. When he made a
donation to someone, he didn't want anyone to know. One guy had something
wrong with his eye. He gave a guy 80,000 córdobas to help a guy with an eye
problem. Then, a reporter wanted Alexis to take a photo with the guy. And
Alexis said, 'No, man, why you do this? This is not the type of person I am. I
don't want to boast or brag.' At the same time, he helped a popular Nicaraguan
singer and Alexis spent 100,000 córdobas to get help for this man. Then Alexis
said, 'I don't want a picture. If we do it, we have to do it.'"

Unfortunately, Argüello's supporters felt the same generous streak that had
made Argüello an icon in Nicaragua would also perpetuate his eventual downfall if they elected him mayor. Since returning to Nicaragua, Argüello had
renewed his friendship with Dr. Roman. There were no lingering effects from
the financial issues that plagued their past. Similar to his role in Argüello's boxing career, Roman returned as the fighter's mentor. Furthermore, Castillo and
Dr. Roman believed in Argüello and his mental capacity to handle the position.

In November 2008, Argüello won 51 percent of the vote at the 2,107 polling stations while CLP candidate Eduardo Montealegre received 46 percent of the votes. The Supreme Electoral Council, affiliated with the Sandinista Party, announced the results of the final tally, which were met with equal amounts of scorn and violence. Ortega's dismissal of impartial international observers to monitor the election's legitimacy and his refusal to conduct a recount or internal investigation stoked the fire of disapproval. At times, the campaign turned ugly, but Argüello, who had gained momentum in the poor districts, never lost his composure. Meanwhile, Montealegre, the Liberal candidate, warned the Nicaraguan people would protest the alleged election fraud. In *Unfinished Revolution*, Kenneth Morris downplays the PLC's charges of corruption, noting, "The high level of distrust and animosity that permeates Nicaragua's political culture is such that even a clean electoral victory would likely have been tainted by accusations of fraud."

Despite the calls for change, Ortega went on with business as usual. Unfortunately, Argüello's reputation remained tainted because of the election controversy, and there was considerable dissent among the hardcore Sandinistas, who felt that Argüello did not truly represent them. Although the Nicaraguan people knew Argüello had nothing to do with any discarded opposition election ballots or other suspicious acts, he could not avoid being embroiled in the negativity and mistrust surrounding them. More importantly, he felt embarrassed and hurt by the debacle, as the marionette strings were already slightly being pulled, just enough so that Argüello knew his place. Despite showing restraint, inside the former champ fumed. As Ortega moved closer to establishing an authoritarian regime, Argüello had no choice but to enter the fray. Still, a strong Nicaraguan contingent never associated Argüello with the Sandinista Party.

"When he was campaigning on the Masaya Highway, guys from the opposition paid people to go against Alexis," said Dr. Henry Castillo. "A sick guy came up to him and yelled at Alexis, 'Fuck you, Alexis.' I was in the backseat, and I laughed. 'What is with this guy?' Alexis asked me. I explained to him, 'Eduardo Montealegre, who ran on the opposing ticket, paid this guy to say that.'

"Another day, we were working for Alexis, and another guy says, 'Bullshit, you fucking sonofabitch. You are trying to do many bad things.' Alexis quickly responded, 'Why do you say to me something like that?' The guy talks to Alexis for 10 minutes, and then he says, 'I am no Sandinista, but I am going to give my vote to you because you are a man with a big heart. Now, I am sorry.' That was Alexis. He had no enemies."

All Nicaraguans knew that Argüello was involved in an illegitimate election. Despite being honest and upfront about his own convictions, a clearly frustrated Argüello had to live with the reality that having cemented his role with the Sandinista Party, he had to blend in with its ugly charade. Thirty years earlier Argüello, a world champion, had the power to question authority and reject what he considered backdoor dealings, but he no longer had leverage. As a former addict rescued by the Sandinista Party, Argüello was powerless, a puppet for Daniel Ortega and First Lady Rosario Murillo to control at their behest.

Sports journalist Edgar Tijerino shed light on the reunion and the subsequent manipulation Argüello endured. According to Tijerino, who clarified that Argüello was in financial ruin when the Sandinistas approached him, "Alexis knew that the Sandinistas were manipulating him. In his mind, Alexis was clear that he was being used and why he was being used. Personally, before he was thrown into the Sandinista problem, I would have asked him, 'Do you know what is going to happen? Do you know that you are going to be used? Do you know that these people are toxic and they will give you a hard time because you are not used to dealing with those types of people?' On the other hand, Alexis knew all of this anyway."

During his several months as mayor of Managua, Argüello knew he was handpicked because he could be controlled. The head of his mayoral campaign, First Lady Rosario Murillo, surrounded him with political "advisers," or personal cornermen to aid him whenever he needed "help." Secretary of City Council Fidel Moreno was his head "trainer." He reeled Argüello in whenever he started to stray and stayed nearby to whisper advice in the mayor's ear. No longer was Argüello allowed to think for himself or act on his own accord. But, as Argüello stated publicly, he didn't care that he was being used, as long as he could help his people. For a short time, he did.

"He was always speaking about the Indian that he was. He said, 'I am an Indian.' He was touched by the poverty of the people and would do whatever he could to help them," said Renzo Bagnariol. "When he was mayor, every morning you would see a big line of people asking for things, and he would never let them down."

Others lauded his accomplishments and willingness to fight for any cause. When Argüello rejoined the Sandinistas, Dr. Roman said, "I was concerned that he would accept everything that he was told to do. But he didn't. He used to argue. Sometimes he would accept and sometimes he didn't. He used to ask me, 'Do I have to do this?' If he didn't think it was right, he wouldn't do it."

Unfortunately, Argüello's trait of "wearing his emotions on his sleeve" hindered him as a political figure and, as many people attest, may have cost him his life.

"Alexis was very important to Ortega because he represented the 'forgive and forget' period," said friend and boxing promoter Ramiro Ortiz. "And Ortega couldn't tolerate it if the people turned against him. [Alexis] used to tell me, 'Ramiro, you can call it whatever you want, Socialism or Communism, but as a rich banker from Miami, you can't relate to the poverty of Nicaragua. I am going to support whoever provides for that poor Indian.' Now, we lived through Castro, so we knew Ortega's bullshit.

"Once I asked him, 'Alexis, what are you going to do when Ortega can't live up to all the bullshit that he promised you?' Then, he got real silent, and gave me this cold look, eyes staring through me, and in a soft voice he whispered like a warrior, 'Then, he has to answer personally to Alexis Argüello.' His forearms were bulging like steel pendants. I'll never forget it. But I knew he was in over his head."

Then, nine months later in July 2009, fifty-seven-year-old Argüello was dead. To his close associates, Argüello had finally turned the corner and put his vices in the past. As Nicaraguans learned that their champion lay in his home with a bullet wound to his chest, all of their collective fears were magnified. The man who had fulfilled their dreams and wishes was now a memory, soon to be the topic of another controversy. Instead of aging gracefully, Argüello had succumbed to something beyond anyone's understanding. Over the coming weeks and months the various theories about his death played out in horrifying stories that graced the pages of the local papers *La Prensa* and *El Nuevo Diario*.

Argüello's widow, Karla Rizo—with whom he had two sons, including an infant, Andrés—became the focus of attention as she tried to field questions from family members, the media, and friends. The ensuing controversy over his death blinded people to the reality that the man whom they hoped would grow old, sit back, and recount his boxing memories to his fans and grandchildren was gone. Nothing could bring him back, a point that would be drowned out by the following days of outrage.

The weekend before his death had been exhausting for Argüello as he traveled to Carolina, Puerto Rico on June 25 to visit Don Kahn, his old friend and trainer. Kahn opened the Alexis Argüello Boxing Academy and called upon his old friend to attend the opening ceremony. Kahn knew that whenever he needed Argüello, Alexis would answer his call. He never hesitated, stopping only to ask the same question, "When do you want me there?" After inaugurating a boxing gym that bore his name, he joked with old friends and boxers and, as Kahn noted, didn't touch a sip of alcohol. Kahn talked about his friend almost as if Argüello had experienced a sort of resurrection and returned to the old, ebullient Argüello everybody knew and loved. If Argüello was suffering at the time, it wasn't apparent to Kahn.

"He trusted me like his father," Kahn said. "He would never hide anything from me, even his maritas [women] or his problems with his wife. He came to me quite often. I could pick up the phone and Alexis would be here."

For most fighters, when taking a trip to the home country of a longtime nemesis, they are often met with open hostility and negativity. Argüello, however, had engendered goodwill all over the world; so, as Kahn noted, he was given a warm welcome in Puerto Rico. Moreover, according to Kahn, Argüello, whose health had deteriorated in previous years, was in better physical shape than he had been when "he fought Scott Walker."

"When I brought him to the opening of the Alexis Argüello Boxing Academy in Carolina, it was like he was a Puerto Rican world champion," said Kahn. "He was the kind of guy who never put down his opponent or made any kind of act, and they respected that."

With all of the political pressure that Argüello faced, coupled with the inner demons that occasionally surfaced, no one in Puerto Rico anticipated the lively Argüello who attended the gym's opening. Argüello also placed flowers on the cenotaph of the late Roberto Clemente, who had died in a plane crash while bringing aid to Nicaraguans devastated by the 1972 earthquake.

Kahn recounted the details of Argüello's last visit: "He left at 5 a.m. for the flight. He was so happy that he was making plans for the future. Then the next day he takes his life? There were no signs. He didn't drink alcohol for those three to four days. He spent most of the days asking for water. He was jumping around and not drinking. . . . [He has] a great day and the next day he dies?"

Friends consoled Kahn, saying that Argüello had come to spend his last days with him and to say good-bye properly. Kahn represented a large contingent of Argüello's friends, associates, and family members who desperately tried to piece together the details surrounding Argüello's death. Kahn tried his best to remember Argüello in high spirits.

"I want people to remember me as a good human being," Argüello told the author in 2008. "I was born a poor guy in a poor neighborhood and because of my dedication and determination, my professionalism and ambition, I made something. God gave me the opportunity to accomplish what I have and to get out of poverty."

The Wednesday after his trip to Puerto Rico, Argüello was confirmed dead at 1:40 a.m. Nicaragua mourned. *La Prensa's* headline read, "Thousands Bid Farewell to Alexis." In *El Nuevo Diario*, one headline said, "An Idol Did Not Die, Only Returned to His Glory." A second admonished the government, "Politics Used and Abused Him," and an article began, "His glory was his curse." The Nicaraguan flag flew at half-mast as thousands gathered in the Plaza de la República (Republic Square) in honor of their fallen hero. Preliminary findings from the Nicaraguan police indicated that Argüello committed suicide. After a chaotic scene at Argüello's home in the early hours of Wednesday, July 1, Argüello's body was taken to the Institute of Legal Medicine, and an autopsy was performed. By the next day, Chief of the National Police Glenda Zavala closed the investigation and confirmed that Argüello had committed suicide from a single gunshot to the chest. The coroner found no drugs or alcohol in Argüello's system.

Argüello's body was taken to the Mount Olivet Funeral Home, where hundreds waited and applauded. A mass was set for 5 p.m. Friday, two days after he was confirmed dead, at the Metropolitan Cathedral in Managua, and the next day his remains were carried through the streets to the National Palace of Culture. Thousands paid their last respects.

Dora Argüello, Alexis's daughter by his first wife, held tightly to her father's coffin as onlookers made their way to bid farewell. In a nearby hallway, Dora told a reporter: "He could have been depressed . . . the simple desire to see a better Managua." As for her father's suicide, Dora added: "If he had it planned, he planned it well, because he never showed it." A. J. was unable to get to Managua for two days, but reflected his and his sister's emotions when he told a reporter: "He was just starting to become the father we all wanted."

That evening, Fidel Moreno refused to talk to a reporter who had heard rumors about his recent confrontation with Alexis. Moreno remained silent, citing the reporter's "lack of respect."

"[I paid my respects] in the church before anyone else," said Roman. "I saw Ortega and his wife and just ignored them."

While Kahn asserted his stance that Argüello was in fine mental and physical condition the previous weekend, it was the details of the following days that have never been uncovered. On Tuesday, June 30, 2009, Argüello came home late in the afternoon. The Argüello housekeeper for four years, Gladys de Jesus López, served Argüello dinner at 7 p.m. He took his dinner to eat in his room and watch TV. According to López, Argüello was a notorious jokester, and he told her, "Every day I feel old and sometimes I want to die." She responded, "Tell me why you want to die?" Argüello playfully responded, "I do not know. I have tried many times, but haven't come up with anything. All that I am suffering from is insomnia. Some nights I can sleep, others I can not."

In retrospect, López did not notice anything odd about Argüello's demeanor that evening. López later went to her bedroom, which was located directly above Argüello's.

Around 8 p.m., Argüello's adviser, Dr. Henry Castillo, visited, but as he noted in various interviews, "I did not see that Alexis was having any emotional problems." Dr. Castillo was one of the few individuals who had remained in Argüello's tight circle of friends for decades. Speaking with Castillo, clearly Argüello was conflicted about his role as mayor of Nicaragua. Dr. Castillo recounted that Alexis had "called me that night and said, 'Can you come here?' I walked to the door and I stand at the front door, which was strange because I walk directly into his home all the time. I talked with the maid, Gladys, and she asked me a medical question. Then, Alexis comes down and said, 'What's happening?'"

Castillo recalled the brief conversation:

"Well, you know tomorrow I definitely quit (as mayor)," said Argüello. "Ok, man. But if you quit, then I have to quit because you are my brother," said Castillo.

Castillo offered to quit his position as well and then asked Argüello to reconsider or at least wait and talk with the president to see if they could fix the problem. But Argüello had said, "I am tired. I am going to do it." Convinced, Castillo assured him that they would resign together. As Castillo exited the Argüello home between 8:30 and 9:00 p.m., the close friends embraced for what would be the last time.

Later that evening, friend and Sandinista Party treasurer Francisco "Chico" López arrived at the Argüello household to speak with him. As noted earlier, the men had known each other from Argüello's rehabilitation stint at Hodera. López was credited with helping Argüello turn his life around and for reuniting Argüello and Daniel Ortega after decades of ill feeling. If anyone knew Argüello's strengths and weaknesses, it was López. The two friends' conversation revolved around Argüello's decision to leave his mayoral position in the Sandinista Party. According to some reports, López tried to coax Argüello to remain as mayor and attempted to bribe him during their contentious meeting. Although he never released details of their conversation, it is plausible that López explained that Argüello had no recourse but to keep his current position or face dire consequences. At some point during their conversation, López contacted First Lady Rosario Murillo to apprise her of their conversation.

López knew that upon returning from his successful weekend in Puerto Rico, Argüello had received news that Murillo had publicly stripped him of his mayoral duties and powers. Although Argüello recognized where he stood within the party, now he felt he was a laughingstock to his people. Threats, bribes, and intimidation tactics were all part of the Sandinista Party's attempt to save face. Those people closest to Daniel Ortega—and anyone remotely following Nicaraguan politics—realized from the outset that Argüello was simply a figurehead whom Ortega, Murillo, and their cronies could nudge toward a camera for a photo-op or strut out during party fundraisers. Every Nicaraguan also knew that when Alexis spoke, he was merely regurgitating the ideas of Secretary-General Fidel Moreno or another high-ranking Sandinista. As long as the kindhearted and good-natured Argüello stayed inside the Sandinista vacuum, they had no cause for alarm. If Argüello ventured too far, the Sandinistas would reel him back in.

Rosario Murillo's decision to strip him of all powers, however, had blindsided Argüello. Those close to him confirmed that hearing the decision left him broken and confused at that moment. *El Nuevo Diario*, on Saturday, June 27, 2009, confirmed that a resolution was passed to create two new districts, which now made seven total, and that they all would respond directly to Moreno. Argüello also would have to answer to Moreno. Luciano Garcia was the only councilman who voted against the resolution, and PLC representative Jimy Blandon believed that the resolution would provide Argüello with more support for the capital city's 500,000 residents. Others realized the resolution's implications: The reforms drastically reduced Argüello's ability to administer his duties. Marginalized again, and this time in a public forum, Argüello was not present at the meeting to argue his case. To many who loved and trusted Argüello, Murillo had leveled a clear shot below the belt.

The day Alexis found out, Dr. Castillo recalled, "Karla comes over with the newspaper and says, 'Do you see what happened in the newspaper? It says in the paper that they stripped your power.' When he found out, he called Secretary Fidel Moreno to find out what was going on. At the same time, they start to argue. Then he called Chico López to see what was going on. When he left, he was really sad. I asked him where he was going, and he responded, 'I don't know. Maybe I will go home.' But he was really sad, and it seemed like he was crying."

That morning, Moreno and Argüello nearly brawled on the municipality premises. They broke several chairs in the office.

Many felt that Murillo and Ortega's decision ignited a domino effect of tragic occurrences that led directly to Argüello's death. Respected journalist Silvio Sirias, who currently resides in Panama, later reported that "to this day, quite a few Nicaraguans, including Alexis's children from previous marriages, claim that the former world champion intended to hold a press conference in which he would denounce Ortega's tampering during the municipal elections." Thus, it was entirely possible that Murillo's suspension of Argüello's duties tied directly to Argüello's threat of uncovering the graft and corruption that the government had been guilty of for years.

Although Don Kahn remembered his close friend and confidant enjoying the last days before his death, Argüello's wife Karla Rizo presented a different portrait. Rizo noted that shortly after midnight, their baby son's crying woke both Karla and Alexis. Karla then told Alexis that she would take care of the baby. "We give him his bottle, I stay with him and walk with him, trying to make him burp," Rizo said. Rizo attempted to quiet the baby, but then after putting him back to bed, he refused to sleep.

Alexis was laying on the bed when she returned. She claims he had removed his Ceska 9mm revolver from a bag and placed it on top of him.

"I manage to take the weapon off him and I try to go away with the baby, but I was running downstairs with the baby in one hand and the weapon in the other," Rizo said. "He manages to take the gun off me, he loads it, he sits down on the bed and in that moment he pointed the gun at himself. . . . He didn't answer me."

Rizo continued to relive the horrific moment. "Even when he had the gun in his hand, he had this look of great sadness. I did not say anything." Then Rizo tried to prevent Argüello from pulling the trigger and screamed wildly, "Put it . . . put it down. Stop, Alexis!" (In other recollections, Rizo claimed that she told Argüello, "Look, the child is looking at you. Put that away, please.")

Argüello did not respond to her pleas, and it is unclear whether Argüello held the gun out or held the gun between his legs and pointed it up at his chest. Rizo called for her mother, Mayra Rizo, and pleaded: "Take the baby, take the baby. Alexis wants to do something."

Rizo then called for López, the housekeeper, to come and help her. López specifically recalled Karla yelling, "Your boss wants to kill himself!"

As the story goes, López was on the second floor of the house, and Rizo came out and started down the stairs, screaming for Argüello to not kill himself. Rizo began to call an unnamed family friend to bring security guards and take the gun from her husband, but it was too late.

"When I was going down the flights of stairs, he pulled the trigger," said Rizo.

The housekeeper was the closest, or outside Argüello's room, when he took his life. Argüello fell over face first, and as soon as Rizo arrived she began to sop up the blood as best she could. As for a stunned López, "I was scared at what I saw, and I stayed watching as he slowly little by little fell to the floor." Rizo and the guards, Clever and Cesar, finally picked up and began to move Argüello's body. When asked later whether they dropped the body at some point, which could have caused the visible trauma to Argüello's face and hand that was noticed at the open-casket funeral, Rizo confirmed that they did not drop him. The source of the bruises on Argüello's nose, finger, and body would become a point of contention. His older children claimed that the bruises were hidden because they were the evidence that a Sandinista hit man had been sent to kill their father.

Later, Rizo would contradict herself and claim that Argüello's bruises came from dropping him as she and the bodyguards carried his body. Gladys López suggested that Argüello's bruises happened when Argüello initially fell from his bed. On several occasions, Rizo reiterated the point that Argüello suffered from a deep depression; however, Argüello's personal physician, Henry Castillo, and López discredited that fact. The details and testimonies that surfaced in the press would soon be scrutinized, disputed, changed, updated, and altered over the coming weeks.

Facing fierce opposition from Argüello's daughter and son from his first marriage, Dora and Alexis Junior (A. J.), Karla Rizo never wavered in her steadfast response to persistent inquiries from the Nicaraguan press regarding her husband's suicide. "This is the truth," she said. "I have no reason to lie. I wish that my husband was still alive, but it was a decision that he took, and I have to live with it. . . . There is nothing to hide."

Alexis Junior, Argüello's son from his first marriage, was dumbfounded by Rizo's indifference after his father's death. When Rizo telephoned Argüello Junior in the early morning of July 1, 2009, he was incredulous at how callous she sounded when she calmly repeated, "Your father shot and killed himself." A bad dream turned into a nightmare when Rizo refused to relinquish his father's championship belts to him. "Where was the sadness and sorrow?" wondered Argüello Junior. If Rizo loved his father, why was she acting as if she was relieved? It is a question that will haunt the Argüello children for years to come.

Although Rizo came under scrutiny from family members, it was hard to disprove her version of events, especially when another reliable witness corroborated her story. The housekeeper, Gladys López, "is a good, honest person," said Dr. Eduardo Roman, who had recommended her to the Argüello family as a cook. "She had no reason to lie. What was there to gain? When I went to the home that evening, they had held her in a room upstairs. I told the police to let her go because she had nothing left to say."

Any conspiracy theory that someone had bought off Lopez can be refuted by the fact that she left the Rizos' employment and went to work a similar job for minimal salary.

Meanwhile, Argüello's ex-wife Alicia Esquivel, who had two children with Argüello, refused to believe that her late husband would have made such a "cowardly decision." She maintained, "For me, he did not take his life." After hearing that the government planned to move Argüello's body to a different location, Esquivel expressed her belief that Rizo, Daniel Ortega, and Rosario Murillo had conspired to use, abuse, and then kill Argüello. She was convinced that the only reason they had to move his remains was to "erase evidence." Esquivel also believed that with the current advanced technology and forensics capabilities that Ortega and Murillo would be indicted for their actions and that one day Argüello's "ashes will speak."

While Esquivel railed at the government's ineptitude, Dora directed her frustration and anger at Rizo. The day following Alexis's death, Rizo had called Dora and said, "Your father always wanted to be cremated. We have to do it now." Infuriated, Dora quickly ordered Rizo not to touch her father's body. Dora had not even seen her father's body yet, and Rizo had already begun the funeral proceedings. In November 2009, Dora Argüello was still fighting for justice as she commented on the inaccuracies of Rizo's testimonies: "[Karla] knows what she told a friend who was close to my father. She knows very well the version that she gave to my brother, and she knows the version she told me," Dora said. She saw a "lot of irregularities" in Rizo's testimony, but Dora felt that the government will never acknowledge or investigate them because they "manipulate everything."

"The investigation is a case that has been closed, and that is also what I think because I lived it," Karla Rizo told the author in 2011. "What people say is what they think or feel. . . . What his children say [is] not what really happened. We all know that it was a personal decision made by him and only God knows why and I don't have anything else to say.

"I have never really cared [what people say]. I don't care what people think about me, and what they think doesn't make an impact on me. Everyone is entitled [to] an opinion and everyone can and has their own opinion. I know what happened and every day I pray and ask God for his [Alexis] forgiveness, because according to our beliefs, I am Catholic, the suicide is a huge sin."

She continued, "At some point I understand the point of view of Alexis's children. I think this is the way they feel because they weren't at the moment of his death and I understand their doubts. But from having doubts to a confirmation. . . they have a lot of imagination. The police investigations are as clear as water and if they are not certain is because that's what they want to think. In any moment I've been against disinterring the body. If Alexis's children want to make any further investigation they can. They say they will bring people from other countries to do it. I don't have a problem with it. I will always give the permission to do it, and that they once and for all are satisfied and calmer about what happened."

Dora Argüello also criticized Eduardo Roman's position, for he refused to believe that the Sandinista Party set up her father for this fall. Argüello had spoken with his former manager Roman the day before he died. Although Roman skirted around the details of the conversation, he did state that Argüello had a problem with the government and planned to revisit it the next morning. Roman and Argüello had a unique relationship. Nearly four decades had passed since Roman had offered newcomer Argüello a contract in 1970, and, unlike most manager-boxer friendships, this one had miraculously stood the test of time. When most people criticized Argüello's move into the political spectrum as another one of his impulsive decisions, Roman had stood by his friend.

"He had a better political mind than one might think," said Roman. "He surprised me a lot. He was very logical. He would always look for reasons why, and he was able to make good decisions. We never had arguments; we had discussions. Even without an education, he had a good mind. I didn't have to tell him to do things. The good thing about argument is to hear the other person before you make a decision. He was a politician in some ways."

They never had the chance to continue their argument. At 2 a.m., Roman received a phone call from a Sandinista Party secretary. Roman quickly tried to silence him so he could go back to sleep.

"My grandmother always told me to let someone finish what they are saying before they jump in," said Roman. "When the secretary, Francisco López called me, he said, 'Dr. Roman, we have a problem with Alexis.' And quickly I jumped in and cut him off to say, 'I know and we will solve it in the morning.' Then he said, 'No Dr. Roman, the problem is that he is dead.'"

Roman quickly dressed and went to the hospital to receive his friend's body and get more information. However, by the time Roman arrived at the hospital, Argüello's body had already been taken to the morgue. Roman then went directly to the house to find out the details. It wasn't long before he heard the various rumors.

"I never thought he would do that," Roman said in 2011 in Nicaragua. "Sometimes he had the idea in his mind, but I never thought he would ever do that. I don't like Sandinistas, but a lot of people think that they killed him. But why would they kill him? He wasn't doing them any damage. If he was going to do something, he would advise them before it. I think he did it because he felt the impulse to do it. If we talked, things could have been different. "

Argüello's closest friend Donald Rodriguez found out about the death on his 4:30 a.m. morning walk when he saw Karla Rizo drive past. Popular sports-writer Edgar Tijerino, who had created the moniker Flaco Explosivo, heard about Argüello's death the next day at his radio station. Bagnariol, one of the closest friends Argüello had, thought it was a cruel joke.

"I was told he died like at 1:30 a.m. and I received a call from his wife just before 5 a.m.," said Rodriguez. "She told me he committed suicide. For me it was incredible that he had committed suicide. But the one who knows and saw what happened is his wife. We just know what she told us."

The official case was closed less than twenty-four hours after Argüello's death. Five months afterward, photographs of the bruises that had surfaced on Argüello's nose, finger, and torso were released to the public. Dr. Zachary Duarte, the director of the Institute of Legal Medicine, analyzed the contusions on Argüello's nose, lower lip, and the first finger of his left hand and determined that they did not prove Argüello had been attacked that fatal evening. However, no one else was allowed to witness Duarte during this examination, and that fact alone had created skepticism regarding his results. So many questions went unanswered over the next week: Why was the autopsy and ballistics report fin-ished within a day of his death? Why was Karla Rizo so swift with the proceed-ings after the death, and so difficult when dealing with Argüello's children? Why was the public not privy to the details of that fateful night? Everything was expe-dited and what turned out to be a confirmed "suicide" had morphed into a debacle—an ugly wart for the Sandinista party.

Dora Argüello claimed again that her father had been assassinated and took her protests to the streets in opposition to Daniel Ortega's fraudulent government. The sign she held showed a photo of Alexis Argüello and the slogan, "No Mas Repression!" Although few were willing to speak their mind because of possible intimidation tactics, many questioned the handling of the case.

"I wasn't suspicious about the death, but the government's posturing after his death made me suspicious," said former member of the Nicaraguan Boxing Commission Sergio Quintero. "For example, when Alexis was dead and they brought him to this Forensics Institute, which was one of the most corrupt institutions in all of Nicaragua, Alexis's body was kept alone for five hours where nobody could see him when they conducted an autopsy. Why wasn't anyone allowed to see him? When Alexis was alive, they used him all the time.

"During the last few weeks of his life, Alexis was showing more instances of frustration and confusion. Also, Alexis was becoming more uncontrollable, to the point where he physically showed his frustration with Fidel Moreno. They almost fought each other. Alexis couldn't take it anymore. At the funeral, Alexis's body was so covered in makeup, so it was nearly impossible to see the bruises on the body."

At a remembrance held by the Nicaraguan Council to mark the anniversary of Argüello's death, Dr. Eduardo Roman stood up and declared, "Alexis never thought about death. . . . He was angry at the municipality" before he died.

After the case was closed, a lawyer and prominent figure in the opposition, Victor Boitano Coleman, quickly pieced together a book that compiled the articles regarding Argüello's death. During an interview, Boitano explained his position on why he thought that Argüello had been assassinated. "Karla Rizo is the only family of Alexis Argüello who says he was not murdered, all the others say . . . he was killed," Boitano said. "The Nicaraguan authorities closed the case in twenty-four hours, without having completed all investigations. It is impossible to close such a case so quickly. The authorities have not allowed family members to conduct independent investigations. As a lawyer and former colonel who worked in military intelligence, I can assure you there are a number of irregularities with this case. Also, the blows to his body are obvious, and forensic experts confirmed that there were signs of violence."

Sirias recognized the power of politics in Nicaragua in contemplating Argüello's death. He said, "When he pulled the trigger, it was neither his addiction to drugs nor to alcohol that provoked the act. Instead, the foul world of Nicaraguan politics, especially as played by the Sandinista leadership, moved him to commit suicide. Every Nicaraguan knows this. The former boxing champion was a man who behaved honorably and who always put his heart into everything he did, even in the brutal world of boxing. The tragic manner in which he ended his life, however, clearly indicates that Alexis Argüello had stopped believing in everyone and everything, including himself. On the night he pulled the trigger, not only did he pierce his own heart, but he wounded those of every Nicaraguan, both at home and away, who saw him as a larger-than-life figure, as one of Nicaragua's noblest offerings to the world."

Many Nicaraguans residing in Miami believe that the evening of Argüello's death, powerful Sandinistas, among them Fidel Moreno and Chico López, strong-armed the champ. Then after punching one of the men during a violent altercation, he was shot and killed by bodyguards, according to one story told to the author during a Nicaraguan wedding. This contingent claims that Argüello was going to reveal the truth of the Sandinistas' complicity during his corrupt mayoral victory.

In the end, it wasn't what the Sandinista brass did, but rather what they didn't do or say that made them appear suspicious. If there was no foul play or coercion, why didn't Francisco López ever reveal what he said to Alexis that fateful night?

"I don't know why he thinks or acts a certain way," said Roman. "He is a politician and I am not." Various organizations held tributes in Argüello's honor on the anniversary of his death in 2011. One tribute was held at the statue that Ortega had erected of Argüello when it was built in 2009; however, most Nicaraguans recognized the statue as nothing more than a weak attempt to save face. But the steadfast devotion to his memory only increased as Dora and Alexis Argüello Junior refused to accept what they considered a fraudulent government's explanation and cover-up of an assassination.

Alexis Junior, who lives in the United States, believes that the former boxer was murdered. "Someone other than Alexis Argüello pulled that trigger," he told a Florida television station.

"They killed my father," Dora Argüello told *El Pais*. Further, she blames President Daniel Ortega for not providing her father with more security. To this day, she fights to reopen a case that the government had sealed in 2009.

Remembering a Hero

You can never replace him.
—Sergio Quintero

In the ring, Argüello exhibited an unmatched patience and control; outside the ring, the man epitomized class and dignity. Between the ropes, Argüello pondered each punch, carefully analyzed each open space, and never rushed to get to the finish line. Later in life, Argüello was unable to fill empty spaces, foundered when faced with adversity, and often forged ahead without proper consideration for his family or the future. In the ring, few could match Argüello's boxing IQ; in the political arena, he was clearly overmatched in debate, didn't have the capacity to think on his feet, and often relied on blanket statements to help serve the poor. When he was successful in the ring, Argüello easily controlled his life outside of it, but when he aged, lost his skills, and regressed, he fell victim to self-pity and recklessness. In both fields, he had thousands of models he could emulate.

In his nearly three decades of boxing, however, Argüello never faced a challenger similar to Daniel Ortega and his Sandinista National Liberation Front acolytes. They didn't use stick-and-run tactics as Vilomar Fernández did or deftly outbox him as Aaron Pryor did, twice, or even attempt to outgun him with a dose of power punching à la Ray "Boom Boom" Mancini. When attempting to maneuver past those opponents, Argüello found ways to be successful, even if they meant he lost by decision or knockout; he was always there when the fight ended. In the 1990s, even before he wrapped his hands, Argüello was reduced to a punch-drunk journeyman when he decided to allow Daniel Ortega back into his life. Although he told himself his decision had to do with aiding the poor or resolving bitter conflict, as he had for his entire life, Argüello instead had reunited with Ortega to please others. When he made his final pact with this devil, though, failure was the only outcome. This was no return to glory as "Forgive and Forget" quickly soured. The savvy Ortega always would be at least three steps ahead of his opponent as they vied for Nicaraguans' approval.

Argüello represented the first of three boxers who died that summer of 2009. Canada's Arturo Gatti, Ireland's Darren Sutherland, and Vernon Forrest of the United States also died violently that summer, with Gatti's death still under investigation as a possible homicide. Since they all had fought in the last decade, the fans were more familiar with their names, records, and accomplishments. For the casual fan, Argüello represented a relic, a rival in one of boxing's monumental battles. The saddest aspect of Argüello's career is that he needed a name fighter, Aaron Pryor, finally to earn real recognition as a boxing icon. To the avid fan or the boxing journalist, though, Argüello was one of the great fighters of all time, and because he was so deft in the ring, some even placed him in their personal top ten.

In actuality, Agrüello symbolized class, consistency, and dedication to the sport for his entire career. He never lost a title in the ring, he became the first of six boxers to win three titles in as many weight classes, and he never, ever avoided an opponent. Unlike his boxing comrades, Argüello always respected the sport, getting in shape and being prepared for every battle; therefore, he rarely experienced the extreme highs and deleterious lows that defined so many careers of his generation of fighters. Argüello never let fans down, so when he finally decided to retire, he had few regrets of how he handled himself in the ring.

The world knew about Alexis Argüello before he faced Aaron Pryor, but most didn't know him. For the multitudes, Argüello's death forced them to search their personal boxing archives to place his name and face, which was undoubtedly alongside Pryor's. Lamentably, even in death Argüello was forced to share center stage.

Gatti and Argüello's death revealed not only their glaring personal flaws but the reality that without regulation or a support system, many more deaths will follow. Ironically, the same people who ran boxing in the days of Argüello's prime still control the sport today. Regulation might never happen because it would mean sharing the gains, curtailing corruption, and wresting control from boxing's upper echelon. Instead of taking the occasion of these boxers' tragic deaths to reflect on the warts and limitations of a sport that uses and abuses and then discards them, the focus has centered on the sordid controversy surrounding Arturo Gatti's death in Brazil. The boxing world should have recognized its complicity in these deaths and initiated debates on necessary change.

Instead, professional boxing went back to "business as usual." That following April, yet another fighter, Venezuela's Edwin Valero, was found hanging in his prison cell.

Everyone I contacted for this project all wanted answers to the questions about Alexis Argüello that they ask themselves on a daily basis. These questions ranged from "Why did he do it?" to "Why did they destroy our hero?" To this day, some fans even refuse to believe that he's gone. People have different approaches to how they mourn the death of an individual who had such a resounding impact, whether directly or indirectly, on their lives. Those people who still have Argüello in their hearts, such as Evelio Areas and Carlos Varela, struggled through the interviews. They became so emotional that they could not finish their sentences. Their love for Argüello was unwavering. Dora Argüello, Alexis's daughter, raged as she heaved herself on her father's coffin, and his eldest son, Alexis Junior (A. J.), kept his composure as he watched the Sandinista facade at the funeral and directed his hateful stare toward Ortega as he walked up to his father's body. Inside he must have thought, my father didn't represent the Sandinistas, he represented Nicaraguans.

Ortega and his wife Rosario embraced Argüello family members, and grieved accordingly. Confidantes of the fighter could hardly mask their disgust at the scene. While A. J. fumed, others kept their distance. As many recall from the proceedings, the pretense and fraudulence was palpable.

During the funeral procession, Dora noticed unusual discoloration on her the bridge of her father's nose and continued to plead her father's case over the next year that the bruises were caused by physical abuse, thus supporting her theory that he was murdered. Several interviewees railed against the country's political instability and blamed the government for Alexis's death. Realizing that Argüello had dealt with personal issues all his life, however, others had accepted his death and moved on. No matter what happened the evening of Argüello's death, something or someone who knew his weaknesses pushed him to the brink, through threats or other intimidation tactics. If he wanted to leave his position, Ortega and the Sandinistas had a lot to lose.

For many Nicaraguans, Argüello had stitched together the fabric of their childhood and adolescent years. The Areas family members, for instance, remembered the "decent young boy" who invited them to his weddings. Even though they had left Nicaragua years ago, they still recalled the innocent boy who would go on to benefit from and be ravaged by fame. Back in Nicaragua, people marveled at his grace as a champion, a man who always knew what he meant to his people. They never forgot. While sitting at home those nights, watching the bouts on television, and waiting for Alexis to enter the ring, they weren't watching a fight but an event. Each punch, each feint reminded them that the world still had heroes, and their hero cared about them as people.

Through all their recollections, they acknowledged the lasting impact that their beloved champion had on their lives. In the midst of this tragedy, it's comforting to know that Alexis touched so many people; it will be impossible to forget him and his engaging smile.

The boxing world weighed in with its praises only days after Argüello died. In an age where news spreads worldwide as rapidly as it occurs, the boxing community learned of his death seconds after his body was found that early morning of July 1.

"Selfishly, I knew that I would miss him. I remember when I heard I wanted to shout out to all those Internet bloggers to tell them about his record and that he never lost a title in the ring," said Showtime boxing analyst Steve Farhood. "I wanted them to appreciate his greatness, and I don't think they did or they do. I don't hear people saying Argüello's name with Roberto Durán's and Sugar Ray Leonard's. He was always a step below. It was frustrating to think, knowing that his greatness would be overshadowed by the tragedy. . . . I envisioned him becoming a grand, old man of boxing."

Former promoter and manager of the Inglewood Forum Don Chargin recalled, "Anybody who knew anything about boxing knew Alexis was the real thing. I think it was common knowledge about his personal downfall. I felt really bad. He seemed to have gotten over the drugs and everything and gotten it together. When he died, I thought of the way he greeted me at the Hall of Fame. Anybody that walked up, he would tell him that I was 'the guy who got me my lightweight title.'"

Said former world champ and West Coast cult figure Danny Lopez, "Alexis was a friend of mine. I was sorry to see he was shot. They say he shot himself, but I don't think so."

The mark of a true, moral man is that he treats everybody in his life the same, with respect. In that regard, Argüello never changed.

"Ever since I was eleven years old, Argüello's been one of my idols. Alexis told me that if I can afford it, I should forget the dealings—I was working fifty-five hours a week—and concentrate on boxing," said former sparring partner Glen Costales from New Jersey. "Some people think that the way he is on TV is just an act. But he's the same all the time. Never in seven days did anyone influence me like that, how to handle myself as a professional inside and outside the ring. If nothing happens in my boxing career, at least I can say I fought with the greatest."

Argüello's agent and manager Bill Miller had grown fond of the fighter during their decade working together. "I miss the camaraderie of boxing. I really admired Alexis," said Miller. "He was strong as an ox. He put the fear of the devil in you. Even if he just hit someone in the shoulder, he wanted out. He was also a wonderful dresser. Everything fit him like a clothes rack. He always looked good.

"We always had a good personal relationship, but it never extended where it would destroy our professional relationship. We lost touch after his comeback. When I heard about his death, I thought that if he committed suicide, someone helped him. Suicide wasn't in his character. It never rang true with who he was."

When Argüello put his arm around Mancini after their title fight in 1981, he let the world know that he wasn't about the money or the fame. Mancini said, "When he died, I was heartbroken. I couldn't believe it. When they said suicide, I said bullshit. He was the happiest guy. He was the mayor of Nicaragua, a guy who loved being around people. I never believed that. It was all horseshit. He was frustrated because he wasn't able to make any decisions. He was just a figurehead. He wanted to represent his people. Here was a guy who was so revered in Miami. People knew him everywhere he went. He wanted so bad to help his people."

Another late-round knockout victim, Rubén Castillo, became close friends with Argüello after their bout in 1980. "I think his best weight was 130 and lightweight," said Castillo. "Can you imagine him at 126? He ruined a whole lot of people's careers. It took people to take drugs to try and beat him. Whenever you fought him, you needed to have a Plan B. He was a legend inside and outside the ring.

"I was sitting at a boxing dinner for the World Boxing Hall of Fame. I was with Ray Mancini and some other fighters who all fought each other. But the common denominator was that we all fought and got knocked out by Alexis. Ray looks over at me and says, 'Ruben, how many rounds did you go against Alexis?' And I said, 'Eleven, why?' And Mancini says, 'Because I went fourteen,' and he starts laughing. I said, 'Well, who's the idiot? You got three more rounds of an ass whipping!' And Argüello was on the floor laughing."

Cuban author Enrique Encinosa spent many hours at the International Boxing Hall of Fame entrenched in endless political discussions with Argüello.

He said, "He was intelligent. He couldn't discuss Mark Twain or Jack Kerouac, but he was exposed to so many strata of society that he had gained polish; even if a lot of his ideas were political clichés, others were solid.

"Also, Alexis had a very charitable side. If he had been able to work for a world organization where he could help bring educational programs to the poor, he would still be alive and content. He had an ideology, but within that ideology he was vulnerable. He was always well meant, but someone who came to him with a good pitch could get him to change sides immediately. All his mistakes were made out of desperation."

Promoter Don Fraser knew Argüello from when the fighter cemented his boxing roots in California. Fraser stressed that Alexis's feelings had gotten "trampled on over the years." Commenting on the lack of appreciation for Argüello after he retired, he added, "Yesterday's cheers have a short echo."

Fraser continued, "First, when he died I remembered what a great boxer he was. How smooth he was. They called José Nápoles 'Mantequilla' or butter, but that could have applied to Argüello. He had duende, or elegance. If Ali did everything in the ring the wrong way, Argüello was a guy who did everything the right way, almost perfectly. He was a great technician, and [in that regard] I would group him with [Wilfred] Benítez."

Dr. Roman knew that Argüello had so much more to give. He said, "He always introduced me as his father, even to a Russian ambassador. I admired him because he knew what he had to do, and then went out and did it. When I see him again, I am going to tell him what he did was wrong. That he should have never shot himself. Not Alexis."

Roman had more access to Argüello than any individual since his boxing debut in 1968. When he thought of his fallen friend, Roman immediately recalled their first meeting.

"I remember when he first came to my office," said Roman. "Nobody could have done what he did. He was one in a million."

While shock was the initial response for Argüello's past opponents, friends, and family members, then anger and sorrow quickly followed. Longtime Kronk trainer Emanuel Steward worked across from Argüello in the rematch with Aaron Pryor.

"I called Aaron when Alexis died, and he said, 'Oh, no.' He was . . . let's just say in the last eight to ten years Alexis's best friend. They were always very close. Think about that type of rivalry. Every time you think about Alexis, you immediately think about Aaron Pryor," said Steward. "Those people only remember

Alexis through his two losses to Aaron. That's unfortunate because he had so many other great fights. That is so unfortunate. That's life, though. People will only remember Aaron through those fights with Alexis. That's just the way history is."

Steward continued: "[Aaron] and Alexis always talked. He and Alexis were close. It had a lot to do with them getting together and being regulars at the Hall of Fame. When Alexis ran for election, Aaron went to help him campaign. He was with him a week before he died. When Aaron found out, he was totally crushed. He said, 'There's no way in the world that that man could kill himself.' He was so happy when we were down there. [Alexis] was always very politically opinionated."

Ironically, both men found solace in their shared experiences in and out of the ring, a dynamic that is typical of such a brutal sport. When people remember Argüello, they must also remember Pryor. The fights changed their lives forever.

"[Argüello] left a legacy that will always be remembered," the then fifty-four-year-old Pryor said. "All I can say is what a friend I had."

"I think that first fight with Pryor had a lot to do with his legacy," said Walter Alvarez. "Even for me as a promoter of the fight—I had been doing fights in Miami since the 1970s—and people introduced me as 'Walter Alvarez, the guy who did the Argüello-Pryor bout at the Orange Bowl.' It defines my career. Whatever those guys did before was a way of getting to that fight. People will remember the trajectory. Common people will ask, 'Who the hell did Alexis Argüello fight?' But they will know his greatness. His past defined his trajectory to get into this one fight."

Sports broadcaster Barry Tompkins called the first fight with Aaron Pryor and emphasized the hostile environment of that bout. He also expressed his admiration for both fighters. As for how he will remember Argüello, he said, "I always liked Argüello and found him to be more complex than what you saw on the surface. All fighters are most introspective. He would think about the questions and give heartfelt answers. A lot of fighters are really complex, and Argüello fell into that category. He was a thinker, extremely sensitive. There was a lot going on and that contributed to his demise. He will always be remembered as a class act. Even when he was living hard, he was still a class act. His legacy will grow, and history will treat him kindly."

Despite only having a brief relationship with Argüello, broadcaster Larry Merchant realized his significance to the sport. His opinion is that Alexis "was a helluva fighter. If Durán was a tough street kid, Argüello was the Spanish gentleman."

Former professional welterweight boxer Armando Muniz reflected on Argüello's career and how he represented the ideal ambassador for the sport: "What boxing lost is that when people met Alexis they had a different view of what boxing was. Alexis represented the opposite, and we need a lot more of him. Alexis was not only a good representative and noble, but he gave assurance that he could fight another day. And he did it the right way."

When Argüello defeated lightweight champ Jim Watt, he earned his third world title in as many weight classes, a feat that grouped him in select company. Watt, meanwhile, is one of the few boxers who found his niche once the final bell sounded on his career.

"It was difficult for a lot of fighters who lived for boxing to finally give it up. For me, boxing was a means to an end," Watt said. "For many fighters, boxing was an addiction, and anything after their career was anticlimactic. He had treatment for depression and attempted suicide. I was shocked, but there were a lot of warning signs."

Conversely, former opponent Alfredo Escalera was dumbfounded when he heard the news. "Alexis was too intelligent and wise. I cannot believe that he killed himself. It is impossible."

When close friend Don Kahn brought Argüello to Puerto Rico to dedicate a boxing gym for amateur fighters that was named in his honor, he never dreamed that it would be the last time he would ever see his friend. Kahn said, "I cannot say but what I heard. He was the one [as mayor], but they dictated what to do. They didn't give him power. That's what I can testify for. Whatever happened, there was no sign of it."

Kahn's echoed the thoughts of thousands who loved the fighter. Argüello left Puerto Rico on a high, and returned home in good health. With the exception of a nagging cold and pain in his leg, Argüello was in fighting shape. When he returned to Managua, his fears were confirmed—it was one thing to be perceived as merely a figurehead, it was another to have it confirmed. Within twenty-four hours of hearing the news of being stripped of his powers, a great man and fighter was gone. The facts about his death may never be revealed, but the suspicion is warranted. With nothing to lose, Argüello became the biggest threat to the same people who claimed to have "saved him." Truth is, they only accelerated the fighter's death, slowly chipping away at the physically imposing, yet fragile and sensitive soul of the greatest Nicaraguan figure who ever lived. The statue stands for the country to visit, a cheap substitute for the real thing.

Trainer and longtime friend Carlos Varela held back tears as he discussed Argüello. Varela said, "I will remember him as a humble guy who put all his efforts and talent into being a champion. He always loved the people of Nicaragua and they loved him back."

As news spread in Nicaragua of Argüello's passing, friends and family members reminisced about the polite and energetic young boy who roamed the Monseñor Lezcano neighborhood and grew into a loving father who doted on his sons. Others recalled a single punch. Alexis Argüello had claimed he was destined to be special, that God had called upon him to do something that only one human could accomplish. He accomplished those goals and so much more. When the news broke on July 1, 2009, no one could deny that one of the great icons had fallen. It was not supposed to end this way for our Alexis, his people thought to themselves. He had dedicated his life to the poor and people who didn't have his advantages. Ever since Alexis experienced the injustice of being kicked out of school at age thirteen, he had sworn that if he had the power he would never let poor people be denied their rights. Despite his flaws, it was impossible to question Argüello's heart. He strove to make his country a better place. He took all the advice his mentors—Dr. Roman, Kid Pambelé, Ratón Mojica, and his parents—had given him and molded his mind and body so that he could be a role model for children and for his people.

In the ring, people remembered, he was disciplined and exhibited an unequaled capacity for compassion. He fought his opponents and then embraced them with the same passion. In an unforgettable moment, he told future champ Ray Mancini, "What you and your father have is something beautiful." Then he put his arm around Mancini and whispered something in his ear. It was a touching moment, and it was vintage Alexis.

Boxing represented one element of his life, humanity another. Argüello eschewed the prefight bluster, instead focusing on his opponent's family and health. Even his opponents had difficulty hating him; they could not muster rage against him. Looking past the knockouts, dramatic victories, and championship belts, they saw the real Argüello. That man was not defined by the glitz and glamour of the limelight but by the relationships that were strengthened once the limelight dimmed. He did not find it easy to handle the fame and the benefits that were allotted world champs. Instead, connecting with people when the fighting finished was what Argüello cherished. Whether it was an arm around a promoter or a former opponent at the International Boxing Hall of Fame, a firm handshake at a celebrity dinner, or even a phone call from a long-time friend, Alexis enjoyed immersing himself in people and relationships.

"Most people can be replaced physically, but Alexis is irreplaceable because of how noble he was inside and outside the ring," said former member of the Nicaraguan Boxing Commission Sergio Quintero. "In the ring, Alexis knew his adversaries and there were rules to abide by. Outside the ring, Alexis couldn't fight that way. You know, below the belt."

As the people mourned, they recognized there never would be another fighter like him and, more important, another man quite like him. He was sensitive, sharp, charming, witty, and, at times, self-indulging. He was pensive, introspective, and, although rarely, boastful. He was a loving son and a loving father. He was a man of contradictions who tried to walk a righteous path. He was the gentleman who would open a door for a lady. He was the champ who walked through his old neighborhood and hailed friends. He was the politician who fought to raise funding for the poor. He was simply Alexis.

In April 2008, Argüello sat in the Intercontinental Hotel and reminisced about his legacy. "I can say that I took the message and responsibility of [all Latin America] because I did it. I can look back and say I did a good job. I stood up to the expectation and represented this country with dignity and respect," he said. "I desired to be somebody. I am not ashamed. If I were born again, I'd do it again. I represented this nation in a positive way. I can tell the youth that I was always the best at my game."

Then he looked into the distance, knowing deep down that he did everything he could for his people, his country, and his family. Someone approached and embraced him, and he once again gave everyone the engaging Argüello smile of old. In a couple of months, he would be elected mayor, fighting for the poor people he refused to leave behind. In or out of the ring, that love and affection will be his lasting legacy.

ARGÜELLO'S BOXING RECORD

Date	Opponent	Location	W/L	KO/Decision/ Number of Rounds
1973				
March 30	Fernando Fernández	Managua, Nicaragua	W	TKO, 2
April 22	Magallo Lozada	Managua, Nicaragua	W	Decision, 10
May 26	Kid Pascualito	Managua, Nicaragua	W	KO, 3
June 30	Octavio Gómez	Managua, Nicaragua	W	KO, 2
August 25	Nacho Lomelí	Managua, Nicaragua	W	KO, 1
October 17	Sigfredo Rodriguez	Managua, Nicaragua	W	TKO, 9
November 27	José Legrá	Masaya, Nicaragua	W	KO, 1
1974				
January 8	Raúl Martínez Mora	Managua, Nicaragua	W	KO, 1
February 16	Ernesto Marcel	Panamá, Panamá	L	Decision, 15
April 27	Enrique García	Managua, Nicaragua	W	KO, 3
May 19	Art Hafey	Masaya, Nicaragua	W	KO, 5
August 29	Oscar Aparicio	Managua, Nicaragua	W	Decision, 12
September 21	Otoniel Martínez	Managua, Nicaragua	W	KO, 1
November 23	Rubén Olivares	Los Angeles, CA	W	KO, 13
1975				
February 8	Oscar Aparicio	San Salvador, El Salvador	W	Decision, 10
March 15	Leonel Hernández	Caracas, Venezuela	W	TKO, 8
May 31	Rigoberto Riasco	Granada, Nicaragua	W	TKO, 2
July 18	Rosalío Muro	San Francisco, CA	W	TKO, 2
October 12	Royal Kobayashi	Tokyo, Japan	W	KO, 5
December 20	Saúl Montana	Managua, Nicaragua	W	KO, 3
1976				
February 1	José Torres	Mexicali, Mexico	W	Split Decision, 10
April 10	Modesto Concepción	Managua, Nicaragua	W	KO, 2
June 19	Salvador Torres	Los Angeles, CA	W	KO, 3
1977				
February 19	Godfrey Stevens	Managua, Nicaragua	W	KO, 2
May 14	Alberto Herrera	Managua, Nicaragua	W	KO, 1
June 22	Ezequiel Sánchez	New York, NY	W	TKO, 4
August 3	José Fernández	New York, NY	W	TKO, 1
August 27	Benjamín Ortíz	San Juan, PR	W	Decision, 10
September 29	Jerome Artis	New York, NY	W	TKO, 2
December 18	Enrique Solís	Managua, Nicaragua	W	KO, 5

Continued

Date	Opponent	Location	W/L	KO/Decision/ Number of Rounds
1978				
January 28	Alfredo Escalera	San Juan, PR	W	TKO, 13
March 25	Mario Méndez	Las Vegas, NV	W	TKO, 3
April 29	Ray Tam	Los Angeles, CA	W	TKO, 5
June 3	Diego Alcalá	San Juan, PR	W	KO, 1
July 26	Vilomar Fernández	New York, NY	L	Decision, 10
November 10	Arturo León	Las Vegas, NV	W	Split Decision, 15
1979				
February 4	Alfredo Escalera	Rimini, Italy	W	KO, 13
July 8	Rafael Limón	New York, NY	W	TKO, 11
November 16	Bobby Chacón	Los Angeles, CA	W	TKO, 7
1980				
January 20	Rubén Castillo	Tuscon, Arizona	W	TKO, 11
March 31	Gerald Hayes	Las Vegas, NV	W	Decision, 10
April 27	Rolando Navarrete	San Juan, PR	W	TKO, 5
August 9	Cornelius Boza Edwards	Atlantic City, New Jersey	W	TKO, 8
November 14	José Luis Ramírez	Miami, FL	W	Split Decision, 10
1981				
February 7	Robert Vásquez	Miami, FL	W	TKO, 3
June 20	Jim Watt	London, United Kingdom	W	Decision, 15
October 3	Ray Mancini	Atlantic City, New Jersey	W	TKO, 14
November 21	Roberto Elizondo	Las Vegas, NV	W	KO, 7
1982				
February 13	James Busceme	Beaumont, Texas	W	TKO, 6
May 22	Andrew Ganigan	Las Vegas, NV	W	KO, 5
July 31	Kevin Rooney	Atlantic City, New Jersey	W	KO, 2
November 12	Aaron Pryor	Miami, FL	L	TKO, 14
1983				
February 26	Vilomar Fernández	San Antonio, Texas	W	Decision, 10
April 24	Claude Noel	Atlantic City, New Jersey	W	TKO, 3
September 9	Aaron Pryor	Las Vegas, NV	L	KO, 10
1985				
October 25	Pat Jefferson	Anchorage, Alaska	W	TKO, 5
1986				
February 9	Billy Costello	Reno, NV	W	TKO, 4
1994				
August 27	Jorge Palomares	Miami Beach, FL	W	Decision, 10
1995				
January 21	Scott Walker	Las Vegas, NV	L	Split Decision, 10

SOURCES

Interviews (all conducted by the author)

Alvarez, Walter (January 2012 phone interview)
Areas, Evelio
Baeza, Carlos
Bagnariol, Renzo (June 2011, Nicaragua)
Baltazar, Tony
Benbow, Hugh
Boitano Coleman, Victor
Buitrago, Mauricio (June 2011, Nicaragua)
Busceme, James "Bubba"
Castillo, Dr. Henry (June 2011, Nicaragua)
Castillo, Ruben (August 2011 phone interview)
Chargin, Don
Costello, Billy
Elizondo, Roberto (June 2011 phone interview)
Encinosa, Enrique
Farhood, Steve
Fletes, Pablo (June 2011, Nicaragua)
Fraser, Don
Garcia, Joe (January 2012 phone interview)
Hafey, Art
Hauser, Thomas
Kahn, Don (August 2011 phone interview)
Lederman, Harold
Lopez, Danny "Little Red"
Maltz, Gerald
Maltz, Katherine
Mancini, Ray "Boom Boom" (December 2011 phone interview)

Marcel, Ernesto (2003, Panama)
Marley, Michael
Mendoza, Ray (June 2011, Nicaragua)
Merchant, Larry
Miller, Bill (Fall 2011 phone interview)
Miller, Yolanda
Mojica, Ratón
Muniz, Armando
O'Grady, Sean
Ortiz, Ramiro (July 2011 phone interview)
Otero, Frankie (July 2011 phone interview)
Palomino, Carlos
Quintero, Sergio (June 2011, Nicaragua)
Resnick, Jimmy
Rizo, Karla (June 2011, Nicaragua)
Rodriguez, Donald (June 2011, Nicaragua)
Roman, Eduardo (interviewed five times)
Ruiz, Paul (Summer 2011 phone interview)
Schuyler, Ed
Steward, Emanuel (June 2011 phone interview)
Tijerino, Edgar
Tompkins, Barry
Tuckler, Dr. Aaron
Varela, Carlos Jr. (February 2012 phone interview)
Varela, Carlos Sr. (February 2012 phone interview)
Watt, Jim (July 2011 phone interview)
Ziegel, Vic

Articles

Ring Interviews

"Arguello's Best." *World Boxing*, March 1983.

"Arguello Bio." *The Ring*, November 1982.

"Arguello Blames Futch for Defeat." *New York Times*, February 21, 1983, ProQuest Historical Newspapers, *New York Times* (1851-2004).

"Arguello Bout Set." *New York Times*, March 4, 1986, ProQuest Historical Newspapers, *New York Times* (1851-2004).

"Arguello Captures Title." *New York Times*, June 21, 1981, ProQuest Historical Newspapers, *New York Times* (1851-2004).

"Arguello Easily Outpoints Fernandez." *New York Times*, February 27, 1983, ProQuest Historical Newspapers, *New York Times* (1851-2004).

"Arguello-Elizondo." *The Ring*, January 1982.

"Arguello Ends Career." *New York Times*, April 12, 1986, ProQuest Historical Newspapers, *New York Times* (1851-2004).

"Arguello Feature." *The Ring*, August 1981.

"Arguello Gives Up Title." *New York Times*, February 16, 1983, ProQuest Historical Newspapers, *New York Times* (1851-2004).

"Arguello May Return to Ring." *New York Times*, June 26, 1985, ProQuest Historical Newspapers, *New York Times* (1851-2004).

"Arguello Rallies, Halts Ganigan in 5." *New York Times*, May 23, 1982, ProQuest Historical Newspapers, *New York Times* (1851-2004)

"Arguello Retains Title by Stopping Navarrete." *New York Times*, April 28, 1980, ProQuest Historical Newspapers, *New York Times* (1851-2004).

"Arguello Stops Alcala." *New York Times*, June 4, 1978, ProQuest Historical Newspapers, *New York Times* (1851-2004).

"Arguello Stops Busceme, Retains Crown." *New York Times*, February 14, 1982, ProQuest Historical Newspapers, *New York Times* (1851-2004).

"Arguello Stops Foe in 7th." *New York Times*, November 22, 1981, ProQuest Historical Newspapers, *New York Times* (1851-2004).

"Arguello Takes Title from Escalera on T.K.O." *New York Times*, January 29, 1978, ProQuest Historical Newspapers, *New York Times* (1851-2004).

"Arguello Trailing, Wins by KO." *Los Angeles Times*, January 21, 1980, ProQuest Historical Newspapers, *Los Angeles Times* (1881-1987).

"Arguello Tribute by Mancini." *The Ring*, October 1982.

"Arguello vs the WBA." *The Ring*, August 1983.

"Arguello-Watt." *The Ring*, September 1982.

"Boxing Is Big; Buyer Beware." *Los Angeles Times*, February 12, 1982, ProQuest Historical Newspapers, *Los Angeles Times* (1881-1987).

Berger, Phil. "Arguello's Victory Bolsters Comeback." *New York Times*, February 10, 1986, ProQuest Historical Newspapers, *New York Times* (1851-2004).

Berkow, Ira. "Arguello Gets Another Shot." *New York Times*, August 1, 1983, ProQuest Historical Newspapers, *New York Times* (1851-2004).

Bradley, John Ed. "For Arguello, Life's a Fight." *Washington Post*, March 16, 1986, ProQuest Historical Newspapers, *Washington Post* (1877-1993).

"Buccaneers: Jackson Will Be No. 1 Choice." *Washington Post*, April 12, 1986, ProQuest Historical Newspapers, *Washington Post* (1877-1993).

Corrigan, Ed. "Arguello Stops Foe in 11th." *New York Times*, July 9, 1979, ProQuest Historical Newspapers, *New York Times* (1851-2004).

"Duran's Most Wanted." *International Boxing*, August 1978.

Green, Ted. "Ray Mancini Is Actually Boom Boom Mancini II" *Los Angeles Times*, December 6, 1981, ProQuest Historical Newspapers, *Los Angeles Times* (1881-1987).

Hall, John. "Mad & Mean." *Los Angeles Times*, November 14, 1979, ProQuest Historical Newspapers, *Los Angeles Times* (1881-1987).

Hawn, Jack. "Nicaraguan Arguello Lifts Olivares' Title on 13th-Round KO." *Los Angeles Times*, November 24, 1974 , ProQuest Historical Newspapers, *Los Angeles Times* (1881-1987).

Hoffer, Richard. "Arguello Tries to Turn Back the Rolex." *Los Angeles Times*, February 8, 1986, ProQuest Historical Newspapers, *Los Angeles Times* (1881-1987).

———. "The Next Title Would Put Arguello in a Class by Himself." *Los Angeles Times*, November 10, 1982, ProQuest Historical Newspapers, *Los Angeles Times* (1881-1987).

Katz, Michael. "Arguello Decides 'The Carnival Is Over.'" *New York Times*, September 11, 1983, ProQuest Historical Newspapers, *New York Times* (1851-2004).

———. "Arguello Fights History Second Time Around." *New York Times*, September 8, 1983, ProQuest Historical Newspapers, *New York Times* (1851-2004).

———. "Arguello Reacting Like a Gentleman." *New York Times*, November 11, 1982, ProQuest Historical Newspapers, *New York Times* (1851-2006).

———. "Arguello Returns to Pay Debt." *New York Times*, August 11, 1985, ProQuest Historical Newspapers, *New York Times* (1851-2004).

———. "Boxing World Faces Staggering Blows." *New York Times*, May 11, 1980, ProQuest Historical Newspapers, *New York Times* (1851, 2004).

———. "Brenner's Lawyer Lays Conspiracy to Sulaiman." *New York Times*, April 8, 1981, ProQuest Historical Newspapers, *New York Times* (1851-2004).

———. "Brenner's Lawsuit May Shake Boxing." *New York Times*, April 5, 1981, ProQuest Historical Newspapers, *New York Times* (1851-2004).

————. "Richest in History." *New York Times*, June 15, 1982, ProQuest Historical Newspapers, *New York Times* (1851-2004).

————. "Unbeaten Pryor Retains Title." *New York Times*, March 3, 1985, ProQuest Historical Newspapers, *New York Times* (1851-2004).

McGowen, Deane. "Arguello, 132, Takes the Measure of Sanchez in 4 Rounds at Garden." *New York Times*, June 23, 1977, ProQuest Historical Newspapers, *New York Times* (1851-2004).

————. "Arguello Stops Artis in 2d Round for 44th Knockout." *New York Times*, September 30, 1977, ProQuest Historical Newspapers, *New York Times* (1851-2004).

————. "Arguello Stops Boza-Edwards." *New York Times*, August 10, 1980, ProQuest Historical Newspapers, *New York Times* (1851).

Montalbano, William D. "Sandinistas' Foe Seeks Money and Supplies." *Los Angeles Times*, February 10, 1984, ProQuest Historical Newspapers, *Los Angeles Times* (1881-1987).

Murray, Jim. "A Mere Triple Crown Isn't Enough for Alexis Arguello." *Los Angeles Times*, October 21, 1982, ProQuest Historical Newspapers, *Los Angeles Times* (1881-1987).

Neumann, Randy. "Will Arguello's Punch Work?" *New York Times*, November 7, 1982, ProQuest Historical Newspapers, *New York Times* (1851-2006).

"Papal Delay for Arguello." *New York Times*, January 30, 1979, ProQuest Historical Newspapers, *New York Times* (1851-2004).

"Pound for Pound the Best." *International Boxing*, August 1978.

"Profile." *The Ring*, August 1980.

"Pryor-Arguello." *The Ring*, January 1983.

"Pryor-Arguello II." *International Boxing*, August 1983.

"Pryor-Arguello Aftermath." *The Ring*, January 1984.

"Pryor-Arguello Predictions." *The Ring*, November 1982.

"Time to Say Goodbye." *World Boxing*, January 1984.

Vecsey, George. "Arguello Wanders into Ring History." *New York Times*, November 16, 1981, ProQuest Historical Newspapers, *New York Times* (1851-2004).

ABOUT THE AUTHOR

Boxing has been a part of Christian Giudice's life since the glory days of the late 1980s when his father took him to the fights in Atlantic City casinos. Ever since then, he was hooked.

Guidice graduated from Villanova University in 1997 with a bachelor of arts in English and completed his master's in journalism at Temple University in 2002. Soon after, he began his writing career as a sports reporter for the *Gloucester County Times* in Woodbury, New Jersey, and published his first book, *Hands of Stone: The Life and Legend of Roberto Duran*, in 2007. Nearly a year later, he traveled to Nicaragua to begin researching *Beloved Warrior*.

Originally from Haddonfield, New Jersey, Guidice currently teaches English at a high school in Monroe, North Carolina. In his spare time, he works as a freelance sportswriter, publishes articles for his new website, belovedwarrior.net, and assists Latin American boxers through his project Golpes y Libros (or Punches and Books).